NATIONALITIES
AND NATIONAL MINORITIES

THE MACMILLAN COMPANY
NEW YORK · BOSTON · CHICAGO
DALLAS · ATLANTA · SAN FRANCISCO

MACMILLAN AND CO., LIMITED
LONDON · BOMBAY · CALCUTTA
MADRAS · MELBOURNE

THE MACMILLAN COMPANY
OF CANADA, LIMITED
TORONTO

NATIONALITIES
AND
NATIONAL MINORITIES

(With Special Reference to East-Central Europe)

By OSCAR I. JANOWSKY
*Department of History
The College of the City of New York*

WITH A FOREWORD
By JAMES T. SHOTWELL

THE MACMILLAN COMPANY
New York · 1945

Copyright, 1945, by
THE MACMILLAN COMPANY.

All rights reserved—no part of this book may be reproduced in any form without permission in writing from the publisher, except by a reviewer who wishes to quote brief passages in connection with a review written for inclusion in magazine or newspaper.

First printing.

PRINTED IN THE UNITED STATES OF AMERICA

TO PAULINE

FOREWORD

Two world wars are the penalty for not having solved the problem with which this volume deals. There is, therefore, no more important, no more compelling problem confronting the world today. And yet it lacks reality for most of us, for the peoples involved are largely foreign to our way of life and live in a part of the world about which few of us have any personal knowledge. Moreover, the problem itself seems to be their problem, not ours: that of local adjustment to neighbors living alongside or to neighboring governments. We have, therefore, a proper reluctance to interfere except when disorders break out which threaten the peace of nations. Then in the clash of interests we become suspicious of the propaganda of hostile factions. What is needed is a clear and definite statement of the problem itself in terms of its own history and proposals for its solution based on parallel experience elsewhere. This is the contribution of this volume.

Although, as Professor Janowsky states in his own preface, "this book faces the future," it deals with an historical process which cannot be understood unless one knows something of the past. That great area which lies between Soviet Russia and Central Europe has been retarded in its political evolution owing to the fact that it has been a borderland between great nations and is composed of what seems to us nondescript races, many of which until recently have lacked full political recognition. The model which all have sought to copy, and this includes the great empires as well, is that of the national state which, from the close of the Middle Ages, has been the outstanding creation of the Western world. But it has now become clear that the process of state formation which was exemplified first in England and France, cannot be copied in east-central Europe without serious modification. The time has passed for that process of unification to be repeated which prevailed in western Europe from the sixteenth to the eighteenth centuries. There was no parallel in eastern Europe during that period of natural formation to the way in which commercial and industrial England took over the task of kings, making all citizens participants in government. Neither was there any parallel in that part of the world of the unification of France under the French Revolution. In contrast with this development in western Europe, three great empires—and a fourth, if we include the Ottoman Empire—extended their bureaucratic sovereignty over the whole area, giving the outward semblance of unity within their frontiers, but suppressing local political action or at best offering it slight and limited opportunities.

When the First World War broke the structure of all three empires, Hohenzollern, Hapsburg and Romanoff, the slogan of the conquerors was self-determination, and this was chiefly applied to the peoples of east-central Europe. The outstanding statesman of this movement of liberation, President Masaryk of the newly created state of Czechoslovakia, had a political philosophy which he hoped to see applied in the whole region extending from the Baltic to the Aegean. It was a democratic polity largely drawn from American sources, especially Jefferson. A recognition of the democratic partnership in government would be the one way to ensure the rights of man and the citizen. Unfortunately, however, the unsettled conditions following the First World War and the inexperience of the citizens in the responsibilities of political independence prevented the successful operation of Masaryk's plan. Instead of a community of like-minded people intent upon the pursuit of happiness under the regime of liberty—the ideal which Masaryk sought to apply—nationalism developed in even more intolerant forms than in the West. The result was social instability within the state due to the dissatisfaction of minorities and more or less unfriendly rivalry with other nations.

There are two lessons, therefore, to be drawn from this history. The first is that nationalist unification of the type of the western European countries does not have the same roots in the history of eastern Europe and that the effort to achieve it becomes an intolerable oppression in the eyes of all but the dominant section of the people. The second lesson is that the processes of representative government must be freed from this centralizing tendency in order not to become ineffective within the state or an invitation to aggression from powerful neighbors.

How then can a multi-national state achieve both efficiency and freedom? Professor Janowsky's answer to this question is straightforward and challenging. The multi-national state must recognize multi-nationalism. This is a new kind of federalism, a development reaching far beyond the federalism of the United States. The best example of it in the past is, as he points out, the unique constitution of Switzerland. But by far the greatest experiment of this form of social and political cohesion is in the Stalinist federalism of Soviet Russia. The chief interest of the book for many people will therefore lie in the analysis of this chapter of Soviet history. Too little attention has been paid to it hitherto because of the concentration of interest upon the economic ideology of Communism. It is hard for us to understand that alongside the great state controls of economic life there is provision for cultural freedom for the many peoples who compose Soviet Russia. Professor Janowsky's analysis of this development is therefore of wider interest than merely in the possible application to the peoples of eastern-central Europe, vastly important as that development might be. He is opening the window upon a new combination of historical forces different from those which have molded western Europe into the state system of today.

In conclusion, it should be pointed out that while Professor Janowsky finds merit in the cultural policy of Soviet Russia, he does not propose that this experiment should be applied to the countries of eastern Europe by the Soviets. His proposal is simply that the method of federalism which has succeeded throughout Soviet Russia might well be tried out by each of these countries on its own behalf. This distinction is important.

The Charter of the United Nations has recognized that human

rights and fundamental freedoms are a matter of international concern, and it has made provision for a Commission to deal with these problems in the future. Important as this achievement is, however, it increases rather than lessens our responsibility as citizens to enlighten public opinion on the complicated question of human and minority rights and to help in the difficult task of devising effective machinery of supervision and enforcement. Professor Janowsky's volume offers an outstanding contribution to the literature of this new movement in international affairs.

JAMES T. SHOTWELL

PREFACE

This book faces the future. It seeks not to commemorate the past but to contribute, in however small a measure, to the fashioning of a more humane, more contented and more stable world. Recent efforts to protect minorities and nationalities are examined with the view of noting achievements and shortcomings, which in turn might help us to find a solution of the troublesome problem. In a word, the book advances a thesis which, in all fairness to the reader, should be stated at the outset.

The minorities and nationalities of east-central Europe do not pose so commanding a problem to world peace as the interests of the Great Powers, or security against aggression, or the unilateral efforts of states to achieve economic well-being. Yet, disaffection and oppression have for many decades contributed to make of east-central Europe a war-breeding zone which repeatedly threatened world peace and, indeed, furnished the immediate occasions in 1914 and 1939 for the precipitation of the First and Second World Wars.

Large masses of people in this wide area, which is bounded by the Baltic, Adriatic and Aegean seas, and by the former Soviet and German-Austrian frontiers, have long been at the mercy of their stronger neighbors. In the nineteenth and early twentieth centuries they were oppressed by Russian Czars, Turkish Sultans, Austro-Hungarian oligarchs and Prussian Junkers. The Peace Settlement of 1919, which reconstructed Europe at the close of the First World War, brought some relief to a large proportion of the nationalities of this region by recognizing them as independent communities. But so complex was the mixture of population that minorities could not be eliminated. In 1939, more than twenty million people were still classed as minorities in a total population of about one hundred million. The League of Nations made the attempt to afford protection against discrimination to members of minorities. But the disloyalty of German and Hungarian minorities, the intolerance of majorities like the Poles and Rumanians, defects in the system of protection and, above all, the deterioration of the international situation during the 1930's, with the consequent weakening of the League, hampered the proper fuctioning of this guarantee.

At the present time, the vast region of east-central Europe is in a state of political and social dissolution. Every borderland, from Trieste to the Curzon Line, from Macedonia and Thrace to Sub-Carpathian Ruthenia, and from Transylvania to Teschen, has its rival claimants, and frontier posts are pulled up and shifted in the interests of a fugitive security by those who have the power to assert their will. However, the juggling of boundaries does not spirit minorities out of sight, and other and more forceful means are apparently being employed to dispose of them. Vague reports emanate from east-central Europe about population transfers, expulsions and warnings that minorities must conform to the cultural standards set by majorities. At best, we are told, minorities might enjoy a status similar to that of the foreign-language groups in the United States.

This book advances the thesis that conditions in east-central Europe are radically different from those of the United States; that the tolerant American attitude to the foreign-born would, therefore, not meet the needs of minorities in the Danubian basin or the Balkans. It is further maintained that forced assimilation can only foment strife and must not be tolerated in a democratic world. Moreover, while population transfers, if humanely administered, might prove expedient in limited areas, so drastic a remedy cannot be applied to the millions of minorities without resorting to some of the savage ways of the Nazis.

East-central Europe, it is argued here, being heterogeneous in population, must become multi-national in its state structure and decentralized at least in educational and cultural functions. National federalism is the solution proposed for the unyielding problem of nationalities and minorities in this area, and the reader is urged to peruse the analysis presented in Chapter VIII. That this is a practicable and workable method of political and social organization is attested by the fact that varying forms of the multi-national state have been evolved and are functioning today in different parts of the world. Part Two of this book surveys the development and operation of the multi-national state in Switzerland, South Africa and the Soviet Union. In particular, the nationality policy of the Soviet Union merits close attention, for it might well serve as the model for national-cultural reconstruction in east-central Europe.

The core of the minorities problem, as envisaged in this book, can be grasped in a few sentences. The states of east-central Europe are not homogeneous in language or culture. A considerable proportion of the citizens of a state speak distinctive languages and cherish diverse historical memories or usages. Therefore national uniformity, which is symbolized by a single countrywide language and a single national culture, is unattainable except through the suppression or elimination of the minorities. Such efforts inevitably engender strife which in turn endangers the peace of the world. If oppression and conflict are to give way to harmony and contentment, the way must be found to recognize cultural differences within a framework of political and economic unity. The multi-national state provides the principle for sanctioning differences, and national federalism furnishes the means of integrating minorities, along with their institutions and customs, in the life of the larger community.

This book is the product of many years of research and investigation, including visits to Geneva, the seat of the League of Nations, and to nearly a score of cities situated in Poland, Czechoslovakia, Austria, Hungary, Rumania, Jugoslavia and Greece. At Geneva I had access to some of the materials filed in the Minorities Section of the League Secretariat. In east-central Europe I collected and read much documentary information and discussed minorities problems with numerous leaders of minorities, government officials, academic scholars, journalists, and simple folk to whom minority difficulties and vexations were hard and near.

The mass of information thus accumulated was a temptation to me to write a bulky and heavily documented account which might have pleased the scholar while ignoring the interest and needs of the general reader. If minorities and nationalities posed only academic problems, like the origins of medieval towns, or, like the Crusades, stirred solely historical interest, I would not have resisted this temptation. But nationalities and minorities are still with us. Their clashes are not the faint echoes of a distant past; their plaints have not yet been muffled by time and forgetfulness. We read of expulsions, plunder and mass murder, not in faded chronicles of bygone days, but in the daily newspaper. In short, we are concerned with the troubles of living human beings and the conflicts of striving groups rather than solely with the record of the past. Such problems of minorities and nationalities require the attention of the statesman to harmonize and adjust clashing interests even more than the cool judgment of the historian who is given to analyze causes and assess methods and accomplishments.

The busy statesmen of our day, however, are preoccupied with the problems of political security, economic welfare and international conciliation. Minorities and small nationalities are therefore apt to be forgotten unless public opinion is alive to the consequences of human oppression and national strife. This book hopes to contribute to the fashioning of an informed public opinion on the subject.

I have made every effort to present an account which might engage the attention of the intelligent and serious general reader as well as the scholar. The book is brief and, I hope, reasonably readable. Details which might have burdened the reader or obscured the main issues have been rigorously excluded. Every quotation from the sources has been carefully weighed, and the ornamental or unessential eliminated. Digressions have not knowingly been indulged in. The emphasis has been placed upon those developments which have relevance to the present problems of minorities and nationalities. And I have not hesitated to draw conclusions and to indicate a course of action for the immediate future.

This book owes its being to the sustained interest and encouragement of Dr. James T. Shotwell, Professor Emeritus, Columbia University, and Director of the Division of Economics and History of the Carnegie Endowment for International Peace. It is difficult to express adequately my appreciation of his concern with the progress of this study. He gave generously of his time, reading the manuscript and discussing with me many of the questions raised therein. He made possible the publication of the book, the preparation of the manuscript for the printer and the compilation of the index. Dr. Shotwell's deep learning and insight made our discussions of subject matter an inspiration to me, and I am particularly indebted to him for the term "National Federalism" and its profound implications.

A timely grant by the Esco Fund Committee rendered possible the completion of research and the formulation of a concrete plan for the international protection of minorities. The grant was made to the Commission to Study the Organization of Peace for the purposes of this inquiry. I am indebted to the Esco Fund Committee and to the Commission to Study the Organization of Peace for thus sponsoring the study. To the Director of the Commission, Clark M. Eichelberger, I am also in debt for his reading of several chapters in manuscript and for his lively interest in the project.

My friend Beryl Harold Levy, formerly Counsel to the Commission to Study the Organization of Peace, read Parts One and Three of the book with painstaking care and a keen critical sense. His many comments and suggestions were invaluable. Professor Max M. Laserson was most helpful in reading the chapter on the Soviet Union.

The late Arthur E. McFarlane, editorial reader of the Division of Economics and History of the Carnegie Endowment, read the entire manuscript despite his failing health, and his editorial suggestions were gratefully accepted. To Mrs. Rose Klima I am thankful for the intelligence and enthusiasm with which she read and typed the entire manuscript, and to Miss Harriet J. Church for her thorough reading of the book and for the preparation of the index.

I owe special acknowledgment for numerous courtesies extended by the staffs of the libraries of the City College, Columbia University, the Woodrow Wilson Foundation and the American-Russian Institute, and to that of the New York Public Library.

My thanks are due to Mr. Corliss Lamont for permission to reprint his excellent chart which appears on pp. 92–95; to the National Council of American-Soviet Friendship for the map reproduced on pp. 70–71; to the American-Russian Institute for the table reprinted on pp. 75–76; and to Survey Associates for permission to use the chart on page 111, which I prepared and first published in *Survey Graphic*.

I need hardly add that the acknowledgment of assistance in no way involves a delegation of responsibility.

OSCAR I. JANOWSKY

The College of the City of New York.
    Spring, 1945

CONTENTS

FOREWORD BY JAMES T. SHOTWELL   vii
PREFACE   xi

PART ONE
The Explosive Nature of the Nationalities Problem in the War-Breeding Zone of East-Central Europe

I. INTRODUCTORY: THE UNIQUE CHARACTER OF THE UNITED STATES   3

II. THE PERENNIAL PROBLEM OF NATIONALITIES AND NATIONAL MINORITIES IN EAST-CENTRAL EUROPE   6
    1. The Present Neglect of the Problem   6
    2. The Dilemma at Paris: National Self-Determination *vs.* Economic Unity   10
    3. A Breeding-Ground of Modern Wars   12

III. THE NATIONAL STATE OF THE WEST UNSUITED TO THE MULTI-NATIONAL POPULATION OF EAST-CENTRAL EUROPE   14
    1. National States in Great Britain and France   14
    2. Multi-National East-Central Europe Prior to the First World War   19
       a. Czarist Russia   20
       b. The Austro-Hungarian Empire   22
       c. The Ottoman Empire   22
       d. Hohenzollern Prussia As an Object Lesson   23

PART TWO
The Evolution of Successful Multi-National States

IV. NATIONAL FEDERALISM IN SWITZERLAND   37
    1. A Composite People   37
    2. Emergence of National Federalism   38
    3. Equality in Law and in Fact   40
    4. Language, Culture and Nationality   41

	5. Pillars of the Multi-National State	42
	a. Democracy	42
	b. Cultural Federalism	43
	c. Decentralization	44
V.	BILINGUALISM IN SOUTH AFRICA	46
	1. The Beginnings of Diversity	47
	2. Anglicization and Its Effects	50
	3. The Boer Emigration	53
	4. The Achievement of Independence	55
	5. Effects of the Boer War	60
	6. The South African National Convention	62
	7. Equality in Practice	65
	8. Conclusion	67
VI.	NATIONAL FEDERALISM IN THE SOVIET UNION	69
	1. A Babel of Tongues and Nationalities	74
	2. Bolshevism and Nationalism	77
	3. The People's Commissariat for Nationalities	81
	4. The Structure of Soviet National Federalism: The R.S.F.S.R. (Russian Soviet Federative Socialist Republic)	83
	5. The Structure of Soviet National Federalism: The U.S.S.R. (Union of Soviet Socialist Republics)	86
	6. The Functioning of Soviet National Federalism: An Appraisal	91
	a. The Soviet Union, a Multi-National, Federal State	96
	b. National Equality	97
	c. Cultural Freedom	99
	7. Conclusion	102

PART THREE

The Bases of a Solution of the Nationalities Problem in East-Central Europe

VII.	THE NEW EXPERIMENT OF THE LEAGUE OF NATIONS: SYSTEMATIC INTERNATIONAL MACHINERY FOR THE PROTECTION OF MINORITIES	110
	1. The Provisions of the Minorities Treaties	112
	2. How the League Enforced the Minorities Treaties	115
	a. The Minorities Petition	117

	b. The Minorities Section	117
	c. The Minorities Committee	118
	d. Official Action by the League Council	120
	3. Was the League System Effective?	122
	a. Accomplishments of the League System	123
	b. Its Weaknesses	125
VIII.	PROPOSALS FOR A SOLUTION IN THE LIGHT OF EXPERIENCE AND EMERGING PATTERNS OF INTERNATIONAL ORGANIZATION	135
	1. Is Transfer of Populations the Solution?	136
	2. The Vague and Impractical Idea of Divorcing National Culture from the Territorial State	144
	3. A New Approach: National Federalism and Economic Unity	145
	4. The Rights of National Minorities	147
	a. Human Rights and National Rights	147
	b. Freedom of Association and Cultural Autonomy	148
	c. The Jews of East-Central Europe as Minorities	150
	d. The Special Problem of the German and Hungarian Minorities	152
	5. International Supervision	154
	a. The Problem of the Sovereign Equality of States	154
	b. The International Guarantee	157
	c. Enforcement Procedure	158
	6. The Critical Character of the Transitional Period	163

CONCLUSION — 165

APPENDICES: THE INTERNATIONAL PROTECTION OF RACIAL, RELIGIOUS AND LINGUISTIC MINORITIES IN EAST-CENTRAL EUROPE

I.	International Instruments Under the Guarantee of the League of Nations	171
II.	The Polish Minorities Treaty	173
III.	The Letter of Clemenceau to Paderewski	179
IV.	Resolutions of the League Council Relating to Minorities Procedure	185

SELECTED BIBLIOGRAPHY — 193

INDEX — 209

PART ONE

The Explosive Nature of the Nationalities Problem in the War-Breeding Zone of East-Central Europe

CHAPTER I

Introductory: The Unique Character of the United States

The history of immigration and national-cultural assimilation in the United States makes it difficult for Americans to grasp fully the complexities of the minorities problem in east-central Europe. We are a composite people, an intricate human pattern of racial, religious, linguistic and cultural strands which can be traced back virtually to every region of the earth. Yet the United States is not a multi-national state in the European sense of the word.

We have in our midst members or descendants of Europe's numerous majorities and minorities—English, Scottish, Irish, French, German, Italian, Russian, Polish, Jewish, Greek, etc.—who have learned the English language and become identified with the American tradition. Old-world associations have been largely severed, and a common citizenship has entailed not only undivided political allegiance but also membership in the all-embracing American cultural community. Our "national" groupings may have a sentimental attachment to the "old country" and continue to read foreign-language newspapers, but they do not aspire to special linguistic or cultural rights, or desire minority status of the east-European variety.

We have, of course, minority problems affecting Negroes, Jews and Catholics; but these can be solved through the normal functioning of democratic processes, without resort to any radical changes in the structure of the state. For the United States, the problem of minorities is one involving *human rights,* that is, civil, political and religious rights, equality of opportunity, the right of association and the elimination of economic and social discrimination. *National rights,* such as the official recognition of minority

3

languages and separate schools, which loom so large in east-central Europe, are not an issue in this country. The United States is a national state, or a national state in the making.

The question then arises, if democracy offers the solution of our minority problems, why cannot the states of east-central Europe follow our example? Why must national-cultural assimilation be abandoned in east-central Europe, when it has been so markedly successful in the United States? In short, why cannot the composite states of east-central Europe become national states after the manner of the United States?

The answer is that only individuals can be assimilated and not conscious national communities. In the immigrant of the nineteenth century the United States was confronted with an individual, whereas it is nationalities or organized segments of nationalities that constitute the European problem, as we shall presently see.

When the immigrant arrived in the United States, he was not a unit in a national community but an individual, or the head of a family, uprooted from his native surroundings and eager to find his place in the new land of opportunity. To be sure, he sought the association of those who understood his language and social habits, but the dynamic character of the American environment and the absence of sustained persecution prevented such groupings from hardening into conscious and self-contained minority nationalities.

The development of the vast resources of the country required the cheap labor of the immigrant, while limitless economic opportunities beckoned to those capable of rapid adjustment. Therefore, agencies of Americanization, such as the public school, were welcomed, especially by the second generation, as the means of advancement. And the public school identified the child with American language and culture.

No such forces of assimilation operated in east-central Europe. There minorities did not consist of individual immigrants but of solid masses who had been conquered and annexed, but had remained true to their immemorial usages. In their compact settlements the minorities found their own languages and customs sufficient to meet their needs. The presence of members of the ruling majority was a reminder of conquest and oppression, while cultural institutions which sought to promote assimilation were resisted as agencies of denationalization. In east-central Europe, both the will and the need for assimiliation were lacking.[1]

Furthermore, Americanization must be sharply distinguished from Prussianization, Russification or Magyarization. Such ideals of iron-clad uniformity and intolerance of differences are alien to the American tradition, and their methods of ruthless and brutal suppression repugnant to American conceptions of freedom. Americanization is positive, requiring all to learn the English language and to become associated with the all-embracing American culture, but not demanding the complete abandonment of supplementary languages or traditions. East-central Europe, however, suffers from a legacy of strife. Minorities have been subjected to cruel persecution, involving deliberate efforts to suppress their cultural individualities. This has stimulated national consciousness, aroused a more passionate desire to maintain intact the cultural heritage, and welded most members of the minority groups into sullen and tenacious national units.

Thus the social processes which have promoted cultural homogeneity in the United States are inoperative in east-central Europe. There the problem remains in all its virulence, and if it is to be solved by means other than violence and extermination, we must find the way not only to tolerate national-cultural differences, but also to unite majorities and minorities organically in the structure of the state. This can be accomplished only by means of a multi-national state containing many recognized nationalities.

[1] For a fuller discussion of this question, see the present writer's chapter entitled "Ethnic and Cultural Minorities," in MacIver, R. M. (ed.), *Group Relations and Group Antagonisms* (New York, 1944), pp. 157–170. See also Levy, B. H., "The Minorities Problem of East-Central Europe in the Prospect of Post-War Reconstruction," *Win the War, Win the Peace* (New York, 1942).

CHAPTER II

THE PERENNIAL PROBLEM OF NATIONALITIES AND NATIONAL MINORITIES IN EAST-CENTRAL EUROPE

1. THE PRESENT NEGLECT OF THE PROBLEM

Immediately before the outbreak of the Second World War, national minorities were very much in the public eye. Czechoslovakia, Poland, Rumania and other states of east-central Europe were rent by national strife. Minorities charged their governments with wilful discrimination and were in turn stigmatized as disloyal, while the intervention of neighboring states like Germany and Hungary converted troublesome local or regional antagonisms into issues of world politics. For a time, minority questions commanded the attention of public opinion overseas, and the echoes of European discussions also reverberated through the American press. More recently, however, the subject has been generally forgotten or ignored. If this lapse of interest were due entirely to the pressures of total war, which must inevitably crowd specific issues into the background, there would be no occasion for alarm. But when national minorities are overlooked in official pronouncements of war aims, and in the peace plans of private organizations, it is important to inquire into the causes of this silence.

Three major reasons may be advanced for the present unpopularity of national minorities, namely, the excesses of nationalism, the exploitation of the minorities issue by the Nazis, and widespread impatience with small political units. First, nationalism is in ill repute today. Identified with Nazism, it raises spectres of hatred, intolerance and savagery which threaten the very foundations of civilization. In the name of nationalism many thousands of human beings have been abused and broken in concentration camps, and millions done to death or reduced to a life of dread and terror. The best of German culture has been driven to exile or suicide. Ideas of freedom and equality have been put under a ban; truth and justice have ceased to exist in a large part of Europe, except as catchwords which conceal personal and national aggrandizement.

For a great part of the world's peoples the word "nation" has ceased to signify a body of individuals and groups whose needs and interests must be harmonized and furthered. No longer is it conceived of as an effort towards common living and common struggle against the ills that afflict man: poverty and insecurity, ignorance and intolerance, privilege and suffering. Under Hitler or Mussolini the "nation" is a mystic entity, an idol which transcends human beings. Men and women must cease to think in terms of human values. They are asked to enhance the power of the nation-state, to glorify its name, to offer up sacrifices to it—human sacrifices, for one must be ready to kill and be killed in its name. Children, too, belong to the state. They are hardened and conditioned to despise equality and humanity, to loathe peace and human brotherhood. Brutality in life and unquestioning readiness to face death, to pass through the fires of the new Moloch, that is the mission of youth, the highest good, the greatest virtue.

When the human beings who compose a nation are battered into insensibility and fused into a graven image—hard, cruel and lifeless; when this image is worshipped; and when maniacs and charlatans arrogate to themselves the roles of priest and prophet, it is difficult to speak constructively of nations and nationalities. And indeed many men and women have despaired of nationalism and abandoned all hope that a movement which could father Nazism might prove a force for civilization. They denounce every manifestation of nationalism as an unmitigated evil, and particularly the nationalism of minorities who are called upon to abandon their claims in the interest of a common humanity, universalist and cosmopolitan.

Yet every concrete statement of war aims, every realistic peace plan, presumes the continued existence of nations; the very term "United Nations" sanctions, as it seeks to harmonize rather than eliminate, national peculiarities. Therefore, if the survival of nations is assured, national minorities will not willingly disappear. They will continue to speak their languages, to cherish their historical traditions, to celebrate their festal days, to remember their heroes and martyrs, to transmit the cultural heritage to their children, to demand that they be governed, judged and led by persons of their own choice. The excesses of nationalism must, of course, be combated, but we should have the perspicacity to distinguish between the vicious extremes of nationalism and self-expression in a people, and its rightful and desirable attachment to its cultural heritage.

The fact that German minorities in east-central Europe became the willing tools of Nazi aggression constitutes a second reason for the present tendency to disdain the claims of *all* minorities. It is true that during the interval between the Treaty of Versailles and the pact of Munich the Germans were the most articulate and best organized of all European minorities, while the readiness of the German Government to champion their cause assured them a respectful hearing before the agencies of the League of Nations. Equally true is the charge that since the triumph of Nazism in Germany, the dominant elements among the German minorities in neighboring states became the spearhead of Nazi aggression, a divisive force which weakened and ultimately aided in the disruption of their adopted countries. Therefore, minority rights have become identified in the popular mind with German irredentism and Nazi pretensions to superiority and dominion.

However, three-quarters of the minorities of east-central Europe were not Germans. The majority of the great variety of national fragments were loyal and law-abiding persons who desired no more than to be assured of the full rights of citizenship and national freedom, including the right to employ the mother tongue and maintain the identity of national cultural groupings. Nor did all

Germans become irredentists or potential Nazis. A considerable element among the German minorities fought Nazism to the end, succumbing only to a violence and intransigence which had its birth in Hitler's Reich and found nourishment in the narrow-visioned policies of most minorities states (that is, states harboring minorities). To abandon the practice of minority protection because it was used for evil purposes would be no more reasonable than to pronounce democracy obsolete when it also yielded to the demagogy and ferocity of Fascism.

Thirdly, minorities are ignored today because of impatience with small political units. The multiplication of small sovereign states at the close of the First World War, when east-central Europe was "Balkanized," undoubtedly contributed to the ensuing political anarchy and economic stagnation. The petty states of east-central Europe were as jealous of their "national honor" and "national rights" as the Great Powers; they were adepts in the intrigues of power politics; they contributed to the general impoverishment and confusion by imitating the practices of economic nationalism in a ridiculous pursuit of an impossible self-sufficiency. But in a crisis, economic or political, they were helpless pawns in the desperate game of the Great Powers. Divided and distracted by petty rivalries, they were a temptation to the aggressor, and the Nazi onslaught quickly reduced them to vassalage or worse.

True enough, the multiplication of petty and unruly sovereignties was a menace to the world and an affliction to the small states themselves. But the alternative is not the *suppression or obliteration* of national cultural peculiarities. The independent political entities of east-central Europe must be pieced together in rational geographic and economic units, without, however, ignoring the peculiar requirements of this nationally intermingled region. To think and plan solely in global terms without regard to the demands and needs of specific areas and groups is to blueprint a vacuum. The way must be found to harmonize local needs with regional prosperity and world security.

2. THE DILEMMA AT PARIS: NATIONAL SELF-DETERMINATION VS. ECONOMIC UNITY

During the First World War, great emphasis was placed on the principle of nationality, and on the rights of small nationalities in particular. The Allied rejoinder to the German "peace note" of December, 1916, declared that no peace was possible without a "recognition of the principle of nationalities, and of the free existence of small states."[1] More specifically, the reply of the Allies to President Wilson's request for a statement of war aims demanded "the liberation of the Italians, as also of the Slavs, Rumanes, and Czecho-Slovaks from foreign domination; the setting free of the populations subject to the bloody tyranny of the Turks. . . ."[2] Elaborating on British war aims in an address to the Trade Unions on January 5, 1918, Prime Minister Lloyd George declared that "a territorial settlement . . . based on the right of self-determination or the consent of the governed" was one of the three fundamental conditions of a permanent peace.[3] Three days later, on January 8, 1918, President Wilson delivered his celebrated message before a joint session of the two Houses of Congress, in which he outlined the "Fourteen Points." No fewer than five of these fourteen points dealt with the rights of nationality and self-determination, the summation proclaiming that

an evident principle runs through the whole programme I have outlined. It is the principle of justice to all peoples and nationalities, and their right to live on equal terms of liberty and safety with one another, whether they be strong or weak. Unless this principle be made its foundation no part of the structure of international justice can stand.[4]

In large measure, the peace settlement which brought the First World War to a close honored the principle of national self-

[1] Great Britain, *Parliamentary Papers*, 1917–1918, XXXVIII, Cmd. 8467. The reply was dated December 30, 1916.
[2] *Ibid.*, Cmd. 8468, Note of January 10, 1917.
[3] *The Times* (London), January 7, 1918.
[4] *The Public Papers of Woodrow Wilson: War and Peace*, ed. by Baker, Ray Stannard, and Dodd, William E. (New York, 1927), I, 155–162.

determination in east-central Europe. The more numerous and nationally more mature peoples like the Poles and Czechs achieved independence, while weaker and less articulate groups, the Slovenes and Slovaks, for example, were united with kindred nationalities to form the Succession States of Poland, Czechoslovakia, Jugoslavia, etc. However, its composite character made it impossible to apply to this area the simple formula: one nationality, one state. The intermingling of peoples and the interpenetration of nationalities inevitably resulted in the creation of numerous national minorities in virtually every state of east-central Europe. The problem of these minorities should not blind us to the fact that the Versailles statesmen sanctioned the liberation of millions of people who had suffered national oppression in Czarist Russia, Germany and Austria-Hungary. Even the national minorities were guaranteed a minimum of national rights, as we shall see in due course.

Yet in centering attention upon the principle of nationality as the foundation of the territorial settlement, the peacemakers of 1919 *sacrificed the values of economic unity.* This was a grievous error. The fifty million subjects of the Austro-Hungarian Monarchy, to cite one instance, had enjoyed the advantages of a unified transportation system and a balanced economy in which agricultural and industrial areas supplemented each other's needs by exchanging freely goods and services. In the hope of putting an end to national strife, the peacemakers sanctioned the dissolution of Austria-Hungary and the alienation of the western borderlands of the Russian Empire. Many new and petty states appeared, cutting the map of east-central Europe into ribbons.

Since no provision was made for economic cooperation, the new, petty states soon began to shift for themselves. Novel currencies appeared which each state manipulated to its own advantage. Tariff walls were erected to protect "infant industries." New railroads were built to serve military as well as economic needs. Old commercial centers like Vienna languished. Long-established trade relations were severed. Producers lost their markets. As a result, poverty and insecurity stalked through east-central Europe, ignoring boundaries and intensifying national hatreds and strife.

Today we recognize that freedom from want, that is, economic prosperity, must occupy a central position in all peace plans. We therefore stress economic welfare; and while the Atlantic Charter expresses a desire "to see no territorial changes that do not accord with the freely expressed wishes of the peoples concerned," the Teheran Declaration is vague on this point. Private organizations, too, think in terms of large economic units with adequate resources to render possible a satisfactory standard of living. We are wary of national self-determination because it raises visions of irrational and air-tight national compartments.

Thus, just as the peace settlement of 1919, in concentrating on nationality, overlooked the needs of economic unity, we run the risk today of reversing the process, by stressing economics to the detriment of nationality. While both economic unity and national freedom are necessary, neither is sufficient unto itself; both are indispensable.

3. A BREEDING-GROUND OF MODERN WARS [5]

It would be tragic to forget that two world wars have been precipitated by hatreds generated in nationality conflicts of east-central Europe. In 1914, a few pistol shots fired by a fanatical youth in distant Sarajevo set Europe ablaze, while the truculence of Germans in the Sudetenland provided Hitler with the excuse for the dismemberment of Czechoslovakia, which in turn led inexorably to the Second World War. On each occasion most Americans felt secure in their isolation, and showed little concern about national squabbles in remote parts of the world. Yet Americans who had not heard of Sarajevo or the Jugoslavs, and who could not locate the Sudetenland on the map, have twice become embroiled in war.

---

[5] See Masaryk, Thomas G., *The Problem of Small Nations in the European Crisis* (London, 1916), pp. 15–16; Brunauer, E. C., "Regional Unions in Eastern Europe," in *Winning the Peace* (Reprinted from the *St. Louis Star-Times*, 1944), p. 45.

If we are to have security, the way must be found to harmonize economic unity with the legitimate claims of nationalities and minorities in east-central Europe, a task which can be undertaken only when the peculiar nature of nationalism in that region is understood.

We shall proceed, therefore, to analyze the national problem of east-central Europe, comparing it with developments in western Europe, and with multi-national experiments in Switzerland, South Africa, and the Soviet Union. Such an analysis will render possible an appraisal of the minorities régime established at the end of the First World War. Finally, the attempt will be made to outline the essentials of a program for east-central Europe which will permit of free development of nationalities and national minorities without sacrificing the requirements of economic unity.

CHAPTER III

THE NATIONAL STATE OF THE WEST UNSUITED TO THE MULTI-NATIONAL POPULATION OF EAST-CENTRAL EUROPE

A national minority consists of a group of persons who differ from the majority in language, religion or culture. Like European nationalism,[1] it is a problem of modern times. The ideal of the Middle Ages was universalism—a universal Church, a universal Empire, and a universal language, Latin, for the literate fraternity. Local dialects and customs, as well as the feeling of kinship born of common ancestry, while prevalent in medieval times, were considered irrelevant, especially in so far as these peculiarities concerned the servile masses.

1. NATIONAL STATES IN GREAT BRITAIN AND FRANCE

The rise of the west-European national states in early modern times was accompanied by a process of economic and administrative centralization. The king, jealous of political power which rivaled his supreme authority, struck down feudal particularism, without regard, however, to the language or usages of the offending locality. The objective was uniformity of allegiance and of obedience to the king's will, not identity of speech or customs. However, so pervasive was the influence of centralizing royal power that the language and intellectual life of the capital, the center of population and wealth, became the model for the entire country. Differences in language and culture gradually faded out. Only in remote and inaccessible regions did distinctive speech and

---

[1] Kohn, Hans, *The Idea of Nationalism* (New York, 1944). See especially the Introduction for an analysis of the nature of nationalism.

customs survive, and even there chiefly among the lowly who were without voice or influence.

The assimilation of minorities of language and culture was facilitated in England and France by a number of circumstances. Mass migration had ceased centuries before the rise of the national state,[2] and common living under an all-embracing religious faith and ritual had laid the foundations for unification. Geography, too, played an important role. The limits of territorial expansion were reached early, obviating the need of absorbing new alien masses. In modern times, too, minorities in England and France could not look beyond the borders for national-cultural influence from large and culturally conscious groups of kinsmen, nor did minorities become irredentas stirred by a desire for unity with such kinsmen. Finally, the unifying process of royal power operated at a time when the linguistic and cultural consciousness of the masses was so rudimentary and inarticulate as to evoke little or no resistance to the forces of assimilation. Thus by the end of the eighteenth century England and France had attained a considerable measure of homogeneity in language and culture.

In the days of royal supremacy, the king was the symbol of national unity, the source of all-embracing national authority, the seat of national sovereignty. When royal absolutism was destroyed by the Puritan and French revolutions, sovereignty was transferred by political theorists from the monarch to the nation, and the word "nation" was associated in France and England indiscriminately with unity of political and legal authority as well as with unity of culture.

In France, the Revolution did much to stamp out lingering differences in language and culture. The Jacobins in particular, who vigorously fought regionalism and provincial autonomy, bestirred themselves to achieve linguistic uniformity along with political centralization. "Citizens!" cried Bertrand Barère, a leading Jacobin, in 1794, "the language of a free people ought to be one

---

[2] Ireland was an exception which proved the rule. It remained a persistent and troublesome problem.

and the same for all . . ."; and the revolutionary leaders took measures to stamp out local dialects and "foreign" tongues, especially through the agency of state-supported teachers and patriotic societies, which were exhorted to branch out into remote and isolated districts.[3] The rigors of revolutionary methods were subsequently relaxed, but the ideal of linguistic and cultural uniformity has remained a cardinal principle of French national life to this day.

The British were neither as rigorous nor as thorough as the French. The government never forbade the use of Gaelic in Scotland, and while Welsh was ousted from official, political and religious circles in Wales during the sixteenth century, no consistent suppression of the minority language ensued. In Ireland, the effort was made to obliterate the native language and culture, but more as a means of countering disloyalty than out of a desire to eliminate cultural differences. Moreover, with the growth of democracy and the concern of the government with public education during the latter half of the nineteenth century, practical considerations led the British Government to assume a friendlier attitude to the language and culture of its minorities. And by the first decade of the twentieth century Gaelic was employed as a language of instruction, and local history and literature were taught in Scotland, Wales and Ireland, wherever local conditions rendered it desirable.[4]

---

[3] Hayes, C. J. H., *The Historical Evolution of Modern Nationalism* (New York, 1931), pp. 63–66.

[4] This tolerant attitude to Gaelic in local affairs prompts C. A. Macartney in his *National States and National Minorities* (London, 1934) to characterize the United Kingdom as an "un-national state," rather than an English national state. (See pp. 465–467.) This results in utter confusion.

In Wales, court records, summonses, processes and notices are drawn in the English language. But judges and registrars of Welsh circuits and districts "understand" the local language, while in many Petty Sessional Divisions, witnesses and advocates employ Welsh. In many local minor courts, too, the proceedings are in that language, and children are taught in the lower grades in the mother tongue. In the view of Mr. Macartney these concessions to local demand have transformed the United Kingdom into an "un-national state."

However, he is obliged to include Czechoslovakia, whose minorities enjoyed far greater language and educational rights, among the "national" states. (See p. 208.) For example, the Germans of Czechoslovakia were represented in the

However, centuries of union with England have left their mark, and English laws, customs, ideas, even language, remain paramount, at least in Scotland and Wales and, of course, England. The English have learned that the preservation of Gaelic has not militated against the diffusion of English.[5]

Thus the concept of nationality which is frequently defined in ethnic and cultural terms, that is, as one's adherence to a people characterized by common ancestry or language or religion or culture,[6] became identified in Britain and France with membership in the nation-state. And just as the king had required undivided allegiance in the days of royal supremacy, so the sovereign nation-state of the nineteenth century expected not only loyalty to the state but also identification with the language, culture and mores of the majority.

Religion alone occasioned serious difficulty and finally achieved an exceptional status. During the sixteenth and seventeenth centuries, the monarchy seeking to unify and centralize the realm

---

two houses of parliament by over 100 members, who employed their language freely in the central legislature; and in local affairs the Germans, and other minorities too, enjoyed even greater national freedom. In parishes or districts where minorities constituted 20 per cent of the population, public documents were bilingual, i.e., they were published in the minority tongue as well as in the official language. Moreover, where a minority numbered more than two-thirds of the population, "all oral and written communications and documents in the State and public offices and courts made or issued to members of a minority are couched in the language of that minority." (Chmelař, J., *National Minorities in Central Europe* [Prague, 1937], p. 22.) The mass of minority children received their entire elementary education in their mother tongues, while numerous secondary, specialized, and continuation schools were likewise provided for minorities. The Germans even had their own university.

On the issue of the "national" and "un-national" state, Mr. Macartney is confused by his own distinctions or, perhaps, by his unfortunate resort to flippancy. (See p. 467.)

[5] The material on Scotland, Wales and Ireland is marshalled in Aucamp, A. J., *Bilingual Education and Nationalism, with Special Reference to South Africa* (Pretoria, 1926).

[6] See Winkler, Wilhelm, *Statistisches Handbuch der europäischen Nationalitäten* (Vienna, 1931), p. 1; Eisenmann, L., "Rights of Minorities in Central Europe," *International Conciliation*, September, 1926, pp. 320–321; Hayes, C. J. H., *Essays on Nationalism* (New York, 1926), pp. 4–5; *Encyclopaedia of the Social Sciences*, XI, 231 ff.; Macartney, *op. cit.*, pp. 4 ff.; Jaszi, Oscar, *The Dissolution of the Habsburg Monarchy* (Chicago, 1929), p. 26, n. 1.

endeavored to maintain religious uniformity. James I of England irately exclaimed at Hampton Court in 1604 that he would make the Puritans conform or "harry them out of the land." Louis XIV revoked the Edict of Nantes in 1685, depriving the Huguenots of civil rights as well as freedom of worship. But religious minorities could not be suppressed. Differences in language and historical traditions yielded to the absorptive powers of the majority, except on the periphery of the kingdom, but the Protestant revolutions threw wide open the floodgates of religious experimentation. The religious non-conformists were not illiterate peasants and mountaineers residing in remote provinces, but merchants and squires, even aristocrats, living in the midst of the majority. A protracted struggle ensued which culminated in the legalization of religious pluralism.

Thus the national state of the nineteenth century, as evolved in France and Great Britain, may be defined as a body politic embracing a territory, a government and a people distinguished by a common language, history, and culture. In France, linguistic and cultural uniformity was jealously guarded, every manifestation of nonconformity being viewed with suspicion as involving the danger of "a state within the state." The English were more tolerant of local differences, but even in England it was assumed that all members of the state shared the common and all-embracing English language and culture.

Both countries were relatively free of nationality conflicts during the nineteenth century—always excepting the special case of the Irish. In each country the theoretical unity of political allegiance with cultural uniformity approximated the actual state of affairs, because the overwhelming majority of the people had become culturally homogeneous. In France few national minorities remained articulate, while the practical tolerance of the English prevented local peculiarities in Wales and Scotland from hardening into minority conflicts. When, however, the ideal of the national state, especially in the form of linguistic and cultural uniformity, was espoused in nationally mixed areas, serious difficulties ensued.

2. MULTI-NATIONAL EAST-CENTRAL EUROPE PRIOR TO THE FIRST WORLD WAR

Eastern and southeastern Europe bristle with nationally mixed areas. The vast region stretching from the Baltic to the Aegean and from the German and Italian borders to that of the Soviets—a region we have referred to as east-central Europe—was, before the present war, the home of more than 100,000,000 people, one-fifth to one-quarter of them being members of minorities. The population of the Soviet Union is even more heterogeneous, nearly one-half of it consisting of non-Russians.

Unlike western Europe, where relative national homogeneity was achieved before the nineteenth century, the East, that is, eastern and east-central Europe, has nurtured differences to the present day. The reasons are manifold. Whereas migrations had ceased in the West at an early date, in the East they continued far into modern times, often in the form of deliberate colonization—the settlement of Germans in southern Russian and Hungary, for example—which repeatedly injected new racial, religious and linguistic elements. The borders of the eastern states, too, remained fluid long after France and England had achieved territorial stability, and each acquisition of territory—as in the case of dismembered Poland—brought masses of people differing nationally and culturally from the dominant state-building groups. Moreover, the influence of Rome, particularly that of the Roman Catholic Church, operated during the Middle Ages to slough off dissimilarities in the West, while in the East it only accentuated distinctive differences as it met and clashed with Byzantine culture and the Greek Church.

The unifying effect of royal power was potent in the West partly because the linguistic and cultural consciousness of the masses was as yet in a rudimentary stage in early modern times. Therefore effective resistance to the process of assimilation failed to develop. In the East, on the other hand, feudal and local particularism did not yield to political and administrative centralization until the nineteenth century, when nationalism was becoming a conscious force. What had been the privileges and prerogatives of local satraps in previous centuries was presumed to be in the nineteenth the birthright of the people, sanctioned by the national ideal and buttressed by the democratic right of self-determination.[7] As a result, royal efforts like those of the Russian Czars to promote national-cultural uniformity encountered passionate and effective opposition from organized nationalities.

Thus the vast area lying between the solid masses of Germans on the west and the Russians on the east remained ethnographically a patchwork. The territories occupied by various religious, linguistic and cultural groups assumed grotesque shapes, bearing no relation whatever to economic or strategic frontiers. Wherever two peoples met, they spilled over into each other's domain, forming national minorities which could not be united with their kinsmen by any conceivable boundary. Moreover, east-central Europe was dotted with national enclaves, far removed from their "homelands" and completely surrounded by "alien" majorities. Such a situation called for a novel approach to the national question, one which the rulers of the territory proved incapable of designing or effectuating.

During the nineteenth century, east-central Europe was divided among three great states—the Russian, Austro-Hungarian and Ottoman Empires—with a fourth, Hohenzollern Prussia, sharing to the extent of some four million Poles. Each constituted an economic unit capable of assuring its population relative prosperity, were it not for the fact that national antagonisms repeatedly threatened political security.

Czarist Russia

Czarist Russia pursued a policy of deliberate and ruthless suppression of its numerous national minorities. Pan-Slavism, which became rampant in government circles during the latter part of

[7] See Jaszi, *op. cit.*, pp. 31–32 ff.; Macartney, *op. cit.*, Chap. III.

the nineteenth century, repudiated Western ideals, pretending that the West was in a state of corruption and decay, Holy Russia alone being capable of rescuing civilization. In fact, however, only the *liberal* practices of the West were denounced,[8] whereas *the ideal of national uniformity,* though inapt for so heterogeneous a population, was favored and pursued with characteristic harshness. The publicist Katkov, a nationalist leader, demanded a unitary Russian national state with a common language and a common faith. "Everything which stands in our way," he declared, "we shall break down. For no one will we show any compassion."

Russification became the order of the day. In the Polish provinces, Polish officials were removed from office, Polish law courts and schools were abolished. Russian became the official language even for religious instruction. Uniate Catholics of the western provinces were forced to unite with the Russian Orthodox Church. Ukrainian books were banned. The autonomy of Finland was severely restricted. Expulsion and massacre were employed to destroy the Jews, Pobyedonostsev, the head of the Holy Synod of the Russian Established church and the high-priest of reaction, declaring cynically: "One-third will die out, one-third will leave the country, and one-third will be completely dissolved in the surrounding population." [9]

Russification and oppression could fashion only the façade of a Russian national state. Behind the false front, the nationalities clung to life, seething with hatred and resentment and offering stout resistance to all efforts to absorb them. With the courage of despair, Poles, Ukrainians, Jews, Finns and a host of others shielded their national heritage, while the bolder and more reckless spirits among them plotted the destruction of the hateful régime. A Russian national state could not be imposed upon a heterogeneous population. In the end, the disaffected nationalities

[8] See Pobyedonostsev, K. P., *Reflections of a Russian Statesman* (London, 1898).
[9] Dubnow, S. M., *History of the Jews in Russia and Poland* (Philadelphia, 1920), III, 10.

contributed materially to the success of the Revolution, which swept the Czarist coterie into oblivion.[10]

The Austro-Hungarian Empire

The Hapsburg rulers of Austria, representing dynastic rather than national interests, did not attempt to convert the Danubian monarchy into a national state. But until the middle of the nineteenth century the absolutist régime fought the national claims of the composite population as disruptive liberal-democratic tendencies. Once the Dual Monarchy of Austro-Hungary was established in 1867, and a constitutional régime was attained, the equality of the various nationalities was proclaimed in the Austrian part of the realm, the maintenance and cultivation of local languages being particularly authorized as an "inviolable right." [11] Indeed, constructive proposals were not lacking for the reconstruction of the Hapsburg realm into a federation of national-territorial units. Nothing, however, came of these plans. The royal court and bureaucracy proved unequal to so radical a transformation. The administration remained centralist to the end, granting concessions to some of the nationalities not so much for the purpose of harmonizing national differences as to play off one nationality against another. The Hapsburgs could not free themselves from the imperial maxim, *divide et impera*, to their own ultimate undoing and the destruction of their state.[12]

The Ottoman Empire

Ottoman Turkey was a Moslem state, in which religion, not language or nationality in the Western sense, was the primary

[10] See Fischl, A., *Der Panslawismus bis zum Weltkrieg* (Stuttgart, 1919); *The Cambridge History of Poland* (Cambridge, 1941), Chap. XVII; Kohn, Hans, *Nationalism in the Soviet Union* (New York, 1933), pp. 37–39.

[11] Autonomous Hungary was far less liberal, maintaining a Magyar national state with a unitary and centralized administration.

[12] See Jaszi, *op. cit., passim;* Renner, Karl, *Das Selbstbestimmungsrecht der Nationen* (Vienna, 1918), second and revised edition of *Der Kampf der Österreichischen Nationen um den Staat;* Bauer, Otto, *Die Nationalitätenfrage und die Sozialdemokratie* (Vienna, 1907: second edition, 1924). Macartney, *op. cit.,* pp. 140–152, contains a good summary of the Austrian problem.

consideration. Various religious groups were organized in *millets,* each enjoying a considerable amount of communal autonomy. The head of each group, the *Millet-Bashy,* was chosen by his community and confirmed by the Sultan. His authority centered in religious and scholastic affairs, but he exercised some civil functions as well. He maintained registers of births, marriages, wills and deaths, established and supervised courts to adjudicate differences among his co-religionists, especially in matters affecting personal status and family relations, and raised taxes for communal purposes.

Had the *millet* system been susceptible of modernization in line with Western ideas of nationality, it might have afforded a means of solving the national question. But the religious state could not recognize the equality of non-Moslems. The westernized Young Turks, who seized power in 1908, were willing to grant equality to Christians and Jews, but they became obsessed with the Western ideal of the national state and succumbed to the temptation of Ottomanizing national minorities.[13]

The resistance of the nationalities, especially in the Turkish part of the Balkans, hampered the Young Turks in their efforts to modernize the State, and the First World War added fresh strains and conflicts. As in the case of Czarist Russia and Austria-Hungary, the inability to harmonize the interests of the various nationalities contributed to the disintegration and partition of the country.

Hohenzollern Prussia As an Object Lesson

The failure of enforced uniformity where a fully conscious national minority persists: Prussia was the least composite of the states which ruled heterogeneous east-central Europe. Compared with the Ottoman Empire, Russia, and Austria-Hungary, it was a homogeneous state, hardly more than ten per cent of its population consisting of non-Germans. One would expect that little diffi-

[13] See Mears, E. G. (ed.), *Modern Turkey* (New York, 1924), pp. 98–99, 121–123, 419–420, n. 502–503; Toynbee, A. J., and Kirkwood, K. P., *Turkey* (New York, 1927), pp. 27–29.

culty would be encountered in fashioning a national state after the Western model. Yet even there bitter strife was the price of enforced uniformity. Prussia offers the clearest evidence that a unitary national state is impossible, where even a relatively small but fully conscious national minority is determined to preserve its individuality. It will be instructive to examine the case of Prussia at some length.

Until the beginning of the nineteenth century, national sentiment had little if any effect upon the policy of the Prussian State. Territories were annexed in the partitions of Poland during the latter part of the eighteenth century for various political, strategic and economic reasons, but in no case was the purpose the extension of the domain of "Germanism." The masses of Poles who became Prussian subjects as a result of the partitions were viewed as a problem, but exclusively in the sense of doubtful loyalty to their new masters.

In the eighteenth century, Prussian officials cared little about Polish nationality, their sole concern being the allegiance and loyalty of the rebellious Polish nobility and higher clergy. The attempt of Frederick the Great to "colonize" the Polish areas had as its objective the creation of a stronghold of royal power through the fostering of an industrious, contented, dependable, and economically capable class of farmers and artisans. In this manner he and his immediate successors hoped to break the power of the Polish upper classes and minimize the danger of rebellion.

The explosive effects of French Revolutionary ideas and the startling victories of Napoleon jolted the Prussian bureaucracy into a realization of the true character of the Polish problem. The rout at Jena in 1806, and the humiliation suffered at the hands of the French, lashed the Prussians into national consciousness, while the readiness with which the Poles yielded to the blandishments of Napoleon revealed to Prussian officialdom for the first time that they were confronted by a national problem in the recently annexed Polish provinces. From that moment until the days of Bismarck, the Prussian Government, torn by divided counsels, vacillated between the policies of Germanization and conciliation.

Encouraged by the English and prompted by the liberal views of Baron Stein and Chancellor Hardenberg, the attempt was made at the time of the Congress of Vienna to respect the national individuality of the Poles. On the other hand, the Polish rising against the Russian Czar in 1830–1831 caused uneasiness at the Prussian Court, too, and resulted in a vigorous turn toward Germanization. For a time limitations were placed upon the Polish language, institutions, and customs which hindered the close union of the Polish districts with the Prussian State. The 1840's saw another effort at conciliation, especially in the matter of language rights in the Polish schools.

The decisive turning point in German-Polish relations was marked by the national upheavals of 1848. Not only had German nationalism come of age, fully conscious of its desire for political and cultural unity, but the very nature and function of the Prussian State were profoundly affected. Until 1848, Poles could entertain the hope of achieving national autonomy within a federal Prussia, composed of Germans, Poles, Lithuanians, Masurians and Wallonians. After 1848, however, the Prussian State and its dynasty became identified with the German national movement, assuming leadership in the cause of German unification, and espousing the "mission" of promoting Germanism on the eastern borders.

The year 1848 disclosed a German national movement in the Polish provinces, hardly less conscious and zealous than that of the Poles. Two national movements, the German and the Polish, had clashed and were soon to lock in combat for the mastery of the Prussian eastern provinces. As the representative of the German nationality, the Prussian State made the cause of Germanism its own, especially in the Polish regions. Polish nationalism must be combated, not only to root out disloyalty but also to extend the sphere of German *Kultur*. Prussia's "destiny" was to build a *German national state*.[14]

The stupendous task of unifying the German states of central Europe absorbed Prussia's energies for two decades after 1848, precluding vigorous anti-Polish measures. However, while the German-Polish national struggle remained generally quiescent during this period, administrative regulations gradually but persistently restricted the use of the Polish language in official circles of the borderlands and otherwise favored the German element at the expense of the Poles. The ideal of a German national state was crystalized during this period, especially in the mind of Bismarck, who was ready to strike with his accustomed vigor, the moment German unity was an accomplished fact.

The issue was squarely joined with the proclamation of the German Empire. At one of the first sessions of the Reichstag in 1871, the leaders of the Poles voiced their national protest against the new order, which had converted them from Prussian subjects enjoying the status of a nationality into unassimilated members of the new German national state. Bismarck's reply to this challenge was the *Kulturkampf*.

The *Kulturkampf* of the 1870's is generally described as a struggle between Bismarck and the Catholic Church. Without minimizing this aspect of the conflict, it may be understood that the danger of Polish nationalism was paramount in Bismarck's mind and that he then regarded Polish and "Romish-clerical" interests as concurrent. In his memoirs, he states categorically: "The beginning of the *Kulturkampf* was decided for me preponderantly by its Polish side."[15] The measures taken in the

[14] Throughout the nineteenth century and until the First World War, Prussian and, later, German foreign policy was greatly influenced by the Polish question. We cannot stop here to consider this matter, but it should be noted that after 1848 the foreign and domestic compulsives of Prussia's anti-Polish policies coalesced.

[15] *Bismarck the Man and the Statesman* (New York, 1899), II, 139. See also pp. 137, 140–148.

It may well be that Bismarck was thus attempting to minimize the non-Polish phase of the *Kulturkampf* which had to be abandoned. Yet anti-Polish legislation was the cornerstone of the *Kulturkampf* in Prussia.

Polish districts warrant the conclusion that the desire to stifle Polish nationalist agitation and guard the German element in the "East" against the inroads of Polonism was at least a major objective.

In the Polish districts of Prussia, the *Kulturkampf* was a struggle for Germanization. The state assumed full control over the schools, removing all clerical (Polish) influence in the choice of teachers and the supervising of instruction. German was made the medium of instruction in all schools, save for the teaching of religion and singing, and then only when no other language was understood. The administration, the police, and the law courts were Germanized, documents in Polish and the use of that language in the witness box being permitted only "by the express will of the sovereign." Numerous place-names were Germanized, and Polish recruits were distributed among German regiments.

When Bismarck made his peace with the Catholic Church, only the confessional aspect of the conflict was abandoned, the national and economic drive against the Polish nationality continuing with even greater vigor. In the 1880's, a regulation barred the employment of teachers of Polish nationality in Polish districts, and another prohibited even the private teaching of Polish. About 30,000 non-naturalized Poles and Jews were expelled from the eastern provinces. And in 1886, a Colonization Commission was established by law, with a preliminary appropriation of 100,000,-000 marks, for the express purpose of purchasing Polish estates and settling upon them German colonists—"Germans, but with German wives, not Polish ones," as Bismarck put it.

The retirement of Bismarck in 1890, with its consequent readjustments in domestic and foreign policies, resulted in a last effort at conciliation. But it was short-lived. The exuberant nationalism of Emperor William II, and of German public opinion too, could not tolerate the continued existence of an "alien" nationality in its midst. For them national unity had become identified with the German national state, which in turn was presumed to require complete national-cultural uniformity.

Moreover, a generation of bitter strife had taught the Germans resident in the Polish regions to think only in terms of domination and subjection. Convinced that their own security depended on the suppression of Polish nationality, extremist elements organized in 1894 with the aid of Bismarck—unrelenting on the Polish question even in his retirement—what later came to be known as the "Association for Defense of the Eastern Marches," or *Ostmarkenverein.* These chauvinists demanded the extermination of Polonism, and their agitation helped seal the fate of the Polish borderlands. Either the Polish nationality would cease to exist in those areas or the Reich would be disrupted.

The foreshadowing of Hitlerism: The policy of the national state, pursued in a region of mixed nationality, led inexorably to catastrophe. For the Prussian leaders, the issue narrowed into "a fight for German nationality," an issue which permitted of no compromise. Said Prince von Bülow, German Chancellor from 1900 to 1909:

> Weak and incapable nations must look on while foreign nationalities gain in number and importance within the borders of their State.
> There is no third course. In the struggle between nationalities one nation is the hammer and the other the anvil; one is the victor and the other the vanquished. If it were possible in this world to separate nationalities definitely and clearly by means of frontier posts and boundary stones, as is done for States, then the world's history and politics . . . would be relieved of their most difficult task. But State boundaries do not separate nationalities. If it were possible henceforward for members of different nationalities, with different languages and customs, and an intellectual life of a different kind, to live side by side in one and the same State, without succumbing to the temptation of each trying to force his own nationality on the other, things on earth would look a good deal more peaceful. But it is a law of life and development in history, that where two national civilizations meet they fight for ascendancy.[16]

This is clear and to the point. Since the struggle for mastery was

---

[16] Von Bülow, Prince Bernhard, *Imperial Germany* (New York, 1914), pp. 290–291.

"a law of life," and since the outcome must be either victory or subjection, only a weak nation would permit the Poles to grow in number and importance within the borders of the German State. And Prussian *Junkertum* was anything but weak. A century-old intermittent policy of Germanization had achieved complete clarity of objective, namely, *ausrotten,* extermination of Polish nationality. Therefore, in 1901 it was decreed that even the religious instruction of Polish children should be given in German. When a general school strike ensued, children were beaten, and parents fined and jailed, in utter disregard of protests throughout Europe. Similarly, in 1908 the Dispossession Act was passed providing for the compulsory expropriation of Polish estates in order to facilitate the colonization of Germans.[17]

Von Bülow says: "The Dispossession Bill was the logical conclusion of the policy of colonisation begun in 1886 . . ."[18] So it was. And one might add that the policy of colonization was a logical development of the practice of Germanization, the latter in turn the "logical conclusion" drawn from the premise that "members of different nationalities, with different languages and customs," could not live side by side in one state without resorting to the compulsory denationalization of the weaker groups.

Prince von Bülow declared before the Prussian Diet in 1902 that ". . . the Prussian state is a German state . . . and its historical mission is to sustain and foster the development of the German spirit."[19] This was the root evil, namely the attempt to impose a German national state upon a mixed population. When combined with the ideal of cultural uniformity, oppression and strife became

---

[17] Summaries and discussions of Prussian-Polish relations will be found in Brackmann, A. (ed.), *Germany and Poland in Their Historical Relations* (Berlin, 1934); *The Cambridge History of Poland, op. cit.,* pp. 344-364, 409-431; Jomard, L., *Le Conflit National et L'école en Pologne Prussienne* (Dijon, 1921); Perdelwitz, R., *Die Posener Polen von 1815-1914* (Schneidemühl, 1936); Guttzeit, J., *Geschichte der deutschen Polen-Entrechtung* (Danzig, 1927); Great Britain, Foreign Office Historical Section, Peace Handbooks, Vol. VIII, No. 45, *Prussian Poland* (London, 1920).

[18] Von Bülow, *op. cit.,* p. 263.

[19] Quoted in Macartney, *op. cit.,* p. 127.

inevitable. In the culturally uniform national state minorities are "aliens," even though—like the Poles of Prussia—they and their ancestors have inhabited the region for centuries. Such "aliens" must be denationalized and eliminated as national minorities at all costs. Through the agency of the school and the administration many might be Germanized and absorbed. The colonization of Germans among the minority would serve to hasten the process of Germanization. As for the bitter-enders, the intrenched and recalcitrant elements who resisted denationalization, the state must stand ready to employ its resources, even to resort to compulsory expropriation, to pry them loose and destroy them.

Equally "logical" was the resistance of the Prussian Poles, for whom the issue was survival or extinction as a national community. They rallied around their national institutions—cultural, religious, and economic—giving no quarter as they received none. The result was an irreparable estrangement between Germans and Poles, so deep and so pervasive as to render understanding and cooperation difficult if not impossible.

When military defeat in the First World War destroyed German might and reversed the majority-minority relationship between Germans and Poles, the latter fell heir to the same ideal—the national state—and substantially the same methods of achieving their objective, until a resurgence of German strength under Hitler again placed the Poles at the mercy of their "hereditary" enemies. This time the Germans arrived at a "logical conclusion" one step beyond that of Bülow, namely, *ausrotten,* or the extermination of the Poles, the human beings, that is, along with Polonism, their nationality.

The savagery of Nazism does not derive exclusively from the distorted mind of a Hitler or a Goebbels. The deliberate and coldblooded manner in which several millions of Jews, Poles, Russians and others have been done to death in Nazi extermination camps, like Maidanek, near Lublin,[20] must not be ascribed solely to the

---

[20] See, for example, Lawrence, W. H., "Nazi Mass Killing Laid Bare in Camp," *The New York Times,* August 30, 1944.

frenzy of hooligans, maddened by the prospect of defeat. The roots of that depravity lie deeply imbedded in the teachings of respectable *Junkers* like Bismarck and von Bülow. It stems from the belief that "members of different nationalities, with different languages and customs," cannot possibly live side by side in one and the same state; that when fate has cast two peoples upon the same territory, one must inevitably be "the hammer and the other the anvil"; that the suppression of the language and culture of the weaker nationality is a legitimate state policy: in a word, that the relentless pursuit of national-cultural uniformity is a law of historical development.

Hitlerism is the policy of Prussianization carried to its most ruthless and implacable extreme. Given a majority that is resolved to tolerate no inroads upon its exclusive and monolithic national state, a national minority becomes a contradiction in terms. We must reiterate that those individuals or groups who betray national characteristics in language, culture, customs and habits, in ideals and aspirations which are at variance with those of the dominant people, are "aliens" to be forcibly absorbed. If, however, such a minority is conscious of its national individuality and determined to preserve it, the technique of the "hammer"—to revert again to Bülow's phrase—must inevitably come into play. The policy of *"ausrotten,"* or extermination of dissident national characteristics, is sanctioned as "a law of life." The "civilized" methods of a Bismarck or a Bülow are legal suppression, expropriation and expulsion. A Hitler resorts to the more rapid and thorough process of the gas chamber or the gallows.

The object lesson: Intolerance and brutality are not exclusively German traits. The Poles, to cite but one example, practiced the "cold pogrom" during recent years, whereby minorities were frozen out of economic life and doomed to slow starvation. The defeat of Nazism may result in the indiscriminate massacre of Germans by Poles and others unless checked by the United Nations. But to check massacre is not enough. It is imperative to snap the cycle of national oppression and terror by a frank recognition that in nationally mixed areas the culturally uniform national state, dominated by one nationality, one language and one culture, is as impossible of attainment as it is unjust. We must invoke the democratic principles of live and let live, of tolerance, of respect for differences, of equality of groups as well as of individuals. Only the *multi-national state* can honor such principles and render possible the solution of the problem of nationalities and national minorities in east-central Europe.

PART TWO

The Evolution of Successful Multi-National States

Americans who will condemn the Prussian method of dealing with a minority might still regard the *multi-national state* with circumspection if not skepticism. The phrase has a novel ring, and some people hesitate to experiment with new institutions and techniques. Often the pronouncement that a plan "has never been tried" in the past serves as the conclusive reason for refusing to test its efficacy for the future. But surely none of us believes that only the agencies which have proved their ineffectiveness hold the key to the solution of troublesome problems.

We must also resist the temptation to equate nationalism with its psychopathic aberrations or to dismiss as academic idealism all proposals for multi-national collaboration. The fact is that many peoples have made the attempt to respect one another's national individuality, and several have succeeded in evolving workable multi-national régimes. This writer is engaged in a comprehensive study of multi-national states, but for the present purposes it will suffice to outline briefly three experiments in national collaboration.

We have selected Switzerland, South Africa and the Soviet Union for several reasons. The three countries represent a variety of political and social conditions: Switzerland is a small, independent community in the heart of Europe; the Union of South Africa is a British Dominion situated on the periphery of Western civilization; the Soviet Union has risen within one generation from the chaos of stupendous upheavals and civil strife to the eminence of a Great Power. The Swiss people comprise three nationalities—German, French and Italian—whose languages and cultures correspond closely to those of three powerful states on the very frontiers of the country. Power and control in South Africa are shared by Britishers who have been accustomed to imperial dominion and Boers whom they long regarded with contempt. The Soviet Union is a conglomeration of racial, religious and linguistic groups ranging from highly civilized and culturally mature nationalities to nomadic tribesmen who have barely emerged from the primitive. Switzerland and South Africa maintain capitalistic economies, while the Soviet Union proscribes private capitalism as a crime.

Yet, differing widely as the three states do, they have one thing in common: each is heterogeneous in population; that is, each consists of two or more peoples who differ in language, usages and historical traditions. And it is most significant that, all alike, they *have abandoned the national state,* in which one people or its culture predominates. Each has recognized that national-cultural uniformity cannot and should not be imposed on a mixed population. *Each has evolved a multi-national state.*

The examples selected have the further merit of presenting three forms or variants of the multi-national state. Switzerland, South Africa and the Soviet Union have all recognized and sanctioned cultural differences, but each has adapted the broad principle of plural nationalism to its peculiar needs. The Swiss have coordinated linguistic and cultural freedom with democratic decentralization; the South Africans have made provision for bilingualism, in an essentially unitary state; and the Soviet authorities have contrived to harmonize nationality rights with the precept and practice of communism. Be it noted, then, that the multi-national state is neither a rigid formula nor a Procrustean remedy. It is inflexible only in requiring that the principles of national freedom and equality be honored. Beyond that, the multi-national state can assume a variety of shapes to conform with the institutions and needs of particular areas.

In describing the multi-national state as functioning respectively in Switzerland, South Africa and the Soviet Union, emphasis will be placed on its historical evolution and on the conditions which made it indispensable. We shall see that the difficulties encountered in South Africa, for example, and the blunders committed, resembled in many instances the contemporary problems of east-central Europe. Particular emphasis will be placed on the development and functioning of the multi-national state in the Soviet Union, not only for its intrinsic importance, but even more because of its relevance to east-central Europe. In national geography, historical experience, and traditions of government, a large part of east-central Europe resembles the Soviet lands to a marked degree. The Baltic and most of the western Slavic areas were for many years ruled by the Russians, while the Balkans yielded to their influence. Therefore, the solution of the nationalities question evolved by the Soviets should be studied with the utmost care, for it may well serve as the model for reconstruction in a region freed from the Nazi yoke by the triumphant arms of the Soviet Union.

Our primary purpose in the following chapters is to show that the multi-national state is far less novel than some of us have supposed; that it is not the artificial concoction of "closet philosophers" but a tried and tested method of government; that we are proposing for east-central Europe, not a visionary ideal fit for the millennium, but a form of political and social organization evolved by practical men to meet the exigencies of common living.

CHAPTER IV

NATIONAL FEDERALISM IN SWITZERLAND

Switzerland is the classic example of the multi-national state. Divided by language, religion and culture, its people have lived in reasonable harmony for more than a hundred years, thus providing incontrovertible proof that linguistic and cultural diversity need raise no insuperable barriers to political unity. The country has remained a political nation, with three major linguistic and cultural communities or nationalities.

1. A COMPOSITE PEOPLE

The Swiss State is a confederation of twenty-two cantons, each enjoying broad powers of local self-government. Its population of approximately four and a quarter millions is further subdivided by language and religion. The census of 1930 showed a distribution of the population according to mother-tongue as follows:

	Per Cent
German-speaking	71.9
French-speaking	20.4
Italian-speaking	6.0
Romansch-speaking	1.1
Others	0.6
	100.0

Within fourteen of the twenty-two cantons German is spoken by over 90 per cent of the people; one canton is overwhelmingly Italian in speech, and three are French. The four remaining cantons are linguistically mixed, as the following table [1] reveals:

[1] Rappard, William E., *The Government of Switzerland* (New York, 1936), p. 9.

Canton	German Speaking (per cent)	French Speaking (per cent)	Italian Speaking (per cent)	Romansch Speaking (per cent)	Others (per cent)
Bern	83.5	15.4	0.8	0.1	0.2
Fribourg	32.1	66.7	0.8	—	0.4
Grisons	53.7	0.5	14.0	30.9	0.9
Valais	32.5	64.9	2.4	—	0.2

The people are further divided by "confessional" differences, 57.3 per cent being Protestant and 41 per cent Catholic. However, the religious and linguistic groupings do not coincide: Protestants are a majority in twelve cantons of which nine are German-speaking and three French; while the Catholics predominate in ten cantons—seven German-speaking, two French, and one Italian.

In accord with modern ideals, Switzerland guarantees religious liberty to all its inhabitants. Moreover, unlike most Western states, provision is made also for linguistic and cultural differences. Thus German, French and Italian are all recognized as official languages in relations with the central government.[2] The individual cantons, too, where the population is sufficiently composite, have assured equality of language: Bern, Fribourg and Valais regard German and French as official, and in the Grisons, German, Italian and Romansch enjoy a similar status.[3]

2. EMERGENCE OF NATIONAL FEDERALISM

It would be futile to seek metaphysical explanations for the national sanity of the Swiss people. Nor will it do to dismiss the matter as a unique and exceptional phenomenon that "goes back to immemorial times." The fact is that the Swiss worked out their nationality problem during the nineteenth century, when com-

[2] In 1938, Romansch, too, was adopted as a national language. See Zurcher, A. J., "The Political System of Switzerland," in Shotwell, James T. (ed.), *Governments of Continental Europe* (New York, 1940), p. 981, n. 1.

[3] Rappard, *op. cit.*, pp. 9–11. See also Brooks, R. C., *Civic Training in Switzerland* (Chicago, 1930), p. 303; and the Constitution of the Canton of Bern, Articles 17 and 59, in Rappard, W. E., *et al.* (eds.), *Source Book on European Governments* (New York, 1937), pp. I:59, 67.

munity of language and culture, if not strait-laced uniformity, was widely held to be indispensable to political unity.

Until the end of the eighteenth century, the Swiss Confederation was a Germanic country, with German as the only official language of government and courts of law. Some of the aristocratic cantons ruled over cultural minorities in conquered provinces; and while there appears to be no evidence that such minorities suffered "to any great extent specifically because of their language,"[4] instances of intolerance are not lacking. For example, during the latter part of the sixteenth century, the public sale of commodities in the French language was subject to a fine in Fribourg, where the Germanic rulers also showed official displeasure with the "barbarous and ear-annoying" French prayers and sermons.

It was the democratic influence of the French Revolution which liberated and assured equality to the French- and Italian-speaking districts, thereby converting Switzerland from a Germanic into a multi-national country. Napoleon, too, despite his penchant for centralization, recognized the unique character of the Swiss population. In a letter addressed to the representatives of the Swiss Cantons whom he had summoned to Paris in 1802, he declared: "Nature has predestined you to become a federal state. No wise man can wish to conquer nature." Moreover, with extraordinary political insight, he grasped the cardinal principle that Swiss federalism must be national as well as territorial. He, therefore, directed that "a federal organization be set up, in which every canton will enjoy a scheme of government adapted to its language, its religion, its customs, its interests and its opinions."[5]

The reaction which set in after the fall of Napoleon produced another attempt to restore the dominant position of the German majority by declaring their tongue the only official language in the country. But it proved unavailing. The reassertion of the liberal forces in the 1830's and 1840's repudiated national intolerance

---
[4] Brooks, *op. cit.*, p. 296.
[5] See Rappard, *et al., Source Book on European Governments, op. cit.,* pp. I:7-8.

as a form of privilege. Thus the constitutions of the cantons of Bern (1831), Fribourg (1831) and Valais (1844) either granted equality to German and French as official languages or otherwise guaranteed the rights of the linguistic minorities.[6]

3. EQUALITY IN LAW AND IN FACT

When the Swiss Federal Constitution of 1848 was adopted, language was no longer an issue; it was recognized as a symbol of nationality and respected. The draft of the Constitution was presented jointly by a German- and a French-speaking member, chosen to act as *rapporteurs,* and an article was included, reading:

> The three principal languages spoken in Switzerland, German, French and Italian, are national languages of the Confederation.

This ideal of linguistic and national-cultural equality has remained the cornerstone of the Swiss multi-national state to this day. The present Constitution, adopted in 1874, incorporated as Article 116 the language provision quoted above, and its requirements have been fulfilled beyond the letter of the law. In all official relations with the federal authorities, the Swiss have the right to employ any one of the national languages, although in practice, the small Italian-speaking minority usually employs French in the federal parliament. Federal laws are published in all three languages, as are also the financial and administrative accounts, the messages of the federal executive to parliament, reports of legislative committees and parliamentary debates.

The Constitution (Article 107) provides further that, in electing the members of the federal judiciary, parliament "shall see to it that the three national languages are represented therein," while custom affords further guarantees of national equality. An unwritten law requires that no more than five of the seven members of the Federal Council or executive be chosen from German-

---

[6] Brooks, *op. cit.,* p. 297, n. 7.

speaking cantons. French-speaking Vaud is always represented on the Federal Council and, in addition, a citizen of another French-speaking canton, or of Italian-speaking Ticino, is chosen. Parliamentary committees, in reporting on important questions, name two *rapporteurs,* one German- and one French-speaking. In the civil service, too, special significance is attached to a knowledge of more than one language. Thus candidates for middle and superior positions in the postal administration and customs service must be bi-lingual, and even in the railway services linguistic attainments are recognized.[7]

4. LANGUAGE, CULTURE AND NATIONALITY

Proficiency in foreign languages is, of course, an asset in the civil service of many European states. It should be observed, however, that in Switzerland language is more than a medium of communication, more than a tool for transacting business or transmitting ideas. The German-speaking Swiss do not regard French or Italian as "foreign" languages, but as the "second" or "third" national language, because the three official tongues are inseparable from Swiss local life and character. The mother tongue is the nexus of a pattern of traditions, customs and loyalties which together lend color and individuality to a group and evoke a sense of kinship. Language is the mark of a people, the symbol of a nationality.

Yet there is political unity despite linguistic and cultural diversity. Boyd Winchester, United States Minister at Bern during the latter part of the nineteenth century, recognized this when he wrote: ". . . an organized nation, and at the same time the

[7] See Rappard, W. E., *The Government of Switzerland, op. cit.,* pp. 6–9, 61, 77–78, 151–152; Brooks, *op. cit.,* pp. 295–298; Friedrich, C. J., and Cole, T., *Responsible Bureaucracy: A Study of the Swiss Civil Services* (Cambridge, 1932), pp. 49–50; Zurcher, *op. cit.,* pp. 992–993.

The Swiss Constitution is reprinted in full in Rappard, *et al., Source Book on European Governments, op. cit.,* pp. I:19–54. Perhaps the best work on linguistic and cultural pluralism in Switzerland is Weilenmann, H., *Die vielsprachige Schweiz* (Basel, 1925).

peoples of the particular Cantons also possessing organic unity; a Swiss nation, and yet a Bernese and Genevese people." [8]

This unity in diversity is all the more remarkable when we note that Switzerland is not an isolated settlement in a remote part of the world. Situated in the very heart of Europe, its national languages coincide with the speech of three powerful neighboring peoples. What is more, each of the three major linguistic communities of Switzerland maintains cultural relations with kinsmen in Germany, France or Italy. The pull of disunity would, therefore, appear to be irresistible. Yet the Swiss are intensely devoted to their common fatherland, and have learned to distinguish sharply between "cultural affinities and essential political loyalties." [9] The nationalities that compose the Swiss State have shared in the literary and spiritual treasures of their prototypes across the borders, but their determination to preserve their unique federation remains unshaken.

5. PILLARS OF THE MULTI-NATIONAL STATE

In the light of the bitter national conflicts elsewhere in Europe, the Swiss achievement appears to many an outsider as a political miracle. The people immediately concerned, however, regard it as a normal requirement of democratic living. What then are the factors which have contributed to the successful functioning of this multi-national state?

Democracy

Loyalty to the democratic ideal is a primary cause of the healthy state of Swiss nationalism. Autocratic governments care little about human rights or the self-expression of the individual. Democracy, however, prizing liberty and equality, must come to grips with the problems of cultural freedom, especially in areas where the population is composite and uniformity of language or culture therefore unattainable. The Swiss recognized in good

[8] *The Swiss Republic* (Philadelphia, 1891), p. 42.
[9] Brooks, *op. cit.*, p. 300. See also pp. 186–187.

time that democracy as a form of government or a way of life could not become a reality, unless each people were permitted to determine its own modes of living; that freedom of expression would be a mockery, if persons were not free to employ the only language in which they could express themselves; [10] that self-determination would ring hollow, if men and women were compelled to conform to standards not of their own choosing. In a word, the Swiss have realized that ". . . a three-language people must form a three-language state in which no nationality shall be considered more than the others." [11]

Cultural Federalism

Democratic government alone would be no guarantee against cultural discrimination, for the impersonal majority, no less than the individual autocrat, is capable of tyrannizing over weak nationalities. This the proponent of democracy often overlooks, for his thinking on the subject of nationalism is apt to be paradoxical. Disturbed by the gross evils of chauvinism, he presumes as a theoretical construction that cosmopolitanism can supplant national loyalties. In fact, however, he frequently falls victim to a subtle form of cultural imperialism. Within his own country, he craves uniformity of language and culture, frowning upon "hyphenates," and sanctioning only the customs and mores of the dominant majority. Even with respect to international comity, his nebulous cosmopolitanism is often dissipated by the strong currents of national patriotism. Despite his better judgment, he cannot help feeling that, if the world were to achieve a single language and culture, should not his own have priority?

[10] Thomas G. Masaryk, who had a profound understanding of the requirements of democracy in multi-national regions, expressed this idea in the following words: "As soon as one admits the rights of the human person, the individual, one admits also his right to his own language (mother tongue); that is a matter of course in uninational states, but in multinational states the official recognition of languages is a matter of national contest and the right to language must be recognized and codified." Masaryk, T. G., *The New Europe: The Slav Standpoint* (London, 1918), p. 21.

[11] H. Weilenmann, quoted in Brooks, *op. cit.,* p. 298.

The ideal of the Swiss for human brotherhood, both international and intranational, appears to be federation rather than cosmopolitanism. Speaking in another connection, M. Calonder, then President of the Swiss Confederation, said:

> National tradition is and remains the most active source of creative power. Our ideal for humanity is federative, not cosmopolitan. And as the international commonwealth of the future will never imply the abandonment of national tradition by the different peoples, it will strengthen and deepen, rather than weaken, the citizen's feeling of duty towards his own State.[12]

The Swiss seem to understand that, while nationalism has unquestionably promoted discord, the solution lies not in visionary hopes for the obliteration of national peculiarities and loyalties, but in tolerance, understanding and mutual respect. They have successfully built and maintained a union of nationalities, because they have striven to federate, while preserving the component peoples. Thus they have been spared the strife which inevitably results when attempts are made to force a heterogeneous population into a common mould.

Decentralization

Swiss federalism rests solidly on the decentralization of government functions and on respect for local sentiment. Cantonal and communal institutions are zealously guarded by the population.

"Our institutions are truly free and popular," said a pamphlet published in 1871, "only in so far as our Communes are free; we move from low to high, the Commune is the centre of our life, and there can be no true development of liberty, except so far as it proceeds from the Communes, from the centre to the circling lines, from the simple to the composite." [13]

The Swiss people do not wish to reduce their communes or cantons

---

[12] Quoted in Bonjour, F., *Real Democracy in Operation: The Example of Switzerland* (New York, 1920), p. 209.
[13] Quoted in Winchester, *op. cit.*, p. 176.

to a "uniform level." Clinging to their ancient usages, local and cantonal communities preserve the character of nationalities.

A centralized government might have operated to cut away differences and fashion a common standard of conduct. But federalism has left to the cantons some of the most essential functions of government—law and order, education and direct taxation. The individual cantons have, therefore, retained a "national character," and "the result of holding different peoples together without transforming them into one nationality has been attained only by allowing each people free course in its local and inner life." [14]

To be sure, the development of industry and commerce has led to a strengthening of the central government. But its sphere of activity has been mainly economic and social. It has occupied itself with railroads, factory legislation, insurance, contracts, sanitary precautions. Educational and cultural affairs remain predominantly the province of the local bodies.

Thus democracy, cultural federalism and decentralization have enabled the linguistic and cultural communities of Switzerland to enjoy the advantages of economic unity, without trespassing upon the unique character or cultural heritage of any group. A less tolerant constitution, or the pursuit of a fugitive uniformity, would unquestionably have resulted in internal national strife and external irredentist pressures. It is the multi-national state which has rendered possible both political unity and cultural freedom.

[14] *Ibid.*, p. 144.

CHAPTER V

Bilingualism in South Africa

At the very time when Switzerland was amicably adjusting its nationality problems, South Africa was seething with resentments, which finally culminated in bitter warfare. Briton and Boer clashed repeatedly during the nineteenth century, over the limits of imperial control. For the Boer, the stakes were the vast expanse of a subcontinent—virgin soil which beckoned beyond a limitless horizon—and the profusion of native labor. For the Briton, it was strategic considerations—the vital route to India—dominion, and, in later years, gold and diamonds, which were paramount. At all times, national irritations contributed to prevent understanding and cooperation.

It would be an oversimplification and a distortion to interpret all South African history in the light of the rivalry between Briton and Boer. Yet this factor must not be minimized. For in South Africa, as a keen interpreter has aptly remarked, "every problem, before it could reach the plane of ethical or economic principles, must run the gantlet of keen racial feeling and social prejudice." [1] Two peoples, speaking distinct languages and accustomed to radically different modes of life, would in any event encounter difficulties. When, in addition, the British as newcomers and conquerors presumed to a position of mastery, dissension was unavoidable. Moreover, given a Boer population of pioneers imbued with the spirit of individual freedom and self-help, and impatient of restraint, governmental controls, no matter how necessary or logical or even benevolent they might appear to the ruling authorities, were certain to provoke resistance. In such circumstances the

[1] De Kiewiet, C. W., *A History of South Africa, Social and Economic* (Oxford, 1941), p. 152.

assertion of authority could not but exacerbate feelings which must inevitably lead to open conflict.

No attempt will be made in this brief survey to trace even the bare essentials of South African history; nor shall we probe into the native problems [2] or all the ramifications of British-Boer antagonism. Our purpose is the more modest one of examining the linguistic and cultural difficulties of the mixed population of ruling whites. Above all, we shall be concerned with the attempts made to cope with these problems, including, of course, the final solution of bilingualism which may be viewed as a species of bi-nationalism.

1. THE BEGINNINGS OF DIVERSITY

For a century and a half, the white population of South Africa, that is of the Cape of Good Hope, had been Dutch in language and national sentiment. Occupied by the Dutch in 1652 and settled mainly by Hollanders, the Cape whites had remained culturally homogeneous until the arrival of the English. Towards the end of the seventeenth century, French Protestant refugees were allowed to settle, but they were interspersed among the Dutch, the use of their language was restricted, and Dutch ministers and teachers were provided to hasten their assimilation. Although constituting one-sixth of the white population, they were quickly merged in the majority. An appreciable number of Germans arrived during the eighteenth century, most of them Westphalians who were somewhat akin to the Dutch and were easily absorbed.[3]

The British seized Cape Colony during the wars of the French

---

[2] Our aim here is to show how two peoples enjoying political and social equality have learned to respect each other's national-cultural individuality through the medium of the multi-national state. The fundamental problems of the "natives" in South Africa are of a colonial nature, involving economic exploitation and political tutelage. The "native" question has, therefore, not been considered.

[3] Botha, C. G., *Social Life in the Cape Colony in the 18th Century* (Cape Town, 1926), pp. 8–9; Aucamp, A. J., *Bilingual Education and Nationalism with Special Reference to South Africa* (Pretoria, 1926), pp. 127, 130–131.

Revolution, securing it in full title after the fall of Napoleon. A British element was immediately introduced into the administration and the armed forces; but the civilian population, which was almost entirely Dutch, occasioned some uneasiness among their rulers. For example, in 1811 some of the leading Dutch inhabitants petitioned the Government to afford asylum to people from Holland, declaring innocently enough that refugees would find conditions, including "nation, religion, language, laws and customs, similar to ancient Holland." The Governor took occasion to inform the London authorities that the "greatest stress" was laid upon the fact that "everything remains Dutch." While the people were outwardly loyal, he felt that hopes entertained for a return to Dutch sovereignty must be dispelled. Security required "the cautious and progressive introduction of the same laws, the same principles, and the same institutions of the parent state."[4] These, of course, were to be English.

These views were shared by the Home Government, and during the following decade the authorities in London as well as Capetown devoted considerable attention to the enhancement of the British character of the colony. In 1820, about four thousand British colonists were aided in settling in South Africa. The primary objective was to relieve distress resulting from dislocations connected with the Industrial Revolution. But the desire to increase the British element was also clearly evident. In fact, a high official reminded the settlers of their "national character as Englishmen," from whom "superior conduct and knowledge" might be expected,[5] a presumption of national superiority as natural and unwarranted as that of numerous other "chosen" peoples.

At the same time, measures were taken to Anglicize the Dutch population, or Boers, as they were popularly called. British clergymen and teachers were sent to the colony to satisfy educational needs and particularly to spread a knowledge of the English lan-

[4] See *Records of the Cape Colony* (London, 1897–1905), VIII, 219–224, 363.
[5] Cory, G. E., *The Rise of South Africa* (London, 1913), II, 58. See also pp. 1–10 ff., 42; *Records of the Cape Colony, op. cit.*, IX, 182–186; X, 206–208, 242; XII, 210–211.

guage. These measures, though not popular, were not likely to arouse vigorous opposition, especially since ministers thus appointed were required to learn the Dutch language as well. Even the decision of the Governor to make proficiency in the English language a qualification for public office would, in all likelihood, have passed without open protest. But the authorities were determined not only to further English ideas and practices, but to discountenance the symptoms of Dutch nationality as well.

There was clearly an intention to have all schools conducted by English masters, in order to win the youth to the English language as well as to improve "the manners and morals of the people." Dutch law was held to be inadequate, especially for matters affecting trade and navigation, and the hope was entertained that the laws of the colony would gradually be assimilated to the "more liberal and enlightened maxims of British jurisprudence." The Dutch language and customs, in fact everything that underscored the old association with Holland, must go.

The British were perfectly clear both as to their objective and to the reason which rendered it necessary. Late in 1821, a high Capetown official wrote that the connection with Holland must be destroyed as rapidly as possible, if the Cape was to remain an integral part of the British Empire. The church, the administration, the law courts, education, all required a new orientation. Language, he thought, was the key to all further reforms. "Community of language," he said, "is the simplest and best security for intimate connection with distant possessions, and by the substitution of the English for the Dutch language in all official proceedings at the Cape, much of what is desired will be obtained." The ultimate objective was "the more rapid assimilation to the institutions and manners of Great Britain." [6]

Aside, then, from a natural and perhaps pardonable assumption that one's own speech, ideas and practices are preferable, the motivation of the British was security and not the "civilizing

---

[6] *Records of the Cape Colony, op. cit.,* XIV, 183–187. See also XIII, 186–187, 386–389, 402–403, 457.

mission" of racial superiority. This rendered possible a flexible policy, determined and vigorous, yet devoid of fantacism and allowing for compromise when necessary.

2. ANGLICIZATION AND ITS EFFECTS

In 1822, the British authorities, both in London and Capetown, were agreed that the time had arrived for the transformation of the Cape into an English-speaking colony. The Governor therefore issued a proclamation on July 5 of that year, informing the people that, since the way had been paved for the diffusion of the English language through the appointment of clergymen of the Scottish Church and of British schoolmasters, the "moment appeared favorable" for the substitution of the English for the Dutch language in all official and judicial business. He ordered that "the English language be exclusively used in all judicial acts and proceedings, either in the supreme or inferior courts of this colony, from the first day of January, 1827; and that all official acts and documents of the several public offices of this Government . . . be drawn up and promulgated in the English language, from and after January, 1825." [7]

In this matter, the British acted with undue haste, consulting only their own convenience. Dutch had been the official language for more than a century and a half, and even two decades of British rule had induced only a handful of people to learn English. We are informed by a contemporary that outside of Capetown, the capital, "there are not 400 who can converse in English, and not 200 if 150 who write it, or can read it." [8] Yet less than three years were allowed for the readjustment in all official business with the Government. Far more important, litigation, even in the inferior courts of the country districts, would have to be conducted in a strange language within less than five years.

[7] *Records of the Cape Colony, op. cit.*, XIV, 452–453. See also XIV, 297–298; XVII, 24–25, 44–45.
[8] *Ibid.*, XIII, 388.

There is no doubt that the Boers resented this high-handed action, for they loved their traditions, customs and language.[9] True enough, the command was received without popular outcry, but that was due to the fact that there were only limited facilities for expression under the despotic rule of the time. The authorities, however, soon had sufficient evidence of public discontent.

A Synod of the Reformed Churches of the colony, held in 1824, discussed the question of language at some length, and the Chief Justice, a Boer in whom the British had confidence, reported to the Governor that "an apprehension is fast spreading among the public that their children will not be allowed to receive any further instruction in Dutch, and that this language is to be totally proscribed." Then, with a show of devotion to the English language, he attacked cautiously but shrewdly the Government's policy at its most vulnerable point. He argued that, since "Dutch is the domestic language in all families . . . religious instruction cannot be given otherwise than in the Dutch language, except at the expense of religion itself." That religious worship, "affecting eternal welfare," must not be interfered with was, of course, self-evident. In the Church, therefore, the English language could "only be introduced in time by degrees and as it were of itself." With the minimum of emotion which a jurist might allow himself, he assured the Governor that, if a moderate policy was pursued, "everyone's own interest will prompt him voluntarily and without any humiliating feeling to give up by degrees the domestic use of the language of his ancestors for that of a new and liberal Mother Country." [10]

Next to the Church, the courts presented the greatest obstacle to the enforcement of the language law. The court of justice at the Cape and two district courts begged to be excused, one of the latter stating with some spirit that, "not having the least knowledge of the English language," they could not continue in service.

---
[9] Cory, *op. cit.*, II, 320.
[10] *Records of the Cape Colony, op. cit.*, XIX, 497–500.

This decision to resign, they said pointedly, was consistent with their loyalty to the British Government and "their bounden duty towards their country and fellow inhabitants." [11]

The British were aware not only of this opposition but also of a widespread assumption that the order would not be enforced, at least in religious institutions and in the courts. They decided to yield, but only with respect to the timeliness of the measure, not the principle of Anglicizing the population. Religious instruction was permitted "for some time to come" in the Dutch language, while the proclamation which postponed the compulsory use of English in the courts empowered the Governor to revert to the fixed policy at his discretion.[12] That part of the law which directed that English be the language of the administration went into effect at the appointed time.

The difficulties encountered had one permanent, moderating effect. The authorities had come to the decision to assimilate the Dutch law, long prevalent in the Colony, to the law of England. In fact a Commission of Inquiry, sent to South Africa largely for that purpose, had favored the immediate introduction of English law.[13] However, in drafting the Charter of Justice (1827) which reconstructed the courts of the Colony, the London Government stopped short with the adoption of British legal procedure. Roman Dutch law remained in force, the Colonial Secretary explaining that the Government found itself "constrained to depart from the immediate adoption of a measure of so much importance and difficulty." He concluded that after all the old law "adequately provides for

[11] *Ibid.*, XXVIII, 447–452.
[12] *Ibid.*, XXII, 182; XXVIII, 427, 445, 479; Eybers, G. W. (ed.), *Select Constitutional Documents Illustrating South African History* (London, 1918), p. 107.
[13] With a self-righteousness characteristic of empire-builders, the Commissioners observed that "the advantages which the mother country desires from the diffusion of her language, her institutions and her laws, in the colonies that she acquires, are at first more perceptible to herself than to the colonists themselves, especially to those who are habitually indisposed to purchase a remote advantage by submitting to a temporary inconvenience." But they were practical enough to propose pensions for judicial officers whose retirement the Anglicizing of the Courts would render necessary. *Ibid.*, XXVII, 502.

the ordinary exigencies of life." The issue was not raised again. In 1845, Roman-Dutch law was established in Natal,[14] irrespective of its British population, and to this day Dutch law prevails in South Africa.

With respect to the language of court procedure, there was more hesitation in London than in Capetown. The Charter of Justice required the exclusive use of English only in the Supreme Court. In the Circuit Courts, said the Colonial Secretary, "it may, perhaps, be necessary for the present to continue the use of the Dutch language." However, the directives issued in South Africa put an end to these doubts by proclaiming English as the language of the inferior courts as well.[15]

3. THE BOER EMIGRATION

The innovations of the British occasioned a deep sense of grievance among the Boers. Their religious preferences were slighted by the appointment of Scottish preachers to their churches. Their children were obliged to learn English, which undeniably had practical value, but failed utterly to prepare the child for membership in the Church, a primary aim of education with the Boers. Their language was cast out of official life, while they, the pioneers, who had subdued the savage land, could not even speak out in open court without the aid of an interpreter. The proud Boers were pained by the arrogance and contempt with which the newcomers regarded them.

These irritants might have been endured. If the Government schools disregarded his needs and desires, the Boer could and did support Dutch schools, especially in the rural districts. The Government, too, might be contemptuous of his ways, but it was distant and aloof. On his farm he was master. His family, servants, neighbors, all spoke his language and respected his customs.

---

[14] Eybers, *op. cit.*, pp. 227–228.
[15] *Records of the Cape Colony, op. cit.*, XXXII, 254–261, 274–292; XXXIV, 116–117, 177–178, 250.

However, other measures taken by the British appeared to the Boers as a threat to their security, indeed to their very existence in South Africa. The depreciation of paper currency, despite protests by the Boers, was regarded as a breach of faith. The emancipation of the slaves in 1834 resulted in heavy losses. British policy on the frontier afforded inadequate protection, the settlers suffering loss of life and property. Particularly vexatious was the effort of the British to apply the same law to blacks and whites, upsetting "proper relations between master and servant," as a Boer manifesto put it. Aggrieved by all these vexations, the Boers were maddened by the successful agitation of missionaries who stigmatized them as oppressors, when, in their view, they were fulfilling a Divine purpose in controlling the black man. If only the Boers could escape from British "tyranny" and rule themselves! Within the Colony, the centralizing policy of the Government, which had swept clean all vestiges of local participation, rendered this impossible. The brooding spirit of resentment saw only one way out—to flee into the wilderness. Large numbers of Boers, therefore, trekked off beyond the frontier, and by the middle of the nineteenth century were sprawled out over the best lands of the interior.[16]

Some historians regard the Anglicizing efforts of the British as a minor cause of the emigration,[17] chiefly because the contemporary pronouncements of the Boers dwell upon the more immediate dangers to life and property. There can be no question, however, that it was a cause of discontent. Moreover, when the emigrants made specific demands, as they did at the time of the annexation of Natal by the British, language figured prominently. The Boers demanded "that the Dutch language shall be used in all courts of law, except where the majority of the inhabitants shall speak English." A knowledge of *either* English *or* Dutch was proposed as a qualification for the suffrage, and a plea was made for permis-

[16] In his brilliant book, *A History of South Africa, op. cit.*, de Kiewiet mentions other primary causes, namely, the hunger of the Boer for land, and his rebellion against the confining effect of a fixed boundary. See pp. 54–55 ff.

[17] See, for example, Theal, G. M., *History of the Boers in South Africa* (London, 1887), p. 70.

sion to name their own church ministers, "without any meddling or interference on the part of Government." [18]

4. THE ACHIEVEMENT OF INDEPENDENCE

For a time the British pursued a vacillating policy with respect to the emigrants. Attempts were first made to induce the Boers to accept British sovereignty, but neither cajolery nor threats prevailed. Natal was annexed because of its strategic importance, the Boers trekking on into the interior. The Transvaal, however, and the Orange River territory were recognized as independent in the early 1850's largely because the Government did not wish to extend its responsibilities in South Africa. Thereafter, the country remained divided, the English predominating in Natal and the eastern provinces of the Cape, as well as in its urban centers, and the Dutch in the two republics of the interior and in the rural districts of the Cape.

Once free of British control, the Boers of the independent republics reasserted the primacy of their language and usages. Both the Orange Free State and the Transvaal established the Roman-Dutch law, "in operation in the Cape Colony at the time of the appointment of English judges," as the law of the land. The Dutch language was likewise made compulsory in all court proceedings and in public business. In 1888, after the discovery of gold had begun to attract foreigners to the Transvaal, its government gave legal sanction to established practice in terms of unconcealed severity. This law read in part as follows:

> The Dutch language shall be the official language of the Country. All other languages are foreign languages.
> All official documents, notices, official correspondence and other writings of officials shall be composed and written in the Dutch language. They may be accompanied by a translation into a foreign language. This translation, however, shall be marked as such. . . .
> In all courts of the State, the Dutch language shall always be used by

---

[18] See Eybers, *op. cit.*, pp. 177–178.

all officials. Those officials shall further see to it that all pleadings are held in that language.

Even auction sales were required to be held in the official language, and violation of the law was punishable by a fine and suspension or dismissal from office. For educational purposes, Dutch was declared the medium of instruction in the public schools, the Transvaal directing the responsible officials in 1884 "to apply the law strictly." [19]

As a rule, national oppression either provokes an impassioned defense of one's way of life, or induces despair and demoralization. In the independent republics, the Boers made good their desire for freedom, but those who remained under British jurisdiction were obliged to submit meekly to Anglicization. In the Cape and in Natal, the English language and culture reigned supreme for half a century. Weakened by the emigration, and unable to offer effective resistance, the Boers of these territories lapsed into indifference. They took no interest in politics, showing little concern for candidates or elections, and even neglected the opportunities of public education. Until the last quarter of the nineteenth century very little was heard of the Dutch section of the population.[20]

Those, however, who took the trouble to study closely the Boer community were aware that the wounds of denationalization were deep and green. A half-century of "suppression, derision and browbeating" had caused the Boer to lose faith in his heritage and in himself. We are told [21] that he

was not particularly proud of his nationality. He hated the Englishman, but he stood in awe of him . . . [and] as the Dutchman feared the Englishman, so the Englishman scorned the Dutchman. Boer stood to him merely for boor. He was made to feel unhappily conscious of his nationality. And he could escape the discomfort of it only in two ways:

[19] See Eybers, *op. cit.*, pp. 295–297, 310, 356, 416–417, 476–477, 482–483.
[20] Aucamp, *op. cit.*, pp. 132–133. See also Barnouw, A. J., *Language and Race Problems in South Africa* (The Hague, 1934), p. 5.
[21] Millin, S. G., *The South Africans* (New York, 1927), pp. 165–166. See also Barnouw, *op. cit.*, pp. 1–2, 71.

either by shunning his despiser, or by shunning that in himself which was being despised. This was especially true of the youth who often expressed their rebelliousness "in a repudiation of the Dutch tradition."

During the last quarter of the century there was a stirring among the Boers, when efforts were made to arouse the masses from their lethargy and to direct their resentment into constructive channels. At first it took the form of a cultural awakening. In the 1870's the people were urged to rally around "Afrikaans," their vernacular, which differed from Dutch, the language of Holland and the official tongue of the independent Republics. Despised by the British, and slighted by the educated Boers as "the language of the kitchen," Afrikaans nevertheless remained the vernacular of the Boers throughout South Africa. By reducing this popular form of speech to writing, it was hoped to stimulate a love for reading and education and thereby to raise the cultural level of the people.[22]

About 1880, the Afrikander Bond was organized and, under the leadership of J. C. Hofmeyr, quickly became a recognized force in Cape politics. Hofmeyr was a moderate, who hoped to retain the good-will and cooperation of the English, even while furthering the interests of the Boers.

For a time it seemed that the national problem of South Africa would be solved, for the British were ready to abandon the policy of uncompromising Anglicization. They were themselves disturbed by the sullenness and apathy of the Boers, their educational commissions particularly expressing concern over the prevailing indifference. When representative government had been introduced in the Cape in 1854, the ruling British had still required that all debates and records of parliament be in the English language. However, in 1882, after responsible government had been secured, and after the Bond had become active, the use of Dutch in parliamentary debates was legalized. Two years later, similar rights were extended to the Dutch language in the central and local courts. The new law provided that "the judges of the superior

[22] See Barnouw, *op. cit.*, pp. 5–10; Aucamp, *op. cit.*, pp. 127–128, 139–142 ff.

courts of justice may," and those of inferior courts "shall, allow the use of the Dutch language equally with the English language . . . when requested so to do" by any of the parties involved. Less generous and less effective was the concession respecting education finally made in the Cape in 1892. Parents were then accorded the right to designate the language of instruction for their children. But examinations and inspections continued to be conducted in English. For this reason, and also because "parents had formed the habit of associating education with the English language," the new law remained virtually a dead letter.[23]

These concessions implied a recognition on the part of the British that South Africa was the home of two white peoples; that an exclusively British national state was, therefore, unattainable if not unwarranted. What is more, influential voices were raised, even in the Boer Republics, in behalf of effective cooperation of all South African colonies. Given time and good will, this augured well for future understanding and cooperation. However, in their anxiety to unify South Africa, the British blundered, and unwittingly jolted Boer patriotism into a more suspicious and intransigent mood.

The British annexed the Transvaal in 1877, rekindling flames of national antagonism which could not be muffled until the Republic was restored seven years later. Out of the seething unrest, recriminations and armed clashes of this period, a new Boer patriotism erupted—an aggressive form of nationalism, rooted in a shared language and way of life and nourished by anti-British feeling, as well as by the delusion of a united and independent Boerdom as the paramount power in South Africa. This movement centered in the Transvaal and its embattled President, Paul Kruger; but even in the Cape, moderates like Hofmeyr found difficulty in steering their followers away from national separatism.

Nor could time assuage aroused feelings. For, with the dis-

[23] For the texts of the laws see Eybers, *op. cit.*, pp. 55, 66, 133–134, 136.

covery of gold on the Rand in the 1880's, a new and dynamic element burst in upon the slow-moving rural inhabitants of the Transvaal. Incompatibility was inevitable.[24]

The Transvaal Boers saw in the newcomers a menace to their hard-won independence and to their traditional way of life. And indeed they were. Modern industry would inevitably work havoc with a stagnant rural economy, while the numerous and aggressive immigrants could not tolerate an exclusively Boer national state.

President Kruger determined to stem the flood of innovations which threatened to engulf his people by piling disabilities upon the newcomers. Severe franchise laws were passed to prevent the intrusion of the "foreigners" into political life. Monopolies and restrictions hampered industrial and commercial activities. Blind to the lesson of the failure of forcible Anglicization in the Cape, the English language was barred from the courts and state schools. And, anticipating a violent British reaction, the aid of European Powers, notably Germany, was invited.

Conflict was inevitable. The immigrants were too strong in numbers, wealth, and influence not to offer resistance. Moreover, the British Government, vigorously imperialistic in the 1890's, was resolved to put an end to disunity and intrigue in South Africa. As Lord Milner put it, a great industry with valuable investments could not remain at the mercy of a "medieval race oligarchy." Even more important, the menace of foreign intervention must be removed from South Africa and the route to the East.

In 1895, the last hope for peace vanished with the Jameson Raid into the Transvaal. Until that ill-fated venture, the extremists of the Transvaal might have hesitated to throw down or accept the final challenge of war. That colossal blunder drove moderate Boers, especially of the sister Republic of the Orange Free State, into the arms of Kruger. The Boer War was the result.

[24] For a profound analysis of the clashing economic forces, see de Kiewiet, *op. cit.*, pp. 107–108, 117–122.

5. EFFECTS OF THE BOER WAR

"South Africa has advanced politically by disasters and economically by windfalls." Nowhere does this astute observation of the historian de Kiewiet apply with greater force than in the case of the national question.

The Boer War taught the white South Africans—Boers as well as British—that their country must remain composite; that neither Boers nor British could be forcibly assimilated or eliminated; and that it was not even possible to separate the two national groups into homogeneous territorial fragments. While Natal was predominantly English and the Orange Free State Boer, the Cape remained the shared home of both peoples, while the Transvaal was a Boer country with its center, Johannesburg, emphatically English. The verdict of arms was final and apparently irrevocable: South Africa was to have uniformity of political allegiance with diversity in nationality and culture,—one state, but two peoples.

Paradoxically, too, the baptism of blood and fire had cleansed white South Africa of much of its arrogance and frustration which had blighted previous efforts at cooperation. As a result of the war, "the aggressive habit of the English, the defensive habit of the Dutch, were toned down." [25] The Briton was less inclined to regard the Boer with contempt; the young Boer, no longer in awe of the English, shed his feeling of inferiority. In this atmosphere, hatreds and resentments might be dispelled, giving way to understanding and compromise.

For a time, the die-hard Tories of Britain threatened to arrest the healing process by lacerating old wounds. The Vereeniging Peace Treaty of 1902 had stipulated:

> The Dutch language will be taught in public schools in the Transvaal and the Orange River Colony where the parents of the children desire it, and will be allowed in Courts of Law when necessary for the better and more effectual administration of justice.

Military administration in the Transvaal and Orange River Colony

[25] Millin, *op. cit.*, p. 185.

will at the earliest possible date be succeeded by civil government, and, as soon as circumstances permit, representative institutions, leading up to self-government, will be introduced.[26]

Despite these commitments, the proconsul, Lord Milner, attempted to rule the former Republics as conquered provinces, and to reassert the supremacy of the British element. English was made the medium of instruction in the public schools and some three thousand young English women were imported to help Anglicize the schools.[27]

The Boers replied in kind. Extremists, who feed on intransigence, paraded before the people the ill-advised words of Lady Curzon: "Capture the Boer children and teach them English only." They warned that "South Africa would not flourish until the children of Boer and Briton sat on the school-benches with equal rights." One resentful Boer exclaimed: ". . . they could not make an Egyptian an Israelite; neither could they make a Boer an Englishman." He demanded with evident popular approval that

the English children must learn Dutch, and the Dutch children must learn English in one school so that the future generation should grow up as one people, each retaining their own traditions, religion, and national sentiments. Then, and then only, could they have permanent peace in South Africa, and they would be better able to understand one another's grievances. They must have equal rights for both.[28]

The moderate Boers, such as Generals Botha and Smuts, avoided provocative language, but they, too, resisted the renewed attempt to Anglicize their children. They established "Christian National" schools, conducted in the Dutch language and in accord with Afrikander ideals and principles.

Fortunately for South Africa, this flare-up was quickly smothered. Conciliatory elements in both camps steered toward a compromise, and the Liberals in Britain, who came to power in 1906,

[26] Eybers, *op. cit.*, p. 346.
[27] McKerron, M. E., *A History of Education in South Africa* (Pretoria, 1934), p. 38.
[28] *Papers Relating to Constitutional Changes in the Transvaal* (London, 1905), Cmd. 2479, pp. 116, 124–125, 136.

soon brought to an end the intermeddling of the mother country in internal South African affairs. By granting responsible self-government to both conquered provinces, they placed the national question in the lap of the South Africans, who were best qualified to find the solution.

Self-government achieved, a vigorous movement was launched by Boers and British alike to effect a union of the South African colonies. Economic needs, in particular those connected with tariffs and railroads, and the native problem, had long dictated such a course. But, aggravated by the national question, differences on these vital matters had hardened into causes of conflict and war. However, once the principle of non-domination had been established, no disagreement was beyond peaceful adjustment. The insoluble problems of the past became simply public issues, susceptible of discussion, investigation and compromise.

6. THE SOUTH AFRICAN NATIONAL CONVENTION

A South African National Convention met during 1908–1909, holding sessions successively at Durban, Capetown and Bloemfontein. Careful preparations had been made, and precautions were taken to prevent untoward incidents. Especially noteworthy was the unity of the Boer and British members of the Transvaal delegation. Mortal enemies a decade before, these men came to the Convention fully agreed on all vital points, and the solid front maintained by them profoundly influenced the deliberations.[29]

The outcome exceeded all expectations. Harmony prevailed at the Convention, which produced a Draft Act for South African union. In little more than a year from the decision to convoke such a body, all four Colonies had accepted the Draft Act. The British Parliament quickly gave its approval, royal assent followed, and on May 31, 1910, the Union of South Africa came into being.

[29] See FitzPatrick, Sir J. P., *South African Memories* (London, 1932), pp. 131–132, 154, 198–202; Brand, R. H., *The Union of South Africa* (Oxford, 1909), pp. 39–41; Walton, Sir E. H., *The Inner History of the National Convention of South Africa* (Capetown, 1912), pp. 18–32 ff.

The language question does not loom large in the Minutes of the Convention. English and Dutch were used freely and interchangeably at the sessions. A number of petitions for equal language rights were received and noted. General Hertzog, Attorney-General of the Orange Free State, introduced a strongly worded resolution; but discussion was quickly adjourned, and when debate was resumed on the following day, an amendment was moved and carried disposing of the troublesome issue in the calm language of what later became Article 137 of the South Africa Act.[30] However, the minutes were deliberately limited to a bare outline of the proceedings, and much transpired at private discussions outside the regular agencies of the Convention.

The language question was one of the "most important" issues confronting the delegates. In fact, some of them regarded it as "the first and most anxious and greatest difficulty," the disposition of which would determine the success or failure of union. Although not put to the fore immediately, it haunted the sessions as "a crux which must be dealt with and settled satisfactorily before any real progress could be hoped for." Once the solution was found, the air was cleared, and the "watchfulness and reserve" of the early days vanished.

It was known that General Hertzog felt strongly on the subject. He was therefore asked unofficially to draft a resolution for private circulation before formal presentation to the Convention. This read as follows:

> In order to effect a closer union of the Colonies represented at this Convention, and in order fully to attain the object of its establishment, it is essential that both English and Dutch be recognized as the National and Official languages of the Union; to be treated on a footing of equality and to possess and enjoy equal freedom, rights and privileges in all the various offices, functions and services of whatsoever kind or nature of or administered by or under the Union; and that every appointment under the Union shall be made with a due regard to the equality of the two languages and to the right of every citizen of the

[30] South African National Convention, *Minutes of Proceedings* . . . (Cape Town, 1911), pp. xvi, 18, 21–22. See also pp. 306, 338, 346, 395–396.

Union to avail himself and to claim either language as the medium of communication between himself and any officer or servant of the Union; and that all the records, journals and proceedings of the Union Legislatures as likewise all Bills and Laws of the Union, and all official notifications of general public importance or interest published in the *Gazette* or otherwise shall be issued and published in both the English and the Dutch Languages.

All were agreed on the basic principle of equality, but many refused to countenance "compulsion," that is, that the holding of public office and appointment to the public services be contingent upon a knowledge of both languages. In deference to these objections Hertzog presented to the Convention a modified resolution deleting the clause relating to appointments.

General Hertzog spoke in support of his resolution "with deep earnestness and some feeling." He warned that the Boers felt strongly about their language; that "they had for a hundred years nursed this feeling." Therefore, a mere paper resolution or an expression of opinion would not do. A real and lasting settlement must be based on genuine equality throughout the public services. Otherwise there would be "a sense of humiliation." These views were strongly seconded. For example, ex-President Steyn of the Orange Free State declared that no unity would be possible if one people labored under a sense of inferiority. He pleaded with the delegates "not to hand down this *hereditas damnosa* to their children, for he believed that it was responsible for most of their troubles."

Feelings might easily have become ruffled, for some of the British delegates took a stand against "any trace of compulsion." However, since both sides feared a deadlock, the debate was adjourned to permit informal discussion by the interested parties. A compromise was reached and a carefully worded resolution drafted, with the full knowledge that "there was no question with regard to which the people were more sensitive." By agreement, the amended resolution was moved the following day by a member of the Transvaal delegation, and it was adopted without a division.

NATIONALITIES AND NATIONAL MINORITIES

With minor stylistic changes this became Article 137 of the South Africa Act:

Both the English and Dutch [31] languages shall be official languages of the Union and shall be treated on a footing of equality, and possess and enjoy equal freedom, rights, and privileges; all records, journals and proceedings of Parliament shall be kept in both languages, and all Bills, Acts, and notices of general public importance or interest issued by the Government of the Union shall be in both languages.

The adoption of this clause was "a great relief to the Convention," and to assure its permanence it was included among the measures which could not be modified except by a two-thirds majority of both houses of the Union Parliament sitting together. All felt that an honorable accord had been reached on the basis of "equality and no compulsion," and all were eager to bequeath the conciliatory spirit to the new Union. There was an understanding among the delegates that education be kept free of political or national passion, and precautions were taken against haste and severity in the enforcement of bilingualism upon public servants. A special article was incorporated prohibiting the dismissal of those already in the service because of deficiency in one of the official languages. It read:

The services of officers in the public service of any of the Colonies at the establishment of the Union shall not be dispensed with by reason of their want of knowledge of either the English or Dutch language. (Article 145) [32]

7. EQUALITY IN PRACTICE

The constitutional solution of the national question was a landmark in South African history, but it was still to be defined and

---

[31] In 1925, an amendment was passed providing that the word "Dutch" included Afrikaans, the Boer vernacular, which was rapidly superseding the older form of Dutch even as the medium of literary expression. For the movement in favor of Afrikaans, see Union of South Africa, *Report from the Joint Committee on the Use of Afrikaans* . . ., March, 1925; Barnouw, *op. cit.,* pp. 10–14, 25–27.

[32] For this discussion, see Walton, *op. cit.,* pp. 33–34, 97–110, 117, 222–224; FitzPatrick, *op. cit.,* p. 19.

tested in the practice of everyday life. It was natural for the British element to try to retain something of its former preeminence, and for the Boers to press for a balanced equality. Difficulties were, of course, encountered.

The first Union elections were fought largely on the language issue, and the first Union Parliament concerned itself with the application of the principle of equality to the schools. In the end, a compromise was effected, on the basis of which the Provinces framed the necessary legislation. The Cape, the Transvaal and the Orange Free State decreed that the home language [33] of the child be the medium of instruction in the primary grades. Thereafter, parents were authorized to designate either or both of the languages as the medium of instruction. Separate Dutch-medium and English-medium schools were established, and in some instances parallel classes were formed in the same school. The second official language, other than the medium of instruction, was to be taught as a subject to every pupil, unless the parents objected. A knowledge of both languages was required in the training of teachers. Natal followed suit tardily and somewhat less generously: in all cases, the parents chose the medium of instruction, and the second language was taught only on the request of parents.[34]

The application of bilingualism to the public services likewise aroused feelings. After 1924, when General Hertzog became Prime Minister of the Union, the Government began enforcing bilingualism "with uncompromising severity." Appointments to the civil service and promotions were made contingent upon competence in both languages, although new appointees were allowed

---

[33] Until 1914, the "home language" of the Boers was assumed to be Holland Dutch. But in that year Afrikaans was included in the term "Dutch," and it soon crowded the older form out of the elementary schools.

[34] For a description and discussion of bilingual education, see Aucamp, *op. cit.*, pp. 10–12, 151–167 ff.; Fife, R. H., *Report on Tendencies in Education in East and South Africa with Particular Reference to Language Questions* (New York, 1932), pp. 42–45; McKerron, *op. cit.*, pp. 127–135; Malherbe, E. G., *Education in South Africa* (Cape Town, 1925), pp. 413–418; Smuts, A. J., *The Education of Adolescents in South Africa* (Cape Town, 1937), p. 68; Nathan, M., *The South African Commonwealth* (Johannesburg, 1919), pp. 111–112, 236–238.

a period of five years to make good any deficiency. The gradual increase of Boer civil servants in English-speaking areas, like Natal, was not liked. In the early 1930's a careful observer found considerable grumbling and tension, but on the whole both parties were attempting to adjust themselves to the requirements of equality.[35]

8. CONCLUSION

South Africa has sought to solve its national problems by means of bilingualism rather than federalism, as in Switzerland. A unitary government has been established in which the central authority is supreme. The former Colonies have become Provinces with designated functions, but the Union legislature may at all times assert its will.

Yet the Provinces enjoy a great deal of latitude, especially in the spheres of education, culture, and purely local affairs. They are entrusted with primary and secondary education, hospitals, charitable institutions, public works and the supervision of local government. Their greatest concern has been with education and its adaptation to the needs of two peoples.[36]

It should be noted, however, that bilingualism is a form of binationalism. To the Boer, his language is the symbol of his nationality, the instrument for the preservation and development of his national culture. The Britisher, too, is keenly aware of his national heritage. Were each to go his own way in quest of a national state and cultural predominance, conflict would be inevitable and interminable.

Since two peoples or nationalities claim South Africa as their homeland, there is no choice but to allow each to maintain and cultivate its characteristic way of life, without, however, cutting itself off completely from the other. South Africa finds in bilingualism the means to this end. Each nationality may thereby conserve its own language and cultural heritage and at the same time

[35] Barnouw, *op. cit.*, pp. 14–17, 27–28, 33–45.
[36] See Nathan, *op. cit.*, pp. 6–9, 17–20, 39–40, 87–112; Brand, *op. cit.*, pp. 43–54, 75–78.

acquire a knowledge and understanding of that of the neighboring group. Thus a channel is cleared for communication and understanding.

To solve a troublesome problem does not mean to put an end once and for all to all differences of opinion, or even overlapping claims. A solution is a guarantee against intransigence, a promise of peaceful settlement of disputes, without resort to force. A quarrel is adjusted when both parties agree to reckon with each other's needs and interests.

In this sense, the South African whites have solved their century-old national question. The Englishman is resigned to a status of equality rather than predominance. The Boer has shed his sense of inferiority, and, therefore,

. . . he feels less sullen towards his English neighbor than ever he has done. With pride has come also serenity. With success, a friendliness of which he is barely conscious himself. Now he seems to feel like a host in his own home, ready to extend the hand of welcome.[37]

Both peoples are learning one another's language, facilitating communication and deepening appreciation of their respective ways of life. With greater confidence in the survival of their culture, the Boers in particular are likely to accept the English language and culture as assets, rather than fear them as a menace. Already, Boers read English books avidly, and their own literature is remarkably free of anti-British bias.[38]

Bilingualism has proved a workable form of binationalism. It has quickened mutual understanding and cooperation, which are indispensable to a permanent union of Briton and Boer.

[37] Millin, *op. cit.*, p. 168.
[38] Barnouw, *op. cit.*, pp. 38–40, 50–57; see also Fife, *op. cit.*, p. 42; Fitz-Patrick, *op. cit.*, pp. 128–130, 134 ff.

CHAPTER VI

NATIONAL FEDERALISM IN THE SOVIET UNION

The national quarrels of South Africa appear almost trivial when compared with the dissensions and violence of Czarist Russia. The British authorities were imperious and arbitrary, and at times arrogant and disdainful. In their eagerness to transform the Boer into an Englishman they often blundered. But there was no deliberate and consistent attempt to stamp out by force the individuality of the Boer. The latter could always retreat into his home and private school, or betake himself into the back country where he could live his own life without serious interference. What is more, the British had the capacity to learn from experience and to compromise when the occasion demanded it.

The Czarist régime was at once determined and inflexible. The ideal of the ruling bureaucracy was Russification—one Czar, one faith, one Russia. The multitude of peoples sprawling over the vast domains of the Empire were to be pressed into a single mould, the motley assemblage of racial, religious, linguistic and cultural groups transmuted into a single nationality—the Great Russian nationality. That the dissident elements constituted a majority of the population, that they embraced scores of millions of human beings, that they ranged all the way from highly civilized and nationally conscious peoples to primitive tribes—all this did not matter. The autocracy willed it, and its will was law.

In 1870 the Russification of the non-Russian population became "the first and most pressing purpose of the elementary schools." [1]

[1] Odinetz, D. M., "Primary and Secondary Schools," in Ignatiev, P. N.; Odinetz, D. M., and Novgorotsev, P. J., *Russian Schools and Universities in the World War* (New Haven: Carnegie Endowment for International Peace, 1929), pp. 22–23.

THE UNION OF SOVIET SOCIALIST REPUBLICS (SOVIET UNION)

BOUNDARY LINES
- —— U.S.S.R.
- —·—· Union Republics
- —··— Autonomous Soviet Socialist Republics
- ---- Other Countries

SCALE OF MILES
0 100 200 300 400 500

Copyright, 1944, National Council of American-

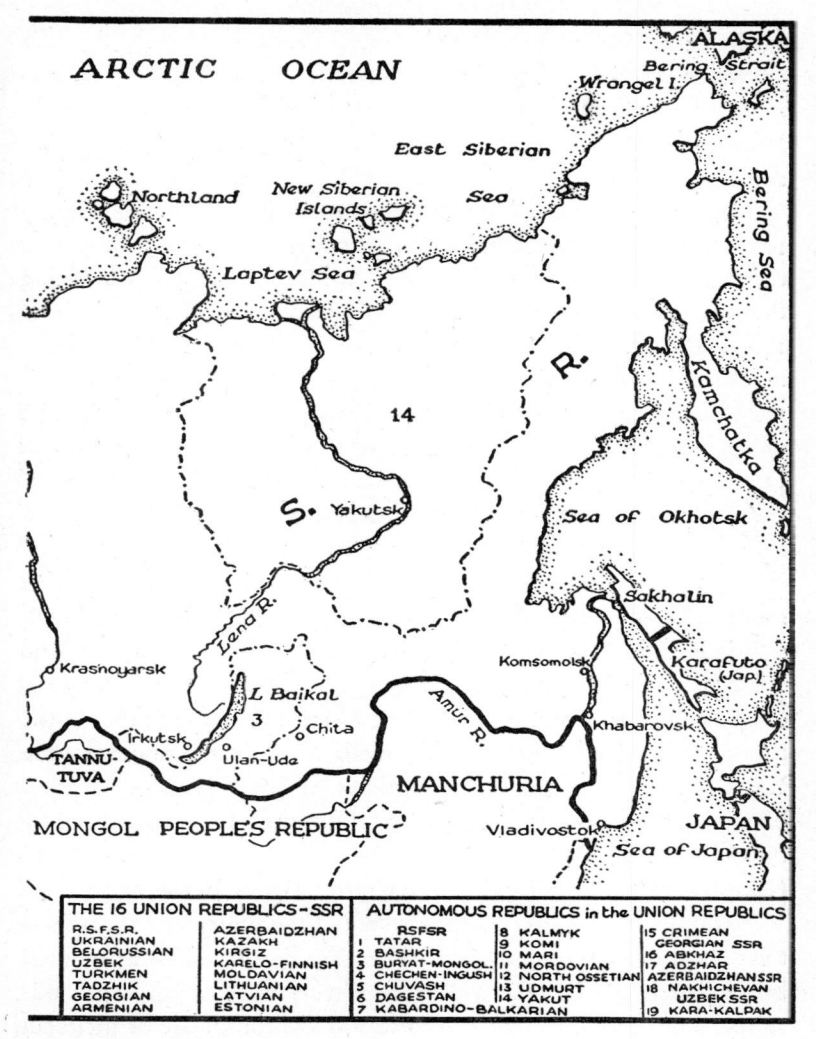

THE 16 UNION REPUBLICS – SSR		AUTONOMOUS REPUBLICS in the UNION REPUBLICS		
R.S.F.S.R.	AZERBAIDZHAN	RSFSR	8 KALMYK	15 CRIMEAN
UKRAINIAN	KAZAKH	1 TATAR	9 KOMI	GEORGIAN SSR
BELORUSSIAN	KIRGIZ	2 BASHKIR	10 MARI	16 ABKHAZ
UZBEK	KARELO-FINNISH	3 BURYAT-MONGOL	11 MORDOVIAN	17 ADZHAR
TURKMEN	MOLDAVIAN	4 CHECHEN-INGUSH	12 NORTH OSSETIAN	AZERBAIDZHAN SSR
TADZHIK	LITHUANIAN	5 CHUVASH	13 UDMURT	18 NAKHICHEVAN
GEORGIAN	LATVIAN	6 DAGESTAN	14 YAKUT	UZBEK SSR
ARMENIAN	ESTONIAN	7 KABARDINO-BALKARIAN		19 KARA-KALPAK

Soviet Friendship. Reproduced by permission.

Therefore, the use of the mother tongue of the children as a medium of instruction was prohibited. Some Russian pedagogues protested that this policy would eventually exclude minority nationalities from the schools: that, in effect, the diffusion of the Russian language would be retarded. But the ruling authorities remained adamant.

The Revolution of 1905–1907 temporarily compelled the bureaucracy to give ground, and new school regulations provided that the mother tongue of non-Russian children be employed during the first two years of primary school. However, the triumph of reaction after 1907 quickly nullified this concession. The officials authorized the use of minority languages only when the pupils were unable to pursue their work in Russian, and the determination of such competence was entrusted not to teachers or parents, but to the narrow and obstructive representatives of the Ministry of Education. This, we are informed, deprived "the conditional privilege . . . of all practical significance." [2]

During the First World War hopes were entertained for a moderation of the policy of Russification. In 1915 the liberal-minded Count Paul Ignatiev was named Minister of Education, and for nearly two years he labored to heal the breach between school officials and the community. Among other reforms, he favored the use of the mother tongue as the medium of instruction for non-Russian children in the primary grades. He had the lively support of public opinion, but could not gain the confidence of the ruling bureaucracy. In December, 1916, he was superseded, and Russification remained the ideal of the Czarist régime to the end.[3]

Naturally, the subject peoples resented the policy of supplanting their local languages and institutions. But disaffection was ignored by the harsh and haughty rulers, and every trace of resistance was sternly suppressed. Czarist Russia was in a chronic state of incipient rebellion, every internal crisis or external danger cheering the victims and inspiring them to fresh efforts at liberation. Vengeance

[2] *Ibid.*, pp. 23–24 ff.
[3] *Ibid.*, pp. 70, 97–98, 101, 116–117. See also pp. xxii–xxiii.

was always swift and cruel, until the despotic régime was eaten away by corruption and defeat.

In 1917 the Russian Empire burst into flame and smoke. The explosive force of revolution tore to shreds the whole fabric of Russian society, the tight cords of unity giving way, along with the decayed bonds of oppression. Pent-up hatreds sought relief in violence which was often deflected upon innocent neighbors, or in a wilful assertion of particularism and sectarianism. Russia became an inferno of strife, ringed by chaos.

It required all the fanaticism and resolute passion of the Bolsheviks to face the colossal task of reconstruction. With a singlemindedness unsurpassed in secular causes, they rallied to the attack, assuaging wounded feelings, curbing the turbulent and intemperate forces, and employing every known device to calm the masses. Where appeals or threats proved inadequate, they did not hesitate to resort to bloodshed to achieve their purpose. In the end, they emerged victorious. They created a new civilization and a new people, hardened, strengthened, revitalized and, above all, united.

From the standpoint of nationalism, the new unity rested to a considerable degree on consent. Gone was the narrow-minded ideal of Russification. Gone, too, was the resentful subservience of the non-Russian peoples. Whatever one may think of Bolshevik methods and achievements in other spheres—and opinions will differ widely—the Soviet leaders attacked the national question in a constructive and statesmanlike manner.

It is important that the national policy of the Soviet Union be understood. Russian influence will, in all likelihood, be paramount in east-central Europe, and the experiment of the Soviet Union may well contribute to a solution of the national question on the western borders. The difficulties encountered and the measures taken to counteract them will be the subject matter of this chapter.[3a]

[3a] For a full treatment of the national question in the Soviet Union, see *The Peoples of the Soviet Union* (Harcourt, Brace and Company), a forthcoming book by Corliss Lamont.

1. A BABEL OF TONGUES AND NATIONALITIES

The Czarist policy of Russification had been a failure; the country remained to the end a vast mosaic of numerous peoples. The collapse of the Empire resulted in the secession of the Western fringe of nationalities; Poles, Finns, Lithuanians and others made good their claims to independence. However, when the new Bolshevik régime took the national problem firmly in hand, there were still 182 distinct nationalities, or fragments of nationalities, speaking 149 different languages.[4]

Only a few of these nationalities were numerically of any consequence; thirteen reached the million mark in 1926, and two of them exceeded five millions. The third largest national group, the White Russians, numbered no more than 4,739,000, or only 3.2 per cent of the total population of over 146,000,000. In fact, only the Great Russians and the Ukrainians (or Little Russians) constituted significant units, the former with a population of nearly 78,000,000—about 53 per cent of the total—and the latter claiming 31,000,000, or slightly over 21 per cent. Both are, of course, Slavic; and if we add to their populations that of the White Russians, we find that the Slavs comprised more than 77 per cent of the people of the entire country. The internationally minded Bolsheviks must have been tempted to ignore the national and "separatist" prejudices of the insignificant peoples. On the face of it, it must have seemed unreasonable to complicate the task of building socialism by recognizing scores of languages and innumerable customs and traditions.[5]

[4] These are the figures of the census for 1926. See Yarmolinsky, A., *The Jews and Other Minor Nationalities Under the Soviets* (New York, 1928), pp. 141, 183. Chapter XII contains an excellent survey of the various peoples in the 1920's.

[5] For the principal nationalities of the U.S.S.R. according to the census of 1926, see Kohn, H., *Nationalism in the Soviet Union* (New York, 1933), pp. 156–157. The 1939 figures are given in the following table.

NATIONALITIES OF THE U.S.S.R. ACCORDING TO THE CENSUS OF 1939

(Exclusive of Western Ukraine and Western Byelo-Russia) *

Nationality	Population	Per Cent of Total
Russians	99,019,929	58.41
Ukrainians	28,070,404	16.56
Byelo-Russians (White Russians)	5,267,431	3.11
Uzbeks	4,844,021	2.86
Tatars	4,300,336	2.54
Kazaks	3,098,764	1.83
Jews	3,020,141	1.78
Azerbaijan Turks	2,274,805	1.34
Georgians (Gruzians)	2,248,566	1.33
Armenians	2,151,884	1.27
Mordvinians	1,451,429	0.86
Germans	1,423,534	0.84
Chuvash	1,367,930	0.81
Tadjiks	1,228,964	0.72
Kirghiz	884,306	0.52
Dagestan peoples	857,371	0.50
Bashkirs	842,925	0.50
Turcomans	811,769	0.48
Poles	626,905	0.37
Odmurts	605,673	0.36
Mari	481,262	0.28
Komi	408,724	0.24
Chechens	407,690	0.24
Osets	354,547	0.21
Greeks	285,896	0.17
Moldavians	260,023	0.15
Karelians	252,559	0.15
Karakalpaks	185,775	0.11
Koreans	180,412	0.11
Kabardins	164,106	0.10
Finns	143,074	0.08

* "Results of the Soviet Census," *The American Quarterly on the Soviet Union* (published by The American-Russian Institute), November, 1940, p. 99. Reproduced by permission.

NATIONALITIES OF THE U.S.S.R. (*Cont'd*)

Nationality	Population	Per Cent of Total
Estonians	142,465	0.08
Kalmuks	134,327	0.08
Letts and Letgauls	126,900	0.07
Bulgarians	113,479	0.07
Ingush	92,074	0.05
Adigeians	87,973	0.05
Karachaevs	75,737	0.04
Abkazians	58,969	0.03
Kakasians	52,602	0.03
Oirots	47,717	0.03
Kurds	45,866	0.03
Balkarians	42,666	0.03
Iranians	39,037	0.02
Lithuanians	32,342	0.02
Chinese	29,620	0.02
Czechs and Slovaks	26,919	0.02
Arabs	21,793	0.01
Assyrians	20,207	0.01
Others	807,279	0.48
Total	169,519,127	100.00

The territorial distribution of the numerous nationalities likewise posed problems which must have appeared all but insoluble. The Great Russians were concentrated in the central and northern zones of the European part of the country, but in varying proportions they were also spread over Siberia, the northern Caucasus, the Crimea, and even distant Turkestan. The Ukrainians were massed in the southern region, to which they gave their name, and, like the Great Russians, were scattered in considerable numbers along the Don, in the Caucasus, Siberia, the Far East, and the region beyond the Caspian Sea. The western borders were peopled by a variety of nationalities—White Russians, Poles, Finns, Moldavians, Karelians, Latvians, Estonians and others. Jews were numerous, especially in the cities of the south and west, to which Czarism had confined them. At least fifteen different peoples lived intermingled in the Crimea, and more than fifty in the Caucasus region, where Georgians, Armenians and Azerbaijan Turks each numbered over a million souls. Along the Volga, south of Saratov, and also in the Crimea were the Germans, who had been settled in the country during the latter part of the eighteenth century, and further north, in the area about Gorki (Nizhni-Novgorod), were the Chuvashes, a Turko-Tartaric people. At Kazan, on the same immense river, and elsewhere in the country, lived nearly three million Tartars. The dominant people of Central Asia were the Uzbeks, about four million strong; and the equally numerous Kazaks roamed over the vast territory stretching from the Volga to the Chinese border. There were, in addition, Tadjiks, Turcomans, Bashkirs, Ossets, Buryats, Yakuts and scores of other peoples.

One would expect that this confusion of racial, religious and linguistic groups would exasperate the highly rational, materialistic, unsentimental and order-loving communists. It would have been so much easier to administer the vast country, and to speed economic and social reconstruction, if national differences were overlooked. Yet the Bolsheviks chose to respect the linguistic and cultural individualities of the innumerable peoples, to so marked a degree, that their penchant for centralization had to be curbed by a large measure of national federalism. The reason for this must be sought in the communist position on nationalism and the national question.

2. BOLSHEVISM AND NATIONALISM

On first thought, the Bolshevik or Communist policy with respect to the national question poses a paradox. Nationalism is denounced as the concomitant of capitalism, but national expression is encouraged among the peoples of the Soviet Union. The class rather than the nation is deemed to be the basis of social differentiation, yet national groupings are recognized. The Dictatorship of the Proletariat is rooted in rigid centralization; structurally, however, the Soviet Union is a federation. At one and the same time, the Soviet leaders anathematize national divisions and champion self-determination as the right of all peoples, even to the point of secession.

These seeming contradictions notwithstanding, the Bolshevik position on the national question has been at once consistent and highly practical. The theoretical foundations were laid by Lenin and Stalin, and the latter must also be credited with the consummation of the policy and the fashioning of institutions. However one might deprecate the widespread adulation of Stalin, or scoff at his contribution to the theory and practice of Communism in the early stages of the Revolution, the prominent role he played in the national question is not the invention of a sycophant. Here he was the collaborator of Lenin, not the blind disciple of the master.

Bolshevik theory did not regard nationalism as an end in itself. It was neither rooted in human nature, nor inherently desirable, nor necessarily ineradicable. A product of historical evolution, nationalism flowered in the competitive era of the bourgeoisie, and would wither when the equality of all peoples had been achieved under socialism.

However, for the time being national differentiation was a fact which one had to reckon with. "One cannot refuse to recognize what is," said Lenin; "one is forced to recognize it." [6] Favoring one people over another, slighting the language or cultural attainments of any group, recognizing a dominant nationality, even if warranted by numbers and influence, would stir up resentments and foment national strife, thus hindering the attainment of class solidarity. National sensibilities must, therefore, be taken into account. If one belonged to the dominant people, one should repudiate all privileges enjoyed by his group; if a member of an oppressed nationality, he must guard against the blandishments of a national unity which defied the class struggle. In a word, national policy was ancillary to the broader aims of social revolution: it

[6] Batsell, W. R., *Soviet Rule in Russia* (New York, 1929), p. 115. This book should be read with the greatest caution, for the author is bitterly partisan and biased. His opinions and judgments are often worthless, but the numerous Russian documents which he reproduces or summarizes are invaluable.

was a means to a higher end, namely, the reconstruction of the social order and the liberation of the working masses.

Bolshevik national policy was to serve the purpose of transition and facilitate the triumph of socialism. It was meant to allay suspicion and permit the proletarian dictatorship to bridge the gulf between dominant and oppressed peoples. Once education and economic planning had achieved substantial equality in the standard of living and cultural level, nationalities would disappear and all groups would be fused into one international and classless society. To quote Lenin again:

> Just as mankind can realize the abolition of classes only through the transitional period of the dictatorship of the oppressed class, so mankind can realize the inevitable fusion of nations only through the period of complete emancipation of all the oppressed nations, i.e., self-determination.[7]

This policy was consistently followed for more than a generation. In 1903, Lenin was instrumental in having party gatherings of the Russian Social Democrats adopt resolutions in favor of the "right of self-determination of all nations included in any state." Ten years later, the central committee of his party reaffirmed its stand on the rights of nationalities and national minorities, specifying this time the free use by each of its "native language in social life and in the schools."[8] Once in power, Lenin and his followers proceeded to give effect to these resolutions.

Critics of the Soviet régime delight in exposing discrepancies between precept and practice in Bolshevik national policy. With bitter sarcasm they point out that cajolery, terror and military force were freely employed to bring recalcitrant nationalities into the fold, at the very time when self-determination was exalted as the right of every people. In the light of Western democratic conceptions such contradictions cannot be harmonized. Lenin, Stalin

---

[7] Quoted in Taracouzio, T. A., *The Soviet Union and International Law* (New York, 1935), pp. 80–81. See also Kohn, Hans, *Nationalism in the Soviet Union* (New York, 1933), pp. 43–48.

[8] Batsell, *op. cit.*, pp. 105–106.

and their colleagues, however, saw nothing inconsistent in their antithetical national program; and, since we desire to understand the Soviet position on the national question rather than commend or condemn it, it is necessary to dwell on this point for a moment.

Communism starts with the premise that the class and not the nation is the fundamental unit of society. In the West, a national group may consist of capitalists, landlords, industrial workers and peasants. Not so in the Soviet Union, where the bourgeoisie and gentry have no right which the government is bound to respect. They are an encumbrance to be cleared away and liquidated at the earliest possible moment. Therefore, the term nationality can apply only to the laboring masses of a given people. Where the outlawed classes take part in national affairs in defiance of communist ideology, every means is deemed legitimate to remove this threat to the class solidarity and class consciousness of the workers. Thus, it was altogether consistent for the Bolshevik leaders to employ force against seceding nationalities, in which the voices of the aristocrats, the clergy, and the middle class had not been silenced.

Moreover, the communist asserts that the working class is itself in need of guidance and enlightenment. Corrupted by capitalist institutions and ideas, the masses, the communist feels, are often incapable of correct judgments. Until the desired economic and cultural progress has been achieved, they must submit to the tutelage or dictatorship of the proletariat. This favored class, or its enlightened "vanguard," the Communist Party, is the guardian of the national as well as the class interests of a people. Therefore, even if the masses of a certain nationality determine to secede from the Soviet state, that decision may be scorned as a symptom of ignorance or heresy. The redemption of the erring masses is the legitimate function, indeed the duty, of the supreme communist authorities at the central seat of government; especially since, truth being absolute and monolithic, the latter can always count on the full approval and cooperation of the "true" proletarian leaders of the nationality.

On this, the Bolshevik leaders minced no words. Writing in 1913, Stalin declared:

> A Nation has the right to arrange its life on autonomous lines. It even has the right to secede. But this does not mean that it should do so under all circumstances, that autonomy, or separation, will everywhere and always be advantageous for a nation, i.e., for the majority of its population, i.e., for the toiling strata.[9]

The final decision would rest with the "Social Democracy," that is, the Communist Party, or, in effect, its supreme leaders.[10] This was the rationale which motivated all measures taken by the Bolsheviks to solve the national question.

3. THE PEOPLE'S COMMISSARIAT FOR NATIONALITIES

The question of nationalities commanded the attention of the Bolshevik leaders the moment they seized power. On November 8, 1917, the morrow of the Revolution, Stalin was named Commissar for Nationalities and assigned the task of working out a solution of the troublesome problem. A Georgian by birth, and at home in the Caucasian "Witches Cauldron," he was familiar with the difficulties and had clearly formulated ideas on the subject. He directed nationality policies with a firm hand, fashioning national republics and regions and welding them into a unit. By 1922, when the Constitution of the U.S.S.R. (Union of Soviet Socialist Republics) had been drafted, his task was complete. The Commissariat for Nationalities was abolished the day after the Constitution came into force, in July, 1923. Its place was taken in the new and federal Soviet Union by the Soviet of Nationalities.

In a broad, general way, the mission of the Commissar for Nationalities was clear. It was twofold: to win the oppressed peoples to the Soviet cause by convincing them that the policy of

---
[9] Stalin, Joseph, *Marxism and the National and Colonial Question* (New York, n. d.), p. 20. This position was affirmed by the central committee of the Bolshevik party in 1913. See Batsell, *op. cit.*, pp. 105–106.

[10] See Stalin, *op. cit.*, pp. 64, 79, 298.

Russification had been abandoned; and, while exalting the right of self-determination, to see to it that this elastic principle did not reach beyond the bounds set by Communist doctrine. With regard to methods, however, the directives were vague, and Stalin had virtually a free hand.

The tried and tested technique of propaganda was, of course, used liberally; appeals, proclamations and manifestoes repeatedly condemned oppression and Russification, and dangled before the wary nationalities the tempting ideal of self-determination.[11] Stalin, however, also employed measures of more constructive and more permanent character—he encouraged and supervised the building of "autonomous republics" and "autonomous areas." To afford constitutional sanction for this policy, he "stretched" the provisions of Article 11 of the Constitution of the R.S.F.S.R. (Russian Soviet Federative Socialist Republic), which dealt with regional unions of soviets, to include autonomous *national* units.[12] Regionalism thus became a conception of nationality as well as of geography.

In May and December, 1920, decrees were issued reorganizing the Commissariat of Nationalities. Its functions were declared to be:

a. The study and execution of all measures guaranteeing the fraternal collaboration of the nationalities and tribes of the Russian Soviet Republic;

b. The study and execution of all measures necessary to guarantee the interests of national-minorities on the territory of other nationalities of the Russian Soviet Federation;

c. The settlement of all litigious questions arising from the mixture of nationalities.[13]

To these broad objectives may be added another implied function, namely, the propagation of communist ideology among the non-Russian peoples—a function which, it need hardly be said, was fulfilled with consummate skill.

[11] See, for example, Bunyan, J., and Fisher, H. H., *The Bolshevik Revolution, 1917–1918: Documents and Materials* (Stanford, 1934), pp. 282–284, 372–374, 394–397, 467–469; Batsell, *op. cit.*, pp. 76–77.

[12] See below, p. 85. See also Webb, S. and B., *Soviet Communism: A New Civilization?* (New York, 1938), I, p. 142; Batsell, *op. cit.*, p. 84.

[13] *Ibid.*, p. 119.

The reorganization also involved the establishment of a "Soviet of Nationalities" at the head of the Commissariat. This consisted of the presidents of delegations from the national areas, who sat with five nominees of Stalin and under his presidency. The Commissar, however, retained full power, for the functions of the new body were advisory and Stalin was also authorized to appoint his own resident agent to the capital of every national region, so as to be able to "watch over" the execution of the decrees of the central authorities.[14]

Thus with power firmly in his hands, and the nationalities mollified by a sense of participation, Stalin was free to fashion the structure of soviet national federalism.

4. THE STRUCTURE OF SOVIET NATIONAL FEDERALISM: THE R.S.F.S.R. (RUSSIAN SOVIET FEDERATIVE SOCIALIST REPUBLIC)

Chapter I of the Constitution of the R.S.F.S.R. (July 10, 1918) reads in part:

> The Russian Soviet Republic is established on the basis of a free union of free nations, as a federation of national soviet republics.[15]

This statement did not appear in the original "Declaration of the Rights of the Laboring and Exploited People," published in November, 1917, over the signatures of Lenin and Stalin, because the prevailing opinion in Bolshevik circles was at that time still unitary and centralistic. Federalism, however, rapidly gained adherents and, when the First All-Russian Congress of Soviets met and confirmed the Declaration on January 24, 1918, the clause quoted above and characterizing the R.S.F.S.R. as a "federation of national soviet republics" was added. It was formally incorporated

---

[14] For another and elaborate decree, that of July 27, 1922, on the Commissariat, see *ibid.*, pp. 184–191.

[15] For the document, see *ibid.*, pp. 80–81 ff. See also Chekalin, M., *The National Question in the Soviet Union* (New York, 1941), pp. 10–11.

as part of the Fundamental Law in July, 1918.[16] At the time, it was no more than an affirmation of future policy, for the Bolsheviks had yet to establish their authority by force of arms. However, efforts were made to redeem the pledge even during the civil war, and the momentum was speeded up once the new régime was firmly in the saddle.

A chronological account of the organization of the numerous nationalities and national minorities would begin with the early days of the Revolution and take us almost to the present. The story would inevitably be lengthy, a good deal of it of academic interest only, and, in part at least, quite confusing. For the purposes of our brief survey it will be best to point out the major trends and achievements.

A considerable number of nationalities were organized during the first few years of the Bolshevik régime. But it was at first difficult to discern any plan in the recognition of "allied republics," "autonomous republics," and "autonomous regions." By 1922, however, a clear pattern had emerged. Larger or stronger nationalities, and those situated on the borders, were allowed a nominal independence, with treaties of alliance to bind them to the R.S.F.S.R., that is, to the Bolshevik leaders at Moscow. Such were the Ukrainians, White Russians, the Azerbaijan Turks, the Armenians, and the Georgians. More tractable peoples were limited to autonomy within the R.S.F.S.R.: those with considerable and concentrated populations, large territories or greater economic and cultural assets, became autonomous republics; less numerous peoples, enclaves within larger nationalities, and semi-nomad aggregations of tribes were declared autonomous regions.[17]

The bulk of the pre-war Russian Empire remained a single entity, the R.S.F.S.R., which reached from the Baltic to the Pacific and from the Polar regions to the borders of Afghanistan and

---

[16] This matter is discussed fully in a forthcoming book on the political evolution of Soviet Russia by M. M. Laserson.

[17] For the treaties of alliance and decrees establishing these national units, see Batsell, *op. cit.*, pp. 137–196, 243–269.

China. Within its broad folds nestled the numerous nationalities organized as autonomous republics or autonomous regions. The total number of national units, and that of each category, has varied during the past twenty-five years, as additional peoples achieved official national status, or as progress resulted in the promotion of a nationality from one category to another. Thus, the Kalmuks and Buryats, both peoples of Mongol stock and Buddhist faith, who live respectively along the Caspian Sea and Lake Baikal, first formed autonomous regions and were subsequently raised to autonomous republics. Similarly, the Karelian peasants situated on the Finnish frontier, and the Kirghiz mountaineers of the Tien-Shan, were elevated from autonomous republics to union republics, independent of the R.S.F.S.R. Article 22 of the new Constitution of 1936 listed seventeen autonomous republics and six autonomous regions in the R.S.F.S.R.[18]

The Constitution of the R.S.F.S.R. did not clarify the relationship of the autonomous republics and regions to the all-Russian central authorities. It left to the nationalities the decision of joining the federation, prohibited the repression of national minorities, and provided for a Commissariat of Nationalities. Article 11, to which reference has already been made, provided the only clue to the actual status of a nationality in the federation. It read:

> The soviets of regions which are distinguished by a particular national and territorial character may unite in autonomous regional unions, at the head of which, as well as at the head of all other regional federations which may be formed in general, stand the regional congresses of soviets and their executive organs. These autonomous regional unions enter into the RSFSR on a federal basis.

In other words, the nationalities constituted regional, provincial or smaller territorial units and enjoyed a status and a political structure similar to other territorial subdivisions. They were represented in the All-Russian Congress of Soviets on the same basis as corresponding territorial units.

[18] See *Constitution of the Union of Soviet Socialist Republics*. These are also given in Chekalin, *op. cit.*, p. 19.

In administrative practice, however, the nationalities enjoyed autonomy in cultural and local affairs. They were encouraged to choose from among their own people teachers, judges, and other local officials who were familiar with the language, customs, and traditions of the people. The vernacular was recognized as the official language in the governmental agencies of the nationality. And the schools employed this language as the medium of instruction. In short, "federalism" in the R.S.F.S.R. meant local government by the native population, and linguistic and cultural autonomy.[19]

5. THE STRUCTURE OF SOVIET NATIONAL FEDERALISM: THE U.S.S.R. (UNION OF SOVIET SOCIALIST REPUBLICS)

In 1922, five republics were in an anomalous position. The Ukraine, White Russia, Georgia, Azerbaijan, and Armenia were nominally independent, but closely allied with the R.S.F.S.R. One War Office and one Foreign Office served them all. Members of the Communist Party occupied the important posts, as in the R.S.F.S.R. Decrees of the Moscow authorities were quickly enacted and enforced in the allied republics. But there was no federal government to give structural unity to what was in fact a united country.

Proposals for a federal union were made in rapid succession during 1922 by all of the allied republics, indicating perhaps prompting by the leaders of the Communist Party. First, the three neighboring Republics of Georgia, Armenia and Azerbaijan were combined in the Transcaucasian Federation. This was accomplished by December 13, 1922. Ten days later, when the R.S.F.S.R. congress of soviets met at Moscow, a resolution in favor of union was introduced by Stalin, and carried. A committee of representatives of the republics affected was thereupon named to draft the terms of union, and the First Congress of Soviets of the U.S.S.R. con-

---

[19] The Constitution of the R.S.F.R.S. is given in Batsell, *op. cit.*, pp. 80–95. See also Webb, S. and B., *op. cit.*, I, pp. 142–144, 154–155.

vened immediately to sanction the instrument. All this was accomplished with rare speed—by December 30, 1922.[20]

Stalin, however, found the document unacceptable because inadequate provision had been made for the needs of nationalities and national minorities. In particular, he favored a bicameral central agency, so as to assure representation by national unit as well as by population. Acting through the Communist Party, he was instrumental in securing a revision, which incorporated his plan for a "Soviet of Nationalities." The revised constitution was accepted by all the interested parties, and ratified by the Central Executive Committee of the U.S.S.R. on July 6, 1923, when it went into force. The second Congress of Soviets of the U.S.S.R. confirmed the action of its executive committee on January 31, 1924.[21]

The Constitution of the U.S.S.R. prescribes the organs of government, the respective powers and functions of the Union and its constituent republics, and the relation between the central and national authorities. According to the Constitution of 1923, the supreme organ of the U.S.S.R. was the "All-Union Congress of Soviets," consisting of delegates from all parts of the country. It was a large and unwieldy body which met once every few years, chiefly to hear addresses on general principles of public policy, and to elect a "Central Executive Committee." The latter, known as "TSIK" for short, was a bicameral assembly convened three or four times a year to supervise and confirm legislation and executive action taken in the intervals between meetings. Its two houses were the "Soviet of the Union" and the "Soviet of Nationalities." The former consisted of 607 members in 1935, representing the constituent republics in proportion to population, while the latter was devised to give representation to the various peoples as national

[20] Stalin's Reports to the All-Russian Congress of Soviets (December 26, 1922) and to the first Congress of Soviets of the U.S.S.R. (December 30, 1922) are given in Stalin, *op. cit.,* pp. 120–136.

[21] The documents are given in Batsell, *op. cit.,* pp. 300–320. See also pp. 270–282 ff.; Webb, S. and B., *op. cit.,* pp. 78–81. Stalin's addresses before the twelfth Congress of the Communist Party are given in Stalin, *op. cit.,* pp. 137–171.

units. The day-by-day powers and functions of government, legislative and executive, were shared by the "Presidium" [22] of the Central Executive Committee and the "Council of People's Commissars (Sovnarkom)," which bore some resemblance to a cabinet. Both bodies were chosen by the Central Executive Committee.

The new Constitution of 1936 has introduced a number of variations. The All-Union Congress of Soviets, the highest organ of state power, has become the "Supreme Soviet or Council," and the Central Executive Committee has been eliminated. The Supreme Council, elected for a term of four years and meeting twice a year, is a bicameral legislature consisting of the "Council of the Union" and the "Council of Nationalities." A "Presidium" of thirty-seven, elected at a joint sitting of both chambers, exercises authority in the intervals between sessions of the Supreme Council, and a "Council of People's Commissars," similarly chosen, functions as the Government of the U.S.S.R., with full executive and administrative power.[23]

The Soviet or Council of Nationalities was the creation of Stalin, who had to fight to maintain it against proposals for the fusion of the nationalities and for a streamlined unicameral legislature. It unquestionably helped to quiet the fears of domination by the Great Russians entertained by the weaker nationalities. The notion of equality of the "sovereign republics" was maintained through equal representation, and even the national units within the formerly "independent" republics had their delegates in the Council of Nationalities. Originally, it consisted of five representatives nominated by each of the republics (the autonomous republics as well as the constituent or union republics), and one representative by each of the autonomous regions. The new Constitution of 1936, however, modified this procedure. All the nationalities are still represented in the Council of Nationalities, but the gradation is more consistent: the union or constituent republics are each allowed

---

[22] This body consisted of 27 members, chosen as follows: 9 from the Presidium of the Soviet of the Union, 9 from the Presidium of the Soviet of Nationalities, and 9 elected in a joint session of the two houses.

[23] Chapters III and V of the Constitution of 1936.

twenty-five deputies; the autonomous republics, eleven each; the autonomous regions, five; and "national areas," one.[24]

The Council of Nationalities enjoys equal rights with the Council of the Union, which is the larger of the two houses of the Supreme Council. No law is considered fully in effect without their joint approval. Moreover, the Council of Nationalities has special functions to guard the interests of the national units, to draft decrees in their favor, and to propose modifications of general laws to suit their needs.

Constitutionally, there is a clear division of powers between the central government and the component republics. Three types of governmental functions are distinguished: those that fall solely within the competence of the All-Union authorities; those that are theoretically the province of the national republics; and a third group shared by both. Until recently, functions such as foreign affairs, defense, and foreign and internal trade were solely within the competence of the U.S.S.R., and the All-Union Commissariats or Ministries had exclusive jurisdiction, naming agents or delegates to the various republics, where they sat as members of the local cabinets. In February, 1944, however, the union or constituent republics were given a share in the administration of military and foreign affairs.[25] Other departments, including internal trade and finance, have been shared by the Union and the republics from the beginning. Each republic has its corresponding commissars, but the central authorities determine general policy and exercise ultimate control. Local and cultural affairs, such as education, health, social welfare and home affairs, are, in theory, left to the national units, there being no such ministries in the U.S.S.R. government. In fact, however, the central authorities formulate "basic principles" which all must follow.[26]

[24] The "national area" was introduced in 1929, as a grade below the "autonomous region."
[25] For an admirable analysis of this action, see Shotwell, James T., *The Great Decision* (New York, 1944), pp. 67–82.
[26] On the structure of government, see Webb, S. and B., *op. cit.*, pp. 81–95; Chekalin, *op. cit.*, pp. 13–16; Brailsford, H. N., *How the Soviets Work* (New York, 1927), pp. 70–75, 104–111.

At the time of its inception (1923), the Soviet Union was a federation of four "independent" or "union republics"—the Russian, Ukrainian, White Russian and Transcaucasian Republics. In 1924, the Turcoman and the Uzbek republics were admitted, and in 1929, the Tadjik republic, all located in Central Asia and bordering on Persia and Afghanistan. The new Constitution of 1936 raised the number of constituent republics to eleven: the Transcaucasian federation of Azerbaijan, Georgia, and Armenia was dissolved and its component states were declared union republics; and two autonomous republics of the R.S.F.S.R. in central Asia—the Kazak and the Kirghiz—were raised to the level of union republics.[27] The annexation during 1939–1941 of the Baltic lands, eastern Poland, Bessarabia, and northern Bukovina resulted in a further increase in the number of union republics. "Western Ukraine and Western White Russia"—the Soviet names for eastern Poland—were incorporated in the Soviet states of corresponding names. The remaining territories became five union republics—the Karelo-Finnish, the Moldavian, the Lithuanian, the Latvian, and the Estonian.[28]

The sixteen union republics are national-territorial subdivisions of the U.S.S.R. Virtually every one of them contains minorities which are recognized as national entities, at least for cultural purposes. Reference has already been made to the autonomous republics and autonomous regions of the R.S.F.S.R. Similar large national units exist in at least six other union republics; the Constitution of 1936 listed a total of twenty-two autonomous republics, seventeen of them in the R.S.F.S.R., and nine autonomous regions, six in the R.S.F.S.R. In addition, there are national counties, districts and

[27] In 1936, Stalin stated the qualifications of an "independent" or union republic. The nationality must be a compact, self-conscious group of at least one million people, and, he added without a trace of humor, its territory must be on the border of the Union so that it might, if it wished, exercise the constitutional right to secede. See Harper, S. N., *The Government of the Soviet Union* (New York, 1938), p. 45.

[28] Note the excellent chart on pp. 92–95. This chart first appeared in *Soviet Russia Today* (July, 1944, pp. 26–27), and is here reproduced by permission of its author, Corliss Lamont.

villages. It has been estimated that in 1935 there were 5,000 national soviets in the U.S.S.R., small enclaves in which national fragments—Bulgarian, Moldavian, Greek, Jewish, Polish, Czech, Swedish, French and scores of others—cultivated their languages and practiced their traditional customs. Of an estimated total population of close to 200,000,000 in 1939, about one-half were not Great Russians,[29] and every appreciable minority group among them possessed or was encouraged to aspire to national status. So far as constitutional pronouncements and governmental machinery can satisfy national claims, the Soviet Union has solved its nationality problem.

6. THE FUNCTIONING OF SOVIET NATIONAL FEDERALISM: AN APPRAISAL

To what extent does practice conform to theory? Do the lofty ideals enshrined in the Constitution actually ensure national freedom and equality? Is the structure of national federalism in the Soviet Union an instrument of self-expression and self-development of the masses, or is it a mechanism to conceal dictatorship?

As might be expected, opinions differ widely, apologists exhausting superlatives in praise of Soviet national harmony, and opponents scoffing at what they regard as a fraud perpetrated upon an innocent world. These extremes might be disregarded, but the understanding of Soviet national policy is not furthered even by respectable and friendly interpreters like Sidney and Beatrice Webb in their *Soviet Communism*. Obsessed with the Western liberal's aversion to nationalism as a totally destructive force, they see in the new Soviet civilization no connection between the state and nationality. The problem, they tell us, has been solved in the Soviet Union "by the novel device of dissociating statehood from both nationality and race." They regard the Soviet Union as an "un-

---

[29] See Hrdlička, A., *The Peoples of the Soviet Union* (Washington, 1942), pp. 1–2, 25–26; Webb, S. and B., *op. cit.*, I, 154–155, 457–459.

CHART OF SOVIET

Republic, Region or District	Date of Formation	Population (Estimated as of July 1, 1941, and based on the 1939 census)	Predominant Ethnic Strain	Total of Dominant Nationality in All U.S.S.R. (1941 Estimate)[2]
RUSSIAN SOVIET FEDERATED SOCIALIST REPUBLIC (R.S.F.S.R.)	1918	114,337,428	Slav	104,833,638
Autonomous Soviet Socialist Republics				
BASHKIR A.S.S.R.	1919	3,304,476	Turco-Tatar	Bashkir 885,747
BURIAT-MONGOLIAN A.S.S.R.	1923	569,713	Mongol	Buriat 249,534
CHECHEN-INGUSH A.S.S.R.	1936	732,838	Japhetic	428,400
CHUVASH A.S.S.R.	1925	1,132,360	Turco-Tatar	1,437,424
CRIMEAN A.S.S.R.	1921	1,184,070	Turco-Tatar	Tatar 4,518,808
DAGHESTAN A.S.S.R.	1921	977,800	Japhetic	900,928
KABARDIN-BALKAR A.S.S.R.	1936	377,485	Japhetic	172,442
KALMYK A.S.S.R.	1935	231,935	Mongol	141,150
KOMI A.S.S.R.	1936	335,172	Finno-Ugrian	429,487
MARI A.S.S.R.	1936	608,904	Finno-Ugrian	505,711
MORDOVIAN A.S.S.R.	1934	1,248,982	Finno-Ugrian	Mordov. 1,525,166
NORTH OSSETIAN A.S.S.R.	1936	345,592	Iranian	372,557
TATAR A.S.S.R.	1920	3,067,740	Turco-Tatar	4,518,808
UDMURT A.S.S.R.	1934	1,281,987	Finno-Ugrian	636,442
YAKUT A.S.S.R.	1922	420,892	Turco-Tatar	324,000
Autonomous Regions				
ADYGEI A.R.	1922	254,055	Japhetic	92,441
CHERKESS A.R.	1928	97,233	Japhetic	172,442
JEWISH A.R.	1934	113,925	Jewish	5,334,824
KARACHAI A.R.	1926	157,540	Turco-Tatar	79,583
KHAKASS A.R.	1930	284,404	Turkic & Mongol	55,274
OIROT A.R.	1922	169,631	Turco-Tatar	Oirot 50,140
National Districts				
AGIN BURIAT MONGOL N.D.	1937	32,000	Mongol	
CHUKOT N.D.	1930	Based on '26 census 14,983	Paleo-Asiatic	*Figures not available*
EVENKI N.D.	1930	38,804	Mongol	
KOMI-PERMIAK N.D.	1925	201,000	Finno-Ugrian	
KORIAK N.D.	1930	12,500	Paleo-Asiatic	
NENETS N.D.	1929	28,125	Mongol	
OSTIAK-VOGUL N.D.	1930	Based on '26 census 102,200	Finno-Ugrian	
TAIMYR N.D.	1930	8,000	Mongol	*Figures not available*
UST ORDIN BURIAT MONGOL N.D.	1937	110,000	Mongol	
YAMALO-NENETS N.D.	1930	12,753	Mongol	
UKRAINIAN SOVIET SOCIALIST REPUBLIC	1919	42,272,943	Slav	37,043,492

(Continued on page 94)

NATIONALITIES

National Origins [1] (In Per Cent of Total as of 1926 Census)	Area (In Square Miles as of 1944)	Location	Capital
Russian, 73.4%; Ukrainian, 7.8% Kazak, 3.8%; Tatar, 2.8%	6,326,395	Soviet Europe and Siberia	Moscow
Bashkir, 23.5%; Russian, 39.9%	54,233	Southwest Urals	Ufa
Buriat, 43.8%; Russian, 52.7%	127,020	Southeastern Siberia	Ulan-Ude
Chechen, 58%; Ingush, 13%	6,060	Caucasus	Grozny
Chuvash, 80%; Russian, 15.8%	6,909	Middle Volga River	Cheboksary
Tatar, 25.1%; Russian, 42.2%	10,036	Black Sea	Simferopol
Gortsy, 64.5%; Russian, 12.5%	13,124	Northeast Caucasus	Makhach-Kala
Kabardin, 60%; Balkar, 16.3%	4,747	Caucasus	Nalchik
Kalmyk, 75.6%; Russian, 10.7%	28,641	Lower Volga River	Elista
Komi, 92.3%; Russian, 6.1%	144,711	Northwest Urals	Syktyvkar
Mari, 51.4%; Russian, 43.6%	8,993	Middle Volga River	Yoshkar-Ola
Mordovian, 37.4%; Russian, 57.3%	9,843	Middle Volga Basin	Saransk
Ossetian, 84.2%; Ukrainian, 6.8%	2,393	Caucasus	Dzaudzhikau
Tatar, 50.4%; Russian, 41.8%	25,900	Middle Volga River	Kazan
Udmurt, 52.3%; **Russian, 43.3%**	15,015	Middle Volga Basin	Izhevsk
Yakut, 81.6%; Russian, 10.4%	1,169,927	Northeast Siberia	Yakutsk
Cherkess, 47.8%; Russian, 25.6%	1,505	Northwest Caucasus	Maikop
Kabardin, 33.3%; Beskesekabaz, 29.7%; Nogaitsi, 16.8%; Cherkess, 7.2%	1,273	Caucasus	Sulimov
Jew, 40% (est. 1936)	14,204	Southern Far East	Birobidzhan
Karachai, 83.3%; Ukrainian, 4.4%	3,821	Caucasus	Mikoyan-Shakhar
Khakass, 51.7%; Russian, 48.3%	19,261	South Central Siberia	Abakan
Oirot and Altai, 37.2%; Russian, 52%	35,936	South Central Siberia	Oirot-Tura
⎫	10,730	Southeastern Siberia	Aginskoe
⎪	254,991	Bering Strait	Anadyr
Figures	209,057	North Central Siberia	Tura
not	8,916	Northwest Siberia	Kudymkar
available	119,968	North Far East	Palana
⎪	82,797	Northeast Soviet Europe	Narian Mar
⎪	293,360	Northwest Siberia	Ostiago-Vogulsk
Figures	286,643	North Central Siberia	Dudinka
not			
available	10,923	Southeastern Siberia	Ust-Orda
⎭	179,876	Northwest Siberia	Salegard
Ukrainian, 80%; Russian, 9.2%; Jew, 5.4%	202,540	Southwest Soviet Europe	Kiev

(*Continued on page 95*)

CHART OF SOVIET

Republic, Region or District	Date of Formation	Population (Estimated as of July 1, 1941, and based on the 1939 census)	Predominant Ethnic Strain	Total of Dominant Nationality in All U.S.S.R. (1941 Estimate)[2]
BYELO-RUSSIAN S.S.R.	1919	10,525,511	Slav	8,595,036
KARELO-FINNISH S.S.R.	1940	512,977	Finno-Ugrian	Karel. 265,431
				Finn 170,341
ESTONIAN S.S.R.	1940	1,120,000	Finno-Ugrian	1,124,102
LATVIAN S.S.R.	1940	1,950,502	Baltic	1,607,925
LITHUANIAN S.S.R.	1940	3,134,070	Baltic	2,697,942
MOLDAVIAN S.S.R.	1940	2,321,225	Romanian	1,624,857
GEORGIAN S.S.R.[3]	1921	3,722,252	Japhetic	2,362,801
ABKHAZIAN A.S.S.R.	1921	303,147	Japhetic	Abkhaz. 61,963
ADZHAR A.S.S.R.	1921	179,946	Japhetic	91,260
SOUTH OSSETIAN A.R.	1922	111,501	Iranian	372,557
ARMENIAN S.S.R.[3]	1920	1,346,709	Japhetic	2,261,207
AZERBAIDZHAN S.S.R.[3]	1920	3,372,794	Turco-Tatar	Azer. 2,390,374
NAKHICHEVAN A.S.S.R.	1924	138,528	Turco-Tatar	Azer. 2,390,374
NAGORNO-KARABAKH A.R.	1923	180,063	Japhetic	2,261,207
KAZAKH S.S.R.	1936	6,458,175	Turco-Tatar	3,256,193
UZBEK S.S.R.	1924	6,601,619	Turco-Tatar	5,090,116
KARA-KALPAK A.S.S.R.	1932	436,995	Turco-Tatar	195,211
TURKMEN S.S.R.	1924	1,317,693	Turco-Tatar	853,009
TADZHIK S.S.R.	1929	1,560,540	Iranian	1,291,399
GORNO-BADAKHSHAN A.R.	1927	41,769	Iranian	41,019
KIRGIZ S.S.R.	1936	1,533,439	Turco-Tatar	929,231
		202,087,877[4]		

[1] It is to be noted that all the chief peoples of the Soviet Union overflow to some extent the boundaries of the territorial divisions bearing their names. Thus each main division has within it a minority or minorities other than the predominant one. *National origin* does not necessarily coincide with *nationality*.

[2] This column, based on the 1939 census, does not include the totals of the following national groups in the Soviet Union: the Poles, 4,158,250; the Germans, 1,495,854; the Greeks, 300,419; the Bulgarians, 269,242; the Koreans, 189,577; the Gypsies, 100,000; the Kurds, 48,195; the Chinese, 31,124; the Czechoslovaks, 30,006; the Arabs, 22,898; the Assyrians, 21,233; the peoples of the National Districts and a few others.

NATIONALITIES (*Cont'd*)

National Origins [1] (In Per Cent of Total as of 1926 Census)	Area (In Square Miles as of 1944)	Location	Capital
Byelo-Russian, 80.6%; Jew, 8.2%	89,300	West Soviet Europe	Minsk
Karelian and Finn, 43%; Russian, 57%	75,656	Northwest Soviet Europe	Petrozavodsk
Estonian, 87.7%; Russian, 8.2% est. 1941	18,050	Baltic Sea	Tallinn
Latvian, 75.6%; Russian, 12.3%	24,700	Baltic Sea	Riga
Lithuanian, 85%; Russian, 2.5%	22,800	Baltic Sea	Vilnius
Moldavian, 70%	13,680	Southwest Soviet Europe	Kishinev
Georgian, 67.7%; Armenian, 11.6%	26,875	Transcaucasus	Tbilisi
Abkhazian, 27.8%; Georgian, 33.5%	3,358	Transcaucasus	Sukhumi
Adzharian, 53.7%; Georgian, 14.5%	1,080	Transcaucasus	Batumi
Ossetian, 69.1%; Georgian, 26.9%	1,428	Transcaucasus	Stalinir
Armenian, 84.7%; Turkic, 8.2%	11,580	Transcaucasus	Erevan
Turkic, 63.3%; Armenian, 12.4%	33,200	Transcaucasus	Baku
Turkic, 84.5%; Armenian, 10.8%	2,277	Transcaucasus	Nakhichevan
Armenian, 89.1%; Turkic, 10%	1,659	Transcaucasus	Stepanakert
Kazakh, 57.1%; Russian, 19.7%	1,059,700	Central Asia	Alma-Ata
Uzbek, 76%; Russian, 5.6%	146,000	Central Asia	Tashkent
Karakalpak, 39.1%; Kazakh, 27%	79,631	Central Asia	Turtkul
Turkmen, 72%; Uzbek, 10.5%	171,250	Central Asia	Ashkhabad
Tadzhik, 78.4%; Uzbek, 17.9%	55,545	Central Asia	Stalinabad
Iranian, 87%; Kirgiz, 13%	25,784	Central Asia	Khorog
Kirgiz, 66.6%; Russian, 11.7%	75,950	Central Asia	Frunze
	8,353,221[4]		

[3] The three Republics of Georgia, Armenia and Azerbaidzhan first united in 1922 in the Transcaucasian Soviet Federated Socialist Republic, which then became one of the four original Union Republics of the U.S.S.R. In 1936 this federation was dissolved and its three constituent members became Union Republics in their own right.

[4] Totals of area and population are reached by adding figures for the 16 Union Republics, abbreviated as "S.S.R."

Copyright, 1945, by Corliss Lamont

national" state, on the theory that it is as independent of nationality as it is of religious faith.[30]

The Soviet Union, a Multi-National, Federal State

The analogy with religion is highly strained. For twenty-five years the Soviet authorities discountenanced religion and encouraged efforts to combat it, whereas national self-expression was sanctioned, and, in fact, nurtured and cradled. Religion was completely excluded from the structure and functioning of the Soviet State, but nationality was and is an important factor both in the theory and in the practice of Soviet federalism.

The confusion has its roots in three circumstances. First, Westerners have overlooked the fact that, when the Soviet authorities thunder against chauvinism and separation, they are denouncing what they regard as symptoms of "bourgeois nationalism." They recognize, in addition, a positive factor in nationality, as has already been indicated. Secondly, people are misled by repeated references to the ultimate fusion of all nations in a common humanity, classless and international. It would be well to note that, like all ultimates, the Soviet variety tends to recede into the distant future, while the transitory hardens into permanence. It is quite true that the Communists hope eventually to achieve an un-national society, just as they expect the state itself ultimately to fade away. For the time being, however, the Soviet state is no more un-national than it is non-existent.

A third cause of confusion is the assumption that the only alternative to the national state is the un-national. Accustomed as Westerners are to the identification of the state with a dominant nationality, they mistakenly believe that the repudiation of Great Russian predominance involves the dissociation of nationality from the state. In the land of the Soviets, the intolerant national state has been superseded, not by the un-national, but by the *multi-national* state. The Soviet leaders are entirely clear on this point, and Stalin himself has repeatedly stressed the fact that the U.S.S.R.

[30] See Webb, S. and B., *op. cit.*, pp. 153-154, 157-158.

is not a "one-nation state" but a "multi-national socialist state." [31]

Soviet federalism likewise requires clarification. If we employed the term "federalism" in the American sense, implying a clear division of powers, with the State and Federal Government each supreme in its own sphere, then, of course, it could not apply to the Soviet régime. No function of government or aspect of life is outside the competence of the central authorities at Moscow. They lay down general principles, supervise all activities, and may veto or disallow any measure taken by the organs of the national regions or republics. National freedom does not extend to the sphere of communist ideology, and there is no federalism in the fundamentals of economics and politics. It is significant that the Council of Nationalities, the highest representative agency of the national units, has never voted differently from the Council of the Union, the second house of the bicameral Supreme Council.[32] The U.S.S.R. is ruled by a dictatorship which permeates all governmental machinery and all public life.

Soviet national federalism means: (1) the recognition of national differences and the encouragement of national languages, institutions and customs; (2) the acknowledgment of the fact that the composite character of the population must be reflected in the state, that is, it must be multi-national; (3) the division of the country into national territorial units; (4) the association of these units as component elements of the state; and (5) a wide latitude in regional and local self-government, so that the organs of the national republics and regions may be manned by natives familiar with the language and customs of the people.

National Equality

Article 123 of the present U.S.S.R. Constitution guarantees equal rights to all citizens "irrespective of their nationality or

---
[31] See Stalin, Joseph, *The New Soviet Constitution* (New York, 1936), p. 10; Chekalin, *op. cit.*, p. 16; Aslanova, C., *The National Question Solved* (Moscow, 1939), p. 36.
[32] Webb, S. and B., *op. cit.*, p. 90.

race." This has been observed fully in letter and spirit. Privileges granted to the factory worker extend to every national and racial group without qualification, and disabilities incident to dictatorship fall equally upon the Great Russian and the tribesman of the steppes. Non-governmental relations, too, are carefully watched, and all forms of national or racial discrimination are sternly suppressed, while a widespread propaganda seeks to promote harmony and mutual respect.

Moreover, this national equality appertains to the group as well as to the individual. The Bolsheviks have no favorites among the nationalities, nor are they constrained by preconceived notions. The Jews are a case in point. In the West, there is much confusion of thought as to whether Jews do or do not constitute a nationality, and some Western writers cherish their dogmas even when dealing with Soviet Jews. The Webbs, for example, declare pontifically that the Jews are an "important and peculiar minority, racial and religious rather than national." [33] Whatever this definition may mean, the Soviet leaders do not subscribe to it. When the present war began, there were several Jewish national areas in the Ukraine and the Crimea, and a Jewish Autonomous Region had been set up in Birobidjan, on the left bank of the Amur River, not far from Khabarovsk. In the Soviet Union, the attributes of nationality are simple and clear. Any and every people with a distinct language or dialect, a territory on which it is concentrated in appreciable numbers, and the desire to maintain its identity, is accorded recognition as a nationality.

"National equality" might be a phrase to conjure with, but it is meaningless if economic and cultural disparity perpetuates actual inequality. The Soviet leaders regard this as the gist of the national question, and they have made determined efforts to raise the economic and cultural level of the more primitive nationalities of the Union. In the prodigious economic transformations of the past two decades, the rate of development of the backward peoples has been far greater than that of the Great Russians.

[33] *Op. cit.*, I, 149.

Tens of thousands of organizers, engineers and technicians, sent into the long-neglected borderlands, have wrought miracles of modernization. Railroads, highways, electric-power stations, mining shafts and industrial cities have sprung up on the steppes where the nomad had roamed, in desolate mountain regions, and in open country which had been broken only by the wooden plow. Irrigation works have brought water and fertility to parched lands in Central Asia and Transcaucasia. Coal, copper and lead mines are now operating in the Kazak country, and textile mills in the Uzbek Republic. Manganese is produced in Transcaucasia, oil in the Bashkir region of the southern Urals, coal in the Kirghiz territory. And Turkestan boasts silk mills, canneries and tanneries. Primitive farming has given way to intensive scientific agriculture and to stockraising, organized in large collectives and aided by modern machinery. Everywhere, natives have been trained in increasing numbers to operate the machines, to share in management and to assume leadership in trade unions and other agencies, thus laying the foundations for a higher standard of living and for genuine equality.

Cultural Freedom

Immediately after the Revolution the Bolshevik leaders declared in a proclamation to the Moslems of Russia:

Henceforth your beliefs and customs, your national and cultural institutions, are free and inviolable. Build your national life freely and unhindered. You have a right to do so.[34]

Understood in the light of Western ideas, this pledge has been but partially made good. National institutions rooted in the older economy have been suppressed, and beliefs and customs associated with religion discountenanced. Soviet leaders, however, glory in the ideal enunciated by this proclamation and insist that it has been realized fully. The discrepancy is due to a difference in point of view. In the Soviet Union the words are interpreted in terms of

[34] Bunyan and Fisher, *op. cit.*, p. 467.

Communist ideology, which recognizes only the right of the "laboring masses" to self-determination, and countenances none but proletarian and "socially useful" beliefs and customs.[35] Stalin has coined a phrase which epitomizes Soviet national policy. Culture in the U.S.S.R., says he, is "national in form and Socialist in content." The Communist rationale is inculcated into every mind; and a common core of aims, ideas and beliefs conditions the thinking of everyone, whatever his nationality. In form, however, culture remains national, reflecting the differences in language and the national characteristics of the numerous peoples.

Another restriction upon cultural freedom should be noted. No nationality or national minority of the Soviet Union may maintain contact or derive spiritual or cultural sustenance from kindred peoples outside the Union. This, too, follows from Communist premises. Since the non-Soviet world disregards the class struggle and tolerates bourgeois institutions and customs, close relations might dim the class consciousness of the Soviet peoples. In other words, the Soviet nationalities must conform to class ideals as well as to national ideals, and class aims always take precedence over national purposes. These restrictions apart, cultural freedom prevails in the Soviet Union; and whatever standard one chooses as the norm, one must own that Soviet national policy has been statesmanlike, and the achievements phenomenal.

Freedom of language is virtually unrestricted.[36] The vernacular of every people is an official language in its regional and local councils, administrative organs, courts of justice, schools, and in all relations between the people and their government. This applies not only to the constituent republics whose languages have official status in the U.S.S.R., but also to the less numerous nationalities and national minorities living in their midst. Local rulers, like the Ukrainians or White Russians, cannot impose their language on

---

[35] See above, pp. 77–81.
[36] The Hebrew language has been frowned upon as a non-proletarian and clerical tongue, primarily because of the prejudices of Jewish communists.

their minorities. Even the most primitive dialects have not been ignored. Alphabets have been invented for numerous peoples like the Bashkirs, with Latin, not Russian, characters as a basis, and printed books have been provided for the first time in their history. In 1935, children and adults were receiving instruction in more than eighty different languages, and newspapers were published in eighty-eight tongues.

Soviet cultural freedom is largely a matter of language, but not exclusively so. Theatres, cinemas, the opera, libraries, publishing houses, newspapers and periodicals, folk songs and dances, national art, customs and costumes, fables and traditions are encouraged and fostered.

In all of this, the backward peoples have made the greatest proportionate progress, more being provided for them in per capita subventions than for the more advanced nationalities. Peoples like the Tartars, Bashkirs, Kazaks, and a host of others, who were practically illiterate twenty-five years ago, now boast hundreds of schools, scores of high schools and colleges, and numerous other mediums of popular education.

Soviet schooling merits special attention. Because of the great variety of conditions, especially in the R.S.F.S.R., the nationalities have been divided into four categories. The languages of the largest and most advanced peoples are the mediums of instruction throughout their educational system, including higher education and research institutes. A second group of nationalities, with substantial populations and their own alphabets, books and an educated class, receive instruction in the vernacular to the age of eighteen. Higher educational institutions employ the Russian language, but there are professional chairs for the study of the native languages and literatures. Thirdly, lesser nationalities for whom alphabets had to be devised, but who live in compact masses, are taught in the mother tongue only in the primary school, while secondary and higher education are given in Russian. The fourth group consists of very small national fragments, dispersed peoples and nomadic tribes, with alphabets in the process of formation, and little culture; these are taught in their dialect in the "pre-school" institutions, but elementary education is in Russian.

These categories must not be visualized in compact territorial terms, for they cut across a large proportion of the population of the country. Practically in every union and autonomous republic will be found national minorities who enjoy a measure of autonomy in education. For example, in 1941, White Russia had 196 Jewish schools, 178 Russian, 107 Polish, and small numbers of Ukrainian, Lettish, German and Lithuanian schools. Georgia has maintained schools taught in Armenian, Greek, German, Jewish, Russian, Turkish, Assyrian, Polish, Kurdish and other tongues. And in the Ukrainian Republic education has been provided in twenty vernaculars.[37]

7. CONCLUSION

One might think that the division of the Soviet Union into national fragments, its multiplicity of languages, and its variety of schools would result in chaos and confusion; that national rivalries would provide the stimulus for national isolation and separatism. In fact, the Soviet Union gives every appearance of order, unity and national harmony. To be sure, allowance must be made for the rigorous discipline of dictatorship, the steel ring of the Communist Party and the cohesive power of a monolithic ideology. Yet it is difficult to believe that repression and propaganda could alone produce the broad base of contentment which seems to prevail in the land of the Soviets. One is forced to the conclusion that the measures taken to solve the national problem have exerted a profound and pacifying influence upon the composite population of the Union.

[37] On Soviet national education and culture, see Hans, N., and Hessen, S., *Educational Policy in Soviet Russia* (London, 1930), especially pp. 177–183; Webb, S. and B., *op. cit.*, II, pp. 893–896; Yarmolinsky, *op. cit.*, Chap. XV; Kohn, H., *Nationalism in the Soviet Union, op. cit.*, pp. 86–114; Chekalin, *op. cit.*, pp. 22–35.

Long regarded with contempt as inferior and subject peoples, exploited economically and forced to submit to Russification, the nationalities have been encouraged by the new régime to maintain their identity, pursue their cultural aspirations, and aspire to equality with the erstwhile dominant Great Russian people. Emboldened to participate in the common tasks of reconstruction, they have acquired a sense of equality, freedom, and personal worth. Old feelings of inferiority and persecution have given way to courage and self-confidence, and self-expression has stimulated a national renaissance even among primitive groups.

Yet the emphasis on national individuality has not resulted in isolation. No longer in awe of the dominant majority, they do not resent its language and culture. Even while cultivating their own heritage, they learn the Russian language and read its literature avidly. Thus a common means of communication, which Czarism failed to impose by force, has been achieved through mutual confidence.[38]

All of this, be it noted, is the product of national federalism. The Soviet Union has not resorted to the transfer or exchange of populations as the solution of the nationality problem.[39] Nor have the Communist leaders attempted to stamp out national feeling,

---

[38] In recent years, national patriotism has been revived, with special emphasis upon the Great Russian people, its language and its traditions of the past. [See Fischer, Louis, *Men and Politics* (New York, 1941), pp. 339–342; Chamberlin, W. H., *The Russian Enigma* (New York, 1944), pp. 105–106, 111–112.] Whether this is a temporary expedient induced by war and the threat of war or a reversal of national policy involving an attempt to fuse all nationalities into one people with a uniform language and culture cannot at this writing be determined. In 1930 Stalin vigorously denounced efforts to ignore national differences as "Pan-Russian Chauvinism." (See "Deviations on the National Question," in *Marxism and the National and Colonial Question, op. cit.,* pp. 256–266.) In 1936 he likewise spoke of the U.S.S.R. as a multi-national state rather than as a "one-nation state" (Chekalin, *op. cit.,* p. 16).

[39] The Soviet Union has transferred masses of people as a punitive measure, or for defense purposes. At the behest of the Nazis, they also agreed to shift some border populations, following the Nazi-Soviet Pact of 1939. [See Dallin, D. J., *Soviet Russia's Foreign Policy, 1939–1942* (New Haven, 1942), pp. 95–100.] Late in 1944, too, fragmentary reports referred to exchanges of populations in the Polish territories. But it was not clear whether this involved compulsory exchanges of minorities or voluntary opting.

even though their early aversion to nationalism might have tempted them to do so. When confronted with a mixed population, they have sought and found a working solution in the multi-national state and national federalism.

PART THREE

The Bases of a Solution of the Nationalities Problem in East-Central Europe

At this writing, the statesmen of the principal Powers are grappling with the overshadowing problem of international security in the post-war world. When the major agencies of world organization have been blocked out, and provision has been made for the indispensable essentials of economic rehabilitation, the question of nationalities and national minorities in east-central Europe will command attention.

In the stress of war, when broad principles are enunciated, it may be sufficient to reaffirm, as the Atlantic Charter does, "the right of all peoples to choose the form of government under which they will live," or, in the words of the Teheran Declaration, to "look with confidence to the day when all the peoples of the world may live free lives untouched by tyranny and according to their varying desires and their own consciences." However, this ideal of self-determination will require clarification when the time comes to precipitate principles into institutions. We shall have to decide whether east-central Europe is to be broken up anew into petty *national states,* or whether *multi-national* economic regions would not better serve the needs of local harmony and world peace. In fine, we shall face the very problem which confronted the peacemakers a quarter of a century ago.

During the First World War, the Allied statesmen did not attempt to define clearly the term "self-determination" or the principle of nationalities or the rights of minorities. They were aware of the intermingling of populations in east-central Europe and apparently assumed that no one formula would assure "justice to all peoples and nationalities." In the pronouncements of January, 1918, already alluded to, the Poles were assured national independence, but both Wilson and Lloyd George categorically stated that the break-up of Austria-Hungary was not contemplated. The Prime Minister promised "genuine self-government on true democratic principles . . . to those Austro-Hungarian nationalities who have long desired it," while the President in his Fourteen Points demanded that "the peoples of Austria-Hungary . . . should be accorded the freest opportunity of autonomous development."

A significant conclusion emerges; namely, that the Allied statesmen did not identify "self-determination" solely with national independence. The century-old injustice to Poland was to be righted by restoring its sovereignty, while commitments to Italy dictated frontier adjustments. The bulk of polyglot Austria-Hungary, however, was not to be dissolved into its component national elements; the heart of east-central Europe, the Danubian region, was not to be Balkanized. Self-determination for this area would, of course, involve the repudiation of the decrepit Hapsburg monarchy and the feudal-minded nobility, but it did not necessarily mean sovereign independence for every nationality. The requirements of self-determination might be met by assuring autonomy and self-government to every people as a component member of a regional federation.[1]

Thus a novel solution of the national question was foreshadowed. Unlike the *national* states of the West, Austria-Hungary, democratized politically and decentralized nationally, would have remained a *multi-national* state, that is, a state in which no national element predominated. In that event, it would have been necessary to evolve a régime in which the German-Austrians, Hungarians, Czechs, Slovaks, Croats, Slovenes, and other nationalities could cooperate in maintaining economic unity, while preserving full self-government in local and national-cultural affairs.

It has become fashionable to attribute to the Western statesmen all the difficulties in the régime set up in 1919 for the protection of minorities. Wilson, Lloyd George, and their advisers, we are often glibly told, were ignorant bunglers whose idealistic and light-headed tampering with the east-European national question aggravated a complicated problem. Yet the caution with which

[1] On "National Self-Determination," see Wambaugh, Sarah, in *Encyclopaedia of the Social Sciences*, XIII, 649–651.

they approached the issue of Austro-Hungarian reconstruction should give one pause.

The evidence warrants the conclusion that the leaders of the eastern nationalities were far more precipitate than the Allied statesmen. Throughout the war, the latter were besieged with pleas for a "Greater Serbia," a "Greater Rumania," and a "Greater Greece," while Poles, Czechs and others pressed their claims for sovereign states with generous boundaries. It was this agitation for national independence which forced the hand of the Allied leaders and prevented more careful consideration of the nationalities question.[2]

Wilson and his colleagues were loath to disrupt the unity of the Danubian basin, until the spring of 1918, when they yielded to the importunate demands of Czechs, Jugoslavs and other nationalities who aspired to complete national independence. A "Congress of Oppressed Nationalities," held at Rome in April, 1918, appears to have been particularly potent, for it was soon thereafter that the Allied leaders promised the Slav peoples freedom from German and Austrian rule. When the Hapsburg Monarchy collapsed, the various nationalities proceeded each to carve out its own national state.

Whether Austria-Hungary could have been salvaged as a democratized and federalized multi-national state is an open question. The fact remains, however, that the leaders of the east-central European nationalities—the Poles, Rumanians, and others—desired no such solution.[3] They thought in terms of the national state of the Western type, in which unity of political allegiance becomes

[2] For a convenient summary of these developments, see Benns, F. L., *Europe Since 1914* (2nd ed., revised, New York, 1937), pp. 113–121.

[3] Some of the Czech leaders were the exception which proved the rule. In the spring of 1919, Dr. Eduard Beneš, Foreign Minister of Czechoslovakia, informed the Peace Conference committee, which was engaged in drafting guarantees for the protection of minorities, that his Government intended "to make of the Czecho-Slovak Republic a sort of Switzerland, . . ." Dr. Beneš and his colleagues were indeed most friendly to the idea of minority rights, but even they favored "reserving a certain special position for the Czecho-Slovak language and element." See Miller, D. H., *My Diary at the Conference of Paris*, XIII, 68–70, 162. A Czechoslovak national state was in fact established.

fused either with complete linguistic and cultural uniformity, as in Prussia, or at least with a recognition of the dominant status of the majority language and culture, as in Britain.

When the Peace Conference met early in 1919, it was confronted with an accomplished fact. East-central Europe had disintegrated into its component national elements, each of the stronger nationalities, and some of the weaker ones too, having taken steps to establish its national state. The Western leaders could no longer experiment with the concept of the genuine multi-national state. They could only arbitrate conflicting territorial claims and attempt to guard minorities against oppression at the hands of the majorities in the new national states.

It is the purpose of Part Three of this book first to describe the measures taken by the Paris Peace Conference to cope with the problem of national minorities, then to appraise the effectiveness of these measures, which were part of the League system, and finally to propose a plan for the consideration of the architects of the new, postwar world. This procedure is employed because we are convinced that current projects in international organization must rest on the foundations of agencies tested in the great laboratory of the League of Nations. The experience of two decades of minorities protection provides the means of estimating the adequacy of the substantive rights prescribed for the minorities and the efficacy of the procedures evolved for their enforcement. We shall draw upon this body of information, underscoring the achievements of the League of Nations in guarding minorities against persecution. We shall stress with equal emphasis the shortcomings which require correction. The plan proposed here for harmonizing the interests of the nationalities of east-central Europe aims, in large measure, to remedy the weaknesses of the League system.

CHAPTER VII

THE NEW EXPERIMENT OF THE LEAGUE OF NATIONS:
SYSTEMATIC INTERNATIONAL MACHINERY FOR
THE PROTECTION OF MINORITIES

The Western statesmen recognized the inescapable need of protecting minorities and took vigorous steps to render such protection effective. But for them, the minorities would have been left to their fate, and millions of human beings, certainly in Poland, Rumania, Hungary and Jugoslavia, would have suffered oppression and forcible denationalization, similar in aim and method to the Prussianization and Russification of the preceding decades.

It must be reiterated that never before in the history of peacemaking was so much attention given to the principle of nationality. The attempt was made to draw frontiers along "ethnic" or nationality lines, and where conflicting claims were encountered, the plebiscite was freely resorted to.[1] Yet, because of the composite character of the population, national minorities remained in every new or enlarged state of east-central Europe, and in not a few in alarming numbers, as the adjoining table reveals. In numerous states it proved utterly impossible to disentangle mixed populations, while in a number of instances economic and strategic considerations were allowed to determine the final territorial decision.

Once they were convinced that minorities would remain, the leaders of the Paris Peace Conference proceeded to draft the minimum guarantees necessary for their protection. With the exception of Czechoslovakia, whose spokesman was Eduard Beneš, the states containing minorities resisted vigorously. But the "Big Three"

[1] See Wambaugh, Sarah, *Plebiscites Since the World War* (Washington, 1933), 2 vols.

MINORITIES IN THE EAST-CENTRAL EUROPEAN STATES *

Country	Year of Census	Total Population	Approximate Number of Minorities	Per Cent of Minorities in Total Population	Principal Minorities in Each State According to Numerical Strength
Albania	estimated	850,000	85,000	10	Greeks, Rumanians
Bulgaria	1926	5,478,741	890,000	16	Turks, Gypsies, Rumanians
Czechoslovakia	[1]	10,000,000	800,000	8	Germans, Jews, Magyars
Estonia	1934	1,126,413	136,000	12+	Russians, Germans
Greece	1928	6,204,684	500,000 to 800,000	8 to 13	Turks, Bulgarian-Macedonians, Rumanians, Albanians, Jews
Hungary	1930	9,723,000 [2]	1,675,000 [2]	17+	Germans, Jews, Slovaks
Jugoslavia	1931	13,934,038	2,500,000	17+	Germans, Bulgarian-Macedonians, Magyars, Albanians, Rumanians, Czechoslovaks
Latvia	1930	1,900,045	500,000	26+	Russians, Jews, Germans, Poles, White Russians, Lithuanians
Lithuania	1923	2,028,971	320,000	15+	Jews, Poles, Russians, Germans
Poland	1931	32,372,000	10,160,000 [2]	31+	Ukrainians, Jews, Germans, White Russians, Russians, Lithuanians
Rumania	1930	18,024,269	5,000,000	28	Magyars, Jews, Germans, Ukrainians, Bulgarians, Turks, Russians

[1] Estimated in 1939 on basis of census of 1930.

[2] This figure includes population acquired from Czechoslovakia.

* This chart was prepared by the present writer. It first appeared in *Survey Graphic*, February, 1939, p. 77, and is reproduced here with permission.

stood their ground, overriding all opposition and compelling every new and enlarged state—except Italy—to assume international obligations to protect minorities. Poland, Czechoslovakia, Rumania, Jugoslavia and Greece, each was obliged to sign a special Minorities Treaty; appropriate articles were incorporated in the general treaties with the defeated states, except Germany; and the Baltic States, as also Albania, made Declarations accepting League supervision of their treatment of minorities.[2]

1. THE PROVISIONS OF THE MINORITIES TREATIES

The provisions for the protection of minorities are best studied by examining the Polish Minorities Treaty, the first to be drafted and the model for all subsequent engagements.[3]

(1) *Human rights.* Life, liberty and religious freedom were guaranteed to all inhabitants of the country (Article 2); and equal civil and political rights, equality before the law in particular, were assured to all citizens, including members of minorities who differed from the majority in "race, language or religion." It was reiterated that members of minorities were to "enjoy the same treatment and security in law and in fact" as the other citizens of the country. (Articles 7–8)

(2) *Citizenship.* There was grave danger that persons belonging to weak or unpopular minorities might be excluded from

[2] See Appendix I, pp. 171–172. For a convenient summary, see Mair, L. P., *The Protection of Minorities* (London, 1928), Chap. IV. Special conventions regulated minority relations in Memel and Upper Silesia. There were also a number of bilateral supplementary treaties respecting minorities.

The drafting of the Minorities Treaties was a complicated process which has no place in this book. The story is told in Janowsky, O. I., *The Jews and Minority Rights* (New York, 1933), Part III; Macartney, *op. cit.*, Chap. VII; Feinberg, N., *La Question des Minorités à la Conférence de la Paix* (Paris, 1929). Miller, D. H., *My Diary at the Conference of Paris,* is a treasure-house of source material.

[3] See Appendix II, pp. 173–177. There were, however, variations and special articles in the other treaties. For the texts of the Minorities Treaties, see League of Nations, *Protection of Linguistic, Racial and Religious Minorities by the League of Nations, Geneva,* 1927 (C. L. 110. 1927. I. Annexe.) The French, German and English texts are given in Schmidt and Boehm, *Materialen der deutschen Gesellschaft für Nationalitätenrecht* (Leipzig, 1929), Nos. 1–13.

citizenship in their native land. It was well known that Rumania had pursued such a policy before the First World War. Although bound by the Treaty of Berlin (1878) to accord equality to religious minorities, the Rumanian Government had successfully evaded its international obligation by declaring its Jewish inhabitants—even those born and habitually resident in the country—"foreigners who are not subject to another power." To prevent such perversion of justice in the future, the Polish Minorities Treaty—and the other minorities treaties as well—included carefully worded and tightly drawn provisions for the naturalization of persons born or habitually resident in the state. However, those who did not wish to become citizens of the new state were permitted to "opt for any other nationality," provided they migrated within a specified period to the state for which they had opted. (Articles 3–6)

(3) *Language rights.* Members of minorities whose mother tongue differed from that of the majority were protected against any such suppression of their language as had been attempted by the Prussian and Czarist Russian governments. The state obliged to sign the Minorities Treaty—Poland, for example—undertook to impose no restriction upon "the free use by any Polish national of any language in private intercourse, in commerce, in religion, in the press or in publications of any kind, or at private meetings." Moreover, regardless of the probable establishment of Polish as the official language, "adequate facilities" must be accorded "to Polish nationals of non-Polish speech for the use of their language, either orally or in writing, before the courts." In like manner, members of minorities were authorized to establish and control, at their own expense, charitable, educational, religious and social institutions, "with the right to use their own language . . . freely therein." (Articles 7–8)

(4) *Scholastic rights.* In a country containing linguistic and cultural minorities, the schools are likely to become a battleground for the youth of the land. If the language, literature, history and national ideals of the majority could be imposed on all children,

the denationalization of minorities would, in time, become inevitable. Fully conscious minorities would naturally resist, and strife would be unavoidable. Therefore, the state was obligated to provide, in towns and districts with "a considerable proportion" of minorities, primary schools in which the children of minorities would be instructed "through the medium of their own language." The state, however, was not prohibited from requiring the teaching of the majority language as an obligatory subject in the minority schools.

It was likewise evident that the scholastic guarantees might be nullified by withholding state funds from minority schools. The Minorities Treaties, therefore, imposed upon the Government the duty of assuring minorities "an equitable share in the enjoyment and application" of public funds which might be allotted "for educational, religious or charitable purposes." (Article 9)

(5) *The Jewish minority*. The Jews were the occasion for two special articles in the Polish Minorities Treaty. (Articles 10–11) This was done because of the fear that the linguistic, scholastic and cultural rights guaranteed to all other minorities might be withheld from the Jewish groups of the east-central European states. The Jews were widely regarded in the West as a purely religious minority, and, in most countries, had readily adopted the language of the majority. There was the obvious danger that a state like Poland might count its Jews as "Poles of the Mosaic Persuasion" and rest content with the assurance of freedom of conscience and worship to them. In east-central Europe, however, the Jews of a country constitute a national-cultural minority, and it would be an injustice to deny to them rights vouchsafed other minorities. The local Jewish communities were, therefore, authorized to appoint "Educational Committees" with power to receive and distribute "the proportional share of public funds allocated to Jewish schools," and to organize and manage such schools.

The devout Jewish masses of east-central Europe also had to be protected from discrimination which might result from their observance of the Jewish Sabbath. For example, if elections were to be held on that day, large numbers of Jews would be deprived of the right to vote. For that reason, provision was made that the observance of the Jewish Sabbath should not become an instrument of persecution.

(6) *The guarantee of the rights of minorities.* The provisions respecting citizenship and human and linguistic rights were to be recognized as fundamental law taking precedence over any other law, regulation or official action. (Article 1) Moreover, the League of Nations was charged with the duty of supervising the enforcement of the treaties.

The stipulations "so far as they affect persons belonging to racial, religious or linguistic minorities" were declared "obligations of international concern" and placed under the guarantee of the League of Nations. They were not to be modified without the approval of a majority of the League Council. Any member of the Council was authorized "to bring to the attention of the Council any infraction, or any danger of infraction" of the obligations; and the Council was empowered to "take such action and give such direction as it may deem proper and effective in the circumstances."

Finally, any difference of opinion "as to questions of law or fact" between a state and any one of the Principal Allied and Associated Powers, or a member of the League Council, was to be recognized as a dispute "of an international character" and referred to the Permanent Court of International Justice on the demand of a member of the League Council or one of the Principal Allied and Associated Powers.

2. HOW THE LEAGUE ENFORCED THE MINORITIES TREATIES

The protection of the rights of minorities was placed under the guarantee of the League of Nations, and the Council of the League was entrusted with the duty of supervision. Therefore it became incumbent upon the Council to formulate adequate procedure to make sure that the stipulated provisions were properly observed.

In devising suitable machinery for enforcement, the Council was mindful of two considerations. In the first place, the purpose of the Minorities Treaties was conceived to go beyond the mere humanitarian desire to guard the weak and heterodox against persecution. It was clear that the maltreatment of minorities would occasion international strife, and the new régime sought to provide such means of peaceful adjustment as would prevent conflicts from endangering the peace of the world. Therefore the Council was eager to avoid the pitfalls of humanitarian intervention which had too often in the past masked imperialist designs. For the same reason, it sought to minimize intercession by interested individual states, especially by neighboring ones whose "racial" or cultural kinsmen might be involved. Any extension to national minorities of the practice of diplomatic protection of citizens abroad would be certain to evoke international strife, and was, therefore, discountenanced.

Secondly, the League Council was exceedingly careful not to offend the sensibilities of the "Minorities States," that is, the states bound by Minorities Treaties or Declarations. Considerations of power politics influenced the attitude of some members of the Council, notably France, toward minority issues, while all assumed that the sovereign dignity of states must at all times be safeguarded as much as possible. The good will of the sovereign Minorities States being a paramount consideration, much was done to meet their wishes, or at least to spare them embarrassment. As a result, the procedure evolved by the Council was a compromise between international supervision and the rights of national sovereignty.

The Minorities Treaties empowered any member of the League Council to bring to the attention of the Council "any infraction, or any danger of infraction," of the stipulated rights of minorities. If supervision were thus left entirely to the state-members of the Council, this provision would have resulted either in neglect and inaction—because disinterested states would hesitate to bring charges against a fellow-member of the international community—or in denunciation of a partisan nature by states actuated by self-interest. Therefore an elaborate preliminary procedure was evolved. This consisted of the "Minorities Petition," the "Minorities Section of the Secretariat," and the "Minorities Committee." [4]

The Minorities Petition

The Minorities Petition consisted of information communicated to the League and alleging an infraction or the danger of infraction of a Minorities Treaty. As information, it was at first unrestricted with respect to source, nature or content. Soon, however, a number of expedient limitations were imposed, namely: it must "have in view the protection of minorities in accordance with the Treaties," it must not request "the severance of political relations" between the minority and its state, it "must not emanate from an anonymous or unauthenticated source," it "must abstain from violent language," and it must "contain information or refer to facts which have not recently been the subject of a petition."

There were no further restrictions. Anyone might submit a petition—an individual member of a minority or a group, an international organization or a state, those directly concerned or interested third parties. The petition was not a legal document nor did it obligate the League Council to take any action. The petitioner was not party to a suit; in fact, he had no legal standing whatsoever before the League or its agencies. The petitioner was no more than a source of information.

The Minorities Section

The petition, addressed to the League of Nations or its Secretary-General, was routed to the Minorities Section of the Secretariat, a

[4] See Appendix IV, pp. 185–192. No attempt will be made here to trace the steps in the evolution of these agencies. The source material is given in League of Nations, *Protection of Linguistic, Racial or Religious Minorities by the League of Nations*, Geneva, 1931 (C. 8. M. 5. 1931. I.), and also in League of Nations, *Documents Relating to the Protection of Minorities by the League of Nations*, Geneva, 1929 (*Official Journal*, Special Supplement No. 73). For a convenient summary, see League of Nations, *The League of Nations and the Protection of Minorities of Race, Language and Religion* (Geneva, 1927), pp. 27–44. The best secondary work on procedure is Stone, Julius, *International Guarantees of Minority Rights* (London, 1932).

small group of officials whose duty it was to gather information respecting minorities and minority areas.

The Director of the Minorities Section determined whether or not the petition was receivable. If it failed to conform to the conditions enumerated above, no further action was taken. If receivable, it moved to the next step of the preliminary procedure, that is, it was dispatched to the Minorities State concerned.

The state was required to declare within three weeks whether it intended to comment on the petition. If the reply was in the negative, the petition was communicated to the members of the League Council. The formal rules required the same procedure when no answer was forthcoming in three weeks, but in practice it was assumed that the state would comment eventually, and transmission to the members of the Council was delayed. If the state concerned replied that it desired to make observations, a period of two months was allowed for the purpose, but on the request of that state the President of the Council could and did grant an extension beyond the two months. Once the comments of the state were received, they were communicated, along with the petition, to the members of the League Council. Thus petitions found receivable ultimately reached the members of the League Council.[5]

The communication of a petition to the members of the League Council did not inaugurate direct and formal action by the Council as a body. The members of the Council as individuals were merely supplied with information to guide their future action. In the meantime, the individual members and the Council as an official body stood aside while a Minorities Committee examined the petition.

The Minorities Committee

This was, as a rule, a committee of three, consisting of the President of the Council and two additional members appointed by him, to consider one or several related petitions. Special care

[5] For a short time, petitions were communicated to all members of the League, but this practice was quickly abandoned.

was taken in the composition of such committees to exclude those who might be prompted by partisan considerations. To acquaint these busy men with the issues involved, and to facilitate their work, the Minorities Section of the Secretariat placed in their hands a memorandum or digest of all the pertinent information at its disposal.

Originally, the purpose of the Minorities Committee was to ascertain whether the question at issue ought to be brought *officially* before the League Council. They attempted to verify claims and counter-claims and to supplement available information. This was still part of the preliminary procedure before the League Council was officially requested by one of its members to deal with an infraction, or the danger of infraction of a Minorities Treaty. The object was to sift the evidence and provide reliable information whereby the individual members of the League Council might decide whether or not to set in motion the formal and judicial machinery as provided in the last article of the Minorities Treaties.

In practice, however, the Minorities Committees devoted their best efforts to dispose of the issues raised out of court, as it were, so that official action would be unnecessary. When alleged infractions were found to be unfounded, or when a satisfactory explanation was made by the state concerned, the question was dropped. When, however, a genuine grievance was involved, instead of taking steps immediately to inaugurate a public discussion in the League Council, the Minorities Committees attempted first to induce the state to redress the wrong. This was done by means of informal, benevolent and unofficial negotiations, either in private conversations or, more often, through the League Secretariat, that is, its Minorities Section. The great majority of complaints were thus disposed of. Only when the case was urgent, or when efforts at conciliation had failed, did the Minorities Committees recommend action by the Council.

When a Minorities Committee concluded the examination of a question, it communicated the result—always, after 1929, and occasionally before that date—to the members of the Council for their information. This done, the Committee automatically went out of existence. When the decision was to bring the issue officially before the Council, the former members of the Committee, acting individually or jointly, requested that the case be placed on the agenda of the Council. Any other member of the Council had the right to do likewise, either at the conclusion or at any stage of these proceedings. But such action was frowned upon because of the danger of partisanship, and was rarely resorted to.

Official Action by the League Council

There were two essential differences between the preliminary procedure and the formal, official action of the League Council. First, in the preliminary steps the attempt was made to ascertain the facts, whereas requests of the Council for further information constituted an invitation to the state concerned to recede from its intransigent position and agree to a settlement. Second, in the preliminary procedure, the Minorities Committees exerted pressure behind the scenes, whereas the Council acted publicly, pressing the recalcitrant state in full view of world opinion.

The League Council did not resort to open dictation. Instead, it applied "persuasion" or pressure by publicity to bring the state to terms. All the known facts in a case were circulated among its members, one of whom, an impartial representative of a Power which had no direct concern with minorities, was named the *Rapporteur*. After consultation with the Minorities Section of the Secretariat and with the state concerned, the latter submitted a Report to the Council. This Report, which summarized the history of the question and brought the issues into focus, was the basis of the Council's discussion. The action of the Council usually consisted of a request that the Minorities State desist from any action which might constitute a *fait accompli*, and an invitation to submit further information. At times the state was able to retreat gracefully by means of a clarification which involved a reversal of policy, an offer of compensation, or a compromise. If accepted by the Council, the issue was settled.

If the state remained obdurate, the Council proceeded, always on the basis of a supplementary statement by its *Rapporteur,* to examine questions of law; that is, whether the state had violated an international obligation through the infringement of its Minorities Treaty. This was done by referring the matter to a Committee of Jurists, and in several instances by submitting the question to the Permanent Court of International Justice for an Advisory Opinion. In this manner, the Council continued to exert pressure until a settlement was reached and consummated.

We cannot burden this account with specific illustrations which would require lengthy elaboration to make the meaning fully clear. But perhaps a mere reference to one celebrated case will exemplify the League's method of enforcement. The German Settlers Case will best serve this purpose, because it passed through practically every step of the League's minorities procedure.

In November, 1921, a petition reached the League charging the Polish Government with having ordered the eviction of several thousand German farmers living in Poland. The problem was a complicated one. The Germans had been settled in the Polish districts under the Prussian colonization law of 1886, to which we have referred in an earlier chapter. The Poles had always regarded these "Settlers" with bitter hatred and, once in control of their government, sought to dislodge them. The peculiar nature of the tenure under which the Settlers held their land provided the opportunity.

Some of the Germans occupied their land under leases which the Polish Government decided to cancel, allegedly because of the low rentals. Others held their land in perpetuity, under a contract known as *Rentengutsvertrag* and requiring a fixed annual rent. Title under this contract was completed by a formal transfer called *Auflassung,* which some had neglected to secure prior to the armistice of 1918. The Polish authorities denied the validity of such titles and claimed the land as state property.

The petition, received in November, 1921, was examined by the Minorities Section and then turned over to a Minorities Committee composed of a Hollander, an Italian and a Japanese. Unable to effect a settlement, the members of the Committee brought the issue before the League Council in March, 1922, in the hope that public notice would stay the hand of the recalcitrant Poles. The Council requested the Polish Government not to create a *fait accompli,* and invited further observations or information. The Poles remaining adamant, the Council decided in September, 1922, to submit the legal issues to a Committee of Jurists. When the Poles refused to accept the conclusions of the Jurists, the Council voted in February, 1923, to refer the matter to the Permanent Court of International Justice for an Advisory Opinion. After the Court had ruled against Poland, in September, 1923, the Council again pressed Poland for a settlement at its sessions in September and December, 1923. Since the Polish Government had in the meantime evicted a large number of Settlers, the Council asked for compensation, designating three of its members—the *Rapporteur* and the representatives of two Great Powers—to negotiate a settlement. During 1924, an agreement was reached on the principle of compensation, and the Council dispatched to Warsaw an "expert delegate," Captain Phillimore, to determine the amount. Poland agreed to pay 2,700,000 *zlotys.*

3. WAS THE LEAGUE SYSTEM EFFECTIVE?

The Minorities Treaties have often been condemned as a failure. This verdict is understandable in the light of the residue of two decades of conflict. The literature of minorities bristles with denunciations. The states which were compelled to assume obligations were never reconciled to the restrictions upon their freedom of action and rarely missed an opportunity to condemn with passion and indignation the idea, as well as the methods, of this international protection of minorities. The minorities, too, bitterly complained that the League régime failed to provide adequate safeguards against injustice. And the disinterested reader, or the traveler in east-central Europe, could not shut his eyes to the fact that the irredentists, especially among the Germans and Hungarians, sought to exploit the minority safeguards for their evil purposes.

However, the condemnation of the League system of minorities protection by Minorities States cannot be regarded as a just appraisal of its value; they would naturally resent any limitations upon their freedom of action, no matter how necessary or salutary. Members of minorities, too, might be prone to generalize from their particular experience. We have mentioned the case of the German Settlers in Poland. Those who lost their lands and homes would naturally denounce the League, even though its efforts had won them some compensation. Likewise, the agitation of disloyal elements, like the Sudeten Germans, should not blind us to the genuine achievements of the League's minorities régime. If the League experiment with minorities is to serve as a guide for the future, its merits as well as its defects must be noted.

Accomplishments of the League System

The League guarantee exerted a restraining and pacifying influence. No state subject even to the limited control of the League's minorities régime dared assume the high-handed manner which Mussolini and Hitler—both free of international obligations with respect to minorities—have employed. Until Fascist aggression reduced the League and its agencies to impotence, compulsory assimilation such as Bismarck enforced in Prussia or Mussolini in South Tyrol was not in evidence in east-central Europe. Minority languages were not outlawed as in Italy; minority schools did not disappear. Nor were minorities stripped of their possessions and subjected to such wholly brutal treatment as in Nazi Germany. The threat of public condemnation by the League Council sufficed to hold in check the worst offenders against minorities.[6]

Similarly, in channeling minority grievances into international machinery, the League prevented intervention by interested and

---

[6] See Janowsky, O. I., "Minorities: Pawns of Power," *Survey Graphic*, February, 1939.

partisan individual states, thus checking local outbreaks which might have endangered world peace. For it is assumed here that the Minorities Treaties must be balanced against the probabilities of the old order as well as the possibilities of a more perfect régime, even though, in doing so, the proponent of collective action must inevitably remain under a disadvantage. Failures can be measured by the high standard of a desired international morality; they loom large in the light of the hopes raised by the League guarantee. The mitigation of suffering and the calming effects of conciliation remain intangibles.

The League régime provided for permanent supervision, with automatic, impersonal and impartial procedure through the agency of the Minorities Petition, the Minorities Section of the Secretariat, and the Minorities Committees. Thus, the attempt was made to prevent smoldering minority disputes from flaring up into open conflict and to discourage individual powers with partisan interest from taking matters into their own hands. This was unquestionably an improvement on the sporadic and often self-seeking efforts of nineteenth-century humanitarian intervention. Rarely was an offending Minorities State menaced openly by an interested neighbor. The champion of a particular minority, Germany or Hungary, for example, was obliged to stand aside while the League agencies tried cautiously to satisfy grievances or effect a compromise. Even when a recalcitrant state was called to account before the League Council, the conflict remained largely impersonal. For only in very few cases was the issue raised by a state directly concerned with minorities. An infraction of the Minorities Treaties was dealt with as an offense against the international community, not as a challenge to a neighboring state. In this manner the League discouraged efforts to extend to minorities the practice of diplomatic protection of citizens or "wards" abroad, and at the same time asserted the right to limit the absolute power of a state over its subjects.

Equally praiseworthy were the efforts to enlist the cooperation of the Minorities States through informal and friendly suggestions, consultations and negotiations. For it is obvious that even an impartial decision would not settle a dispute unless the state concerned chose to enforce it, and particularly so when the sanctions of the international body were still in a rudimentary stage. The League's minorities machinery, often condemned as slow and ponderous, was calculated to afford the maximum facilities for amicable settlement.

Its Weaknesses

Expediency: However, the laudable desire to mollify the Minorities States had an invidious effect upon the minorities régime of the League of Nations. The emphasis upon negotiation and conciliation rendered necessary a strongly political procedure, and once political considerations predominated, *expediency* assumed paramount importance. Always fearful of unfriendly results, the Council acted on the assumption that the less minorities were discussed the better. Therefore secrecy became a fetish, nourishing the suspicion that the plaints of the minorities were ignored. The League diplomats "never went deeply into the facts and neither controlled nor disproved assertions made by Governments." [7] They tolerated prolonged negotiations even when the purpose was obviously dilatory, as in the case of the thirty-four peasants of Russian origin in Lithuania; [8] or when delay might result in a *fait accompli,* as in the case just mentioned, and in the celebrated case of the German Settlers in Poland, already recounted.

The anxiety lest a minority issue become the cause of conflict

[7] Kaeckenbeek, G., *The International Experiment of Upper Silesia* (London, 1942), p. 239. The author is immediately concerned with Upper Silesia, but his remark applies with even greater force to the general minorities procedure.

[8] In August, 1928, the thirty-four peasants charged, in a petition to the League, that the Lithuanian Government had confiscated their lands and rendered them destitute. It was nearly a month and a half before the petition was forwarded to the Lithuanian Government for "observations," and even then the latter ignored the request. A Minorities Committee, formed in December, 1928, was informed by the Lithuanian Woldemaras that the time was inauspicious for explanations. When the case was brought before the Council in June, 1929, Lithuania was given time to study the issues until September, 1929. In September, Woldemaras challenged the procedure of the Council and a further delay was allowed. In January, 1930, the matter was again before the Council, with Woldemaras still obdurate, and one month later the case was dropped.

between two neighboring states dominated minorities proceedings before the League. The supreme objective became some sort of peaceful settlement, regardless of the clear demands of justice or the welfare of the minority involved. Any "amicable" settlement was regarded with satisfaction by the politically minded and preoccupied members of the League Council. Those, however, who are concerned with a more comprehensive and more permanent solution of the minorities question must appraise each settlement in terms of justice as well as pacification. This the League procedure failed to achieve, for, to quote a report by a study group of the Royal Institute of International Affairs, "the acceptance of a settlement has been more often proof that it offends no important interest than that it secures justice." [9]

It can, of course, be argued that the cause of peace is of such overwhelming moment as to claim priority over every other consideration. Without questioning this premise, it must, however, be urged that the maltreatment of minorities is itself a fundamental cause of strife which has repeatedly endangered world peace. The League procedure attempted to dispose of complaints and charges, often shutting its eyes to the injustice which provoked them. Yet the cause of peace is menaced not by the outcry of the minority but by the persecution of which it is the victim. Peace will be served through impartial adjudication of disputes as they arise, rather than by appeasing the strong or condoning injustice. Minority grievances must not be permitted to provoke war, but a conflict cannot be resolved by ignoring the needs of one party. To promote understanding and pacification, the international protection of minorities will require a procedure that affords continuous supervision with a minimum of friction.

The violation of the theoretical equality of states: The Minorities Treaties were attacked from the very first as a negation of the principles of sovereignty and equality of all states. To be sure, the Minorities States (that is, Poland, Rumania, Jugoslavia and others) agreed to assume the international obligation to respect the rights

[9] *Nationalism* (London, 1939), p. 292.

of minorities. But most of them did so under compulsion and resented bitterly the fact that they were singled out for special treatment.

As early as 1919, the small states protested that their sovereignty "was being invaded, that their good intentions were being doubted. . . ." They were ready, they said, to assume obligations equally with all other states, and would accord to minorities all the rights guaranteed such groups by the Western Powers. But to require special commitments from some states, after the Great Powers had refused to incorporate a religious liberty clause in the League Covenant, was denounced as inequality.[10]

The Minorities States never receded from this position and lost no opportunity to press the claim for equality with vigor and rancor. Time and again, the League was troubled with proposals to generalize or universalize the Minorities Treaties, that is, to apply their provisions to all states indiscriminately.[11]

To mollify the Minorities States, the victorious Great Powers advanced the telling argument that safeguarding the rights of minorities did not constitute an innovation, but rather followed an established tradition in the public law of Europe. They called attention to the fact that during the nineteenth century, the formal recognition of new states, or of "large accessions of territory" by established states, had been made contingent upon the acceptance

---

[10] See Janowsky, *The Jews and Minority Rights, op. cit.*, pp. 353–355 ff.

[11] However, only Poland went so far as to repudiate even a part of a Minorities Treaty. On September 13, 1934—eight months after the conclusion of his non-aggression pact with Berlin—Colonel Joseph Beck, the Polish Foreign Minister, formally served notice upon the League diplomats that his country would no longer tolerate League supervision of its minorities policy. He said:

"Pending the introduction of a general and uniform system for the protection of minorities, my Government is compelled to refuse, as from today, all cooperation with the international organizations in the matter of the supervision of the application by Poland of the system of minority protection.

"I need hardly say that the decision of the Polish Government is in no sense directed against the interests of the minorities. These interests are and will remain protected by the fundamental laws of Poland, which secure to minorities of language, race and religion free development and equality of treatment." League of Nations, Records of the 15th Ordinary Session of the Assembly, *Official Journal*, Special Supplement No. 125, pp. 42–43.

of certain principles of government, and then asserted that the novel features of the Minorities Treaties were dictated by changed circumstances.[12]

This would have been a compelling argument, if the precedent of the nineteenth century had been followed more consistently. In practice, however, a distinction was made between Great Powers and lesser states. No guarantees were required of Italy, which had annexed a considerable minority population. Even vanquished Germany was treated with special consideration, being obliged to assume obligations only for the minorities of her share of Upper Silesia, and that, too, for a limited period.

Given the legal precept of the equality of all states in international law, this discrimination was intolerable. The "lesser" states could not concede that their politics were suspect and required international supervision, while only the Great Powers were sufficiently civilized to be exempt from definite engagements. The Great Powers, on the other hand, in defending the Minorities Treaties were obliged to appeal at one and the same time to the realities of international relations and to a fiction of international law.

It was realism to say to the small states, as Wilson did, that the military might of the Great Powers had won their independence or accessions of territory; that the maintenance of peace and the security of the new frontiers would devolve upon the Great Powers; and that they were, therefore, justified in taking measures to prevent oppression and conflict which might endanger world peace. "If we agree to these additions of territory," said Wilson pointedly, "we have the right to insist upon certain guaranties of peace." Yet this realism was bedeviled by the legal fiction that all states, great or small, are equal in international law, just as the principle of equality was belied by the fact that the small states were held in leash by the Great Powers. This was a fundamental contradiction in the minorities régime of the League of Nations.

[12] See Letter of June 24, 1919, addressed by Clemenceau to Paderewski, Appendix III, pp. 179–184.

The plaint of inequality might have been countered if the Great Powers had argued, as is argued here, that the special treatment of the east-European states was dictated by the special conditions obtaining in that area; that the mixture of population, nationally and culturally, required a régime radically different from that of the Western world. But this basic factor was studiously ignored. It was assumed, on the one hand, that the culturally homogeneous national state of the West could be achieved in eastern Europe, and, on the other hand, that the cultural and human rights of minorities must be safeguarded. These contradictions, first, the abstract equality of all states yoked with practical domination by the Great Powers, and second, the ideal of nationally homogeneous states linked to the reality of special cultural and linguistic rights, constituted fatal weaknesses which militated against the proper functioning of the Minorities Treaties.

Ambiguity of aim and purpose: Another crucial weakness in the minorities régime of the League of Nations was the failure to resolve the issue whether the guarantees were to be utilized to protect and strengthen the national-cultural individuality of a minority, or prepare the ground for its gradual assimilation—in other words, whether the Treaties were to be regarded as a temporary measure to facilitate absorption or as permanent instruments which might enable a minority, if it so desired, to remain indefinitely a distinct cultural community.

Members of minorities were emboldened to hope that their protection was meant to be permanent, because the Minorities Treaties had no time limit, and no provision was made for their renunciation. Yet the remarks of responsible statesmen at Geneva encouraged majorities to believe that the international régime was a temporary makeshift. For example, in December, 1925, M. de Mello-Franco of Brazil, one of the most important authorities on minorities questions among the members of the League Council, remarked:

> It seems to me obvious that those who conceived this system of protection did not dream of creating within certain States a group of

inhabitants who would regard themselves as permanently foreign to the general organisation of the country. On the contrary, they wished the elements of the population contained in such a group to enjoy a status of legal protection which might ensure respect for the inviolability of the person under all its aspects and which might gradually prepare the way for conditions necessary for the establishment of a complete national unity.[13]

These cautious words might have been interpreted as a rebuke to the irredentists among the minorities, but Sir Austen Chamberlain, then British Foreign Minister, proceeded with more enthusiasm than discretion to second the views of the Brazilian delegate in the following words:

It was certainly not the intention of those who had devised this system . . . to establish in the midst of nations a community which would remain permanently estranged from the national life. The object of the Minority Treaties, and of the Council in discharging its duties under them, was . . . to secure for the minorities that measure of protection and justice which would gradually prepare them to be merged in the national community to which they belonged.[14]

Applauded by the official spokesmen of the Minorities States, and roundly condemned by leaders of minorities,[15] these views are characteristic of the lack of clarity among the League statesmen with respect to the future of the minorities guarantees. Sir Austen's position is particularly instructive. He subsequently qualified his words, declaring that he had not meant that minorities were to be assimilated culturally. He favored cultural freedom, but merely looked forward to the time when League supervision would no longer be necessary.

In all likelihood the British Foreign Minister had spoken honestly but clumsily and had, therefore, been misunderstood. He thought in terms of British conditions with which he was familiar. Britain was a national state, with a dominant and all-embracing

[13] League of Nations, *Official Journal* (1926), p. 142.
[14] *Ibid.*, p. 144.
[15] See, for example, *Sitzungsbericht des Kongresses der organisierten nationalen Gruppen in den Staaten Europas*, Geneva, 1926, pp. 28–29; 1928, pp. 17, 29, 40–41; 1929, p. 33.

English language and culture, which, however, did not preclude the enjoyment of local cultural freedom by small Welsh or Scotch groups. Envisaging the east-European situation in a similar light, he innocently expressed the hope that, in time, all minorities would enjoy the status of the small and isolated Gaelic-speaking fragments of Great Britain, and that loyal minorities and tolerant majorities would render international guarantees superfluous.

Sir Austen's words, however, evoked an altogether different meaning in eastern Europe. There the expression "to be merged in the national community" meant cultural assimilation, which memories of Prussianization, Russification, and Magyarization predisposed people to regard as forcible absorption. Moreover, the clear implication that League supervision was a temporary and distasteful expedient encouraged majorities to withhold full cooperation and predisposed minorities to look for protection to their cultural kin beyond the borders, rather than to the League of Nations.

Failure of the League's leaders to recognize that the minorities guarantees required the abandonment of the ideal of national-cultural uniformity nourished unrealizable hopes in majorities and exaggerated fears in minorities. Therefore, the very safeguards which were meant to eliminate national-cultural conflicts, and thus promote understanding and cooperation, frequently served to estrange minorities from majorities. An assurance of the permanence of the international guarantee might have induced the dominant and dissident elements in the states of east-central Europe to accommodate themselves to the new situation. But uncertainty about the future led to aloofness which nourished discord.

The paradox of attempting to protect minority groups while denying group status to minorities: The most fundamental weakness in the League régime for the protection of minorities was this ambiguity of aim and purpose. The Western statesmen were aware that the numerous minorities of east-central Europe required protection, and they took measures to safeguard the linguistic and cultural as well as the human rights of those who differed from majorities in "race, language or religion." The proper observance of these provisions was bound to promote and perpetuate differences in language and culture. And yet the Westerners apparently expected that the minorities of a state would in time become identified with the culture of the majority.[16] They therefore discountenanced proposals which might interfere with the eventual development and functioning of a single and all-embracing or dominant national culture in each state.

The Minorities Treaties explicitly authorized the establishment of an official language (i.e., that of the majority) and to make its teaching obligatory in all schools. With rare exceptions the use of a minority language as the medium of instruction was limited to *primary* schools, while control of the cultural agencies of minorities was lodged in the state.

Whether or not minorities were to be recognized as "legal entities or public corporations," that is, as collective units endowed with governmental functions, especially in cultural affairs, was an important issue in the drafting of the Minorities Treaties. The Western statesmen resolved the issue by deciding to grant rights to *individuals* as members of minorities rather than to minorities as groups.[17]

It was individuals—nationals of a state who differed from the majority in "race, language or religion"—who were guaranteed against discrimination in linguistic and cultural as well as in their religious and civil rights. But the rights of language, education and culture are really *group* rights, requiring social institutions for their implementation and realization.[18] Such institutions became the bulwark of a minority in the struggle to preserve its nationality and culture. Yet the minority *as a group was legally non-existent* and could therefore exercise no effective control over its cultural agencies. The state, required by the Minorities Treaties to provide

[16] See Royal Institute of International Affairs, *Nationalism, op. cit.* p. 293.
[17] Janowsky, *op. cit.*, Chap. IX, especially pp. 349–352.
[18] See the interesting Opinion rendered by a majority of the Permanent Court of International Justice in the Albanian Minority Schools case, *Judgments, Orders and Advisory Opinions*, Series A–B, Fascicule No. 64.

adequate educational facilities for the children of minorities, retained full control of the public schools. And the state, as the embodiment of the national-cultural aspirations of the majority, would naturally favor the dominant culture. In east-central Europe, with its heritage of forced assimilation, of which we must never lose sight, such a relationship was bound to result in strife.

An illustration should clarify this point. The Minorities Treaties provide that in allocating public funds for educational, religious, or charitable purposes, an "equitable share" should be allotted to minorities. The term "proportional share" was urged upon the peace-makers as both equitable and far less susceptible to evasion or misinterpretation. But the more indefinite expression was preferred, apparently to avoid even the implication that the members of a minority constituted a unit throughout the country. As a result, the states which were none too eager to subsidize competing cultural agencies had virtually a free hand in determining what facilities minorities were "equitably" to enjoy. To the latter, the stipend always appeared niggardly and inadequate, while the majorities, who thought in terms of the national state with a uniform culture, regarded every such appropriation of public funds as an encouragement to disunity. This was once expressed graphically when in reply to a criticism of the government's appropriation Titulescu, the well-known Rumanian politician, remarked provocatively that even one *leu*, equal to one cent, might be considered an "equitable share."

The root difficulty lay in the fact that the Minorities Treaties assumed the existence of *national* rather than *multi-national* states in east-central Europe. The provisions for freedom of language and culture sought to prevent the establishment of *intolerant* national states, such as Hohenzollern Prussia, which suppressed cultural differences. The national state, however, remained, with a dominant majority culture supposedly embracing all inhabitants of the state, but with adjustments to meet the special needs of local groups. Where, as in England, cultural minorities are both few in number and largely identified with the language and customs of the majority, such a status is equitable and workable. In eastern Europe, however, where minorities are numerous, nationally conscious, cohesive and frequently well organized, and where the prestige of minority languages and literatures (such as German and Hungarian in Rumania) is often greater than that of the majorities, the national state is an imposition which must provoke resentment and strife. In eastern Europe the *tolerant* national state is not enough. Large and articulate groups should be equal partners in the state, rather than minorities. They should share with the majority in the maintenance of a multi-national state.

CHAPTER VIII

Proposals for a Solution in the Light of Experience
and Emerging Patterns of International
Organization

All discussions of the minority problems of east-central Europe begin and end with an unyielding fact; namely, the population lacks national-cultural homogeneity. Numerous nationalities differing in ancestry, language, religion and historical traditions live side by side in compact settlements on the land, or entirely interspersed in the urban centers. Practically every territory which might be designated as a geographic, economic or historical unit will comprise several peoples or segments of peoples, each determined to guard its home as the national homeland.

We of the Western world are partial to the ideal of national-cultural uniformity. In our minds, the state is identified with the culture of the majority, and political allegiance becomes fused with loyalty to the prevailing language and usages of the country. We assume that a given territory should harbor one and only one national community, with a common language, history and literature, with shared national ideals and aspirations, national heroes and festive days. The national body, envisaged as a cultural as well as a political unit, is regarded as one and indivisible.

We have already shown that east-central Europe cannot be reconstructed along the lines of the culturally uniform national states of the West. "Ethnic" frontiers would be the obvious means of eliminating minorities. But such frontiers are impossible both because national enclaves live in the midst of alien majorities, and because the web-like populations of border areas cannot be disentangled.

1. IS TRANSFER OF POPULATIONS THE SOLUTION?

The composite character of the population, the impossibility of devising "ethnic" frontiers, and the dismal record of attempts at forced assimilation in the past should be conclusive reasons for abandoning further efforts to carve out national states of cultural uniformity in the war-breeding zone of east-central Europe. Yet so strong is the desire to emulate the homogeneous state of the West that a drastic plan has been proposed as a solution of the problem of national minorities; namely, the exchange or transfer of populations. If history and geography have created over the years a Babel of tongues and peoples in east-central Europe, man is to step in and set things aright by sorting out and redistributing many millions of people according to national-cultural symptoms or labels.

Although such a project might strike one as too stupendous to be practicable, it must be examined with the utmost care, for with it has become associated the name of no less distinguished a statesman than Eduard Beneš, President of Czechoslovakia. The eminence of this humane and liberal-minded statesman, and the very good record of his country in the treatment of minorities, require that his position on this question be analyzed thoroughly and understood clearly.

In September, 1941, President Beneš wrote as follows:

> The problem of national minorities will have to be considered far more systematically and radically than it was after the last war. I accept the principle of the transfer of populations. Populations were exchanged, successfully and on a large scale, between Greece and Turkey after the war of 1922. . . . If the problem is carefully considered and wide measures are adopted in good time, the transfer can be made amicably under decent human conditions, under international control and with international support.[1]

On the face of it, one would assume that President Beneš is definitely committed to the principle of population transfers; that he

---

[1] "The New Order in Europe," *The Nineteenth Century and After*, September, 1941, p. 154.

regards it as capable of solving the problem of national minorities; and that he would apply it indiscriminately wherever minorities are to be found, so as to achieve national-cultural homogeneity in every state of east-central Europe. In point of fact this is not so.

Dr. Beneš is both a student and a great political leader. He sees in national minorities "one of the most momentous" problems of reconstruction. As a student, he is probing for a solution; as a political leader, he is testing the reaction of public opinion to various proposals, including the transfer of populations.

Dr. Beneš knows that the compulsory transfer of large masses of people can create injustices, and he does not relish any method which would involve brutality or violence. In October, 1941, he referred to this proposal with considerable caution. "*It may be,*" he said, "that we shall—*if this principle will be applied in the other countries*—carry out *to a certain extent* an emigration and exchange of the non-Czech speaking population." (Italics mine.)[2] Again in January, 1942, he said: "Perhaps it will be necessary to undertake this time the transference of minority populations." He speculated also on the possibilities of solving some minority problems by changes in frontiers, and others by resettling minorities within the borders of the same state, presumably to remove them from the frontier.[3] The same qualified approval is found in his address before the Foreign Press Association in London, April 28, 1942: ". . . if a minority problem is likely to be intractable I am prepared," he said, "for the grim necessity of population transfers."[4] In a lecture at Manchester University, December 5, 1942, we see again Beneš the student grappling with a difficult problem, and in a few words he stated it clearly:

> We cannot altogether rule out the possibility of certain population transfers as a condition for establishing the equilibrium of a permanent peace.

[2] "Czechoslovakia's Struggle for Freedom," *The Dalhousie Review*, October, 1941, p. 269.
[3] Beneš, E., "The Organization of Postwar Europe," *Foreign Affairs*, January, 1942, pp. 237–238.
[4] Holborn, L. W. (ed.), *War and Peace Aims of the United Nations* (Boston, 1943), pp. 427–428.

Transfers are a painful operation. They involve many secondary injustices. The framers of the peace settlement could not give their consent unless the transfers were humanely organized and internationally financed.[5]

Thus the approval by President Beneš of population transfers is highly qualified and circumscribed.[6] Even more significant is the fact that he recognizes that this drastic remedy *cannot solve the problem of national minorities*. On this point he is thoroughly clear:

Even after this war it still will be impossible in Europe to create states which are nationally homogeneous, since there are cases in which certain countries cannot exist at all as states without a certain region of mixed populations (for instance, Czechoslovakia without the German and mixed districts in Bohemia and Moravia).[7]

Not only is this the opinion of a student and thinker, but of Beneš the political leader as well. In a message to the Czechoslovak State Council he courageously declared that Germans would remain in his country after the war, and strongly warned against any premature decision on the nationality question.[8]

The present writer is forced to the conclusion that when President Beneš speaks of population transfers he has in mind not a solution of the problem of national minorities, but the elimination of those Germans and Hungarians who as disloyal irredentists plotted the destruction of the Czechoslovak State. He is properly incensed against the cynical exploitation of minority difficulties by the brutal Nazi régime, and no doubt embittered by the false charges of oppression leveled against his country, which was finally dismembered on the pretext of rendering justice to minorities.

One can share his resentment aroused against the unscrupulous

---

[5] *Ibid.,* p. 446.

[6] In an interview published in *The New York Times,* February 19, 1943, President Beneš is represented as more emphatically in favor of population transfers. Even there, the Germans and Hungarians are uppermost in his mind, but he would allow minorities, "democratic" rather than "national" rights.

[7] *Foreign Affairs,* January, 1942, p. 238.

[8] Holborn, *op. cit.,* pp. 443–444.

elements among the pre-war German and Hungarian minorities, as well as his disgust with the short-sighted policy of appeasement pursued by the Great Powers in the face of hypocritical Nazi pretensions. Granting the difficulties and inadequacies of the pre-war system of minorities protection, it is still necessary to reiterate that the mass transfer of minority populations cannot be regarded as a solution of the nationalities problem, and to insist that emphasis upon the idea of population transfers can result only in discouraging efforts to find a genuine solution.

The exchange of minorities between Greece and Turkey and between Greece and Bulgaria in the 1920's is often adduced as evidence that large populations can be transferred successfully. But a careful reading of Stephen P. Ladas's definitive study [9] should give one pause. Properly speaking, only about 150,000 of the Greeks resident in Turkey were exchanged. The overwhelming majority—almost a million Greeks—had been obliged to flee for their lives after the collapse of the Greek invasion of Asia Minor in 1922, and before provision had been made for an orderly transfer. Some 400,000 Moslems, compelled to leave Greece under international supervision, likewise suffered hardships, and protested vigorously against what was really expulsion from their ancestral homes. And a great many of these people, Dr. Ladas assures us, were not a troublesome minority, but loyal to Greece, speaking, as a rule, the Greek language and sharing many of the customs of the majority. The exchange of Greek and Bulgarian minorities was termed "voluntary," but, in fact, pressure was widespread; and even compulsion did not succeed in clearing Greece of Bulgars, a minority of about 80,000 remaining in the country.

If an orderly transfer of populations implies compensation for property left behind, the Greek, Turkish and Bulgarian exchanges were a failure. The Greco-Turkish Mixed Commission failed altogether to indemnify the people affected, and payment in bonds of

[9] Ladas, Stephen P., *The Exchange of Minorities: Bulgaria, Greece and Turkey* (New York, 1932). See especially pp. 122–123, 441–442, 465, 720 ff.

a large part of the Greco-Bulgar sums resulted in heavy losses through depreciation.

Suffering, too, was widespread and intense. Many thousands perished. The peaceful life of masses of people, rooted in their surroundings for centuries, was shattered. The cost of settling refugees imposed upon the Greek people a heavy burden of indebtedness. And many of the Greek traders and artisans, unable to achieve economic usefulness in their new homes, became an unemployed and pauperized urban proletariat. Writing in 1931, Dr. Ladas expressed concern about the disposal of Greek "surplus population" and looked to the old homes of the refugees as probable outlets.[10]

This experience gained from the Near Eastern experiments with population transfers should serve as a warning. To remove a minority from its home requires compulsion, for "voluntary" transfers have not been effective, and forced migration means expulsion, at least to the people concerned. An unbiased student has correctly remarked that the transfer of populations is "a remedy so drastic when attempted in the Near East that one shudders at the thought of its application to European peoples so much more firmly rooted." [11]

The transfer of populations has long been the policy of Pan-Germanism, the inspiration of present-day Nazidom. During the First World War the great Thomas G. Masaryk, founder of the Czechoslovak State, wrote:

> The Pangermans often proposed the transmigration of quite large national minorities. . . . It is doubtful whether it may be carried out without compulsion and injustice. *De facto,* Pangerman politicians intend by this proposal to weaken non-German minorities, not to satisfy their national aspirations.[12]

These statesmanlike words are as true today as they were a

[10] *Ibid.,* pp. 733-734.
[11] Stephens, J. S., *Danger Zones of Europe: A Study of National Minorities* (London, 1929), p. 32.
[12] Masaryk, Thomas G., *The New Europe: The Slav Standpoint* (London, 1918), p. 28.

generation ago. So ruthless a policy can solve the minorities problem only in a Nazi "new order" which is insensible to human suffering. Democratic states and statesmen must regard the compulsory transfer of minorities as a "surgical operation," to be performed only when every other remedy has been tried and found wanting.

The exchange of minorities may be possible in special areas and on a small scale. For example, where farming communities live interspersed on the frontier, adequate international supervision should find it possible to disentangle a mixed population with a minimum of suffering. Where exchange of land holdings is not possible, the transfer of a farming population would involve uprooting a mass of people and casting them adrift in overcrowded cities. And the transfer of urban minorities presents even greater difficulties. Petty traders or artisans who perform a useful economic function and earn a livelihood in their old homes are likely to be ruined by removal to a new environment. Laborers, too, might not find their skills in demand when transferred to a new country. If urban minorities are shifted, provision must be made for retraining and other economic readjustments.

Even the transfer of relatively small groups of people requires stable, peaceful conditions, with a maximum of international supervision. But, to solve the minorities problem, it would be necessary to shift many millions of people under the least favorable circumstances. Are we then prepared to direct colossal transmigrations at the close of the war, when our energies will be taxed to the utmost in demobilizing huge armies, in repatriating millions of war prisoners and millions more whom the Nazis have dragged off to Germany for forced labor?

There is a widespread but mistaken belief that the shuffling of populations decreed by Hitler has already disposed of many minority problems; that the numerous German minorities have already been transferred to the Reich. The fact is that these Nazi efforts have by no means solved even the problem of the Germans. Before the war, nearly seven million Germans were scattered as minorities in east-central Europe. Only about 600,000 of them were summoned "home" by Hitler, and these, too, were not settled within the former borders of Germany. The great majority were established in conquered territories, like the Polish regions of Poznan, West Prussia, the Lodz district and Pomerania. If the transferred Germans survive the fall of Hitler, they will still remain minorities, albeit with a change of habitat.[13]

We are forced to the conclusion that the minorities problem will not be solved by the elimination of minorities through forced migration. This conclusion is shared by Štefan Osuský, for many years Czechoslovak Minister to Paris, for a time a member of the Czechoslovak Government-in-Exile, and a man who is thoroughly conversant with the merits and deficiencies of the League's system of minorities protection. He says:

> In my opinion the attempt to introduce national uniformity in that part of Europe could only lead to a catastrophe. . . . It is folly to imagine that national uniformity could be brought about by a vast transfer of populations. No doubt this method could be used here and there to overcome local frontier difficulties; but, broadly speaking, the map of Europe cannot be ethnographically remade.[14]

If, therefore, minorities remain in east-central Europe, and national states of the Western type are formed, it would be necessary to condone compulsory assimilation. But this too, as we have shown, offers slight prospects of a genuine solution. For the national fragments are no longer pliant and assimilable. Each is more or less conscious of its national individuality, each determined to retain its identity as a people. The attempt to impose a national state upon a mixed population can only result in oppression, strife, and, in the end, failure.

Finally, it should be noted that the quest for non-existent ethnic boundaries, the willingness to resort to forced migration, and the tendency to tolerate oppressive assimilation, all spring from the

---

[13] For these transfers, see Kulischer, E. M., *The Displacement of Population in Europe* (Montreal: International Labour Office, 1943), Chap. I.

[14] "Liberty or Uniformity in Eastern Europe," *The Contemporary Review*, November, 1941, p. 280.

desire to see east-central Europe partitioned into national states. But thus to dissect the region is to "Balkanize" it, and to sacrifice economic welfare to the fetish of national uniformity.

If in favoring ethnic boundaries, transfer of populations, and forced assimilation, the objective is to divide east-central Europe into numerous small, sovereign states, then general impoverishment and international strife will be promoted thereby. If, on the other hand, the aim is to encourage the peoples of the area to unite into regional federations, then these expedients are both unnecessary and dangerous. The compulsory denationalization of minorities within a federation will strain unity to the breaking point, for the national kinsmen of the minority of one province will constitute the majority in another. The transfer of population, too, would be out of harmony with the spirit of federal union. A federation is hardly conceivable without freedom of movement for the people of a federated area, especially in an industrial age with adequate means of transportation and communication. But transferred minorities might desire to return to their old homes unless restricted to their new location. Would pacification and harmony be furthered if a section of the population of a federal union were denied freedom of movement?

The very idea of federation presupposes national-cultural diversity within large economic units. For example, if Serbs, Croats, Bulgars and Rumanians live together harmoniously in a Balkan federation, freedom of language and culture must prevail in the enlarged federal area; and once national freedom is assured to Bulgars or Rumanians as component members of the federation, it can hardly be denied to the lesser groups or minorities living in Transylvania or the Banat.

The dislocations and suffering involved in compulsory, large-scale transfer of populations, or in forced assimilation, are not only painful and harmful, they are unnecessary. The solution of the problem of minorities must be sought not in centralized uniformity, but in the decentralization of the cultural functions of government and in national federalism.

2. THE VAGUE AND IMPRACTICAL IDEA OF DIVORCING NATIONAL CULTURE FROM THE TERRITORIAL STATE

Before proceeding with the discussion of national federalism, a word must be said about a theory recently propounded to solve the minorities problem by divorcing the territorial state from the "religion" of nationalism.[15] It is argued that just as the dissociation of creed from territory has rendered possible pluralism of faith and religious freedom, so national freedom must wait upon the separation of culture from territory.

This position is sound when interpreted in the sense that territorial unity must not involve cultural uniformity; that residence in a territory must not entail the forced acceptance of the language and culture of its majority. But the analogy with religious faith can be strained. It is possible to separate church from state and leave to the individual the decision whether or not he is to participate in denominational affairs. But the sentiment of nationality is, as a rule, intertwined with language and historical traditions, which in turn depend upon the school for their proper development. And education as well as language cannot be divorced from government.

When education was left to individual or group initiative, the masses remained illiterate. It was state action which rendered possible universal elementary education. This achievement cannot be sacrificed even to the ideal of non-territorial nationalism. Therefore, if the analogy with religion implies that the state should withdraw from the educational field, or that cultural needs must cease to be the concern of government, it is unacceptable. If, on the other hand, what is meant is merely that the state is to delegate to the cultural group the function of education, then drawing the parallel only confuses the issue.

[15] See, for example, Guérard, A., "Culture and Territory," in Kingsley, J. D., and Petegorsky, D. W., *Strategy for Democracy* (Longmans, 1942), pp. 85–100; *idem*, in *Menorah Journal*, October–December, 1941, pp. 249–265. See also Guérard's proposal for an international auxiliary language, in *The American Scholar* (Spring, 1941), pp. 170–183.

Language, too, is as inseparable from government as from culture. Such prosaic matters as the communication of the government with its citizens in a multilingual region, the medium of intercourse in the administration and courts of law, the provision of post and telegraph facilities, cannot be left to the individual who "carries his own tradition wherever he goes." These are group functions which can be regulated only through the cooperation of majorities and minorities.

The term "cultural pluralism" is itself a cause of confusion, in so far as it implies disorganized, individualistic, and casual relations between national groups. "National federalism" [16] characterizes far more clearly the relationship necessary for a solution of the problem of national minorities.

3. A NEW APPROACH: NATIONAL FEDERALISM AND ECONOMIC UNITY

We have seen that the European national state has assumed two forms, namely, the intolerant state of strict cultural uniformity like the Prussia of Bismarck's time, and the tolerant national state like Great Britain, in which one language and a national culture predominate, but minorities enjoy the freedom to cultivate locally their languages and customs. Since neither variation of the national state is suitable to conditions in east-central Europe, it is here proposed that the region be reorganized on the basis of national federalism. In essence this means that minorities are not to be endowed with special privileges, that their status is not to be an exceptional one involving toleration, but that they be organically incorporated in the structure of the multi-national state.

No state can enjoy domestic tranquillity when some of its minorities entertain hopes of its destruction. During the past quarter century, many of the states of east-central Europe failed to win the loyalty of some of their minorities, and the resulting insecurity

[16] The writer is indebted to Dr. James T. Shotwell for this clarification. The term "national federalism" has the added virtue of suggesting unifying centripetal, rather than disruptive and centrifugal tendencies.

vitiated the entire League régime for the protection of minorities. Plans for the future must rest on the foundations of loyalty and cooperation. But the devotion of minorities will not be achieved through injunctions or threats. Nor will toleration suffice, for it implies a measure of exclusion and inferiority. Loyalty is best rooted in a sense of belonging, and minorities will regard the state as their homeland when they, along with their institutions and customs, are fully integrated in the life of the larger community.

National federation can function within the framework of regional federations, thus satisfying at the same time the national requirements of minorities and the economic needs of all. Early in this war steps toward federation were taken by several governments-in-exile. For example, on November 11, 1940, the Polish and Czechoslovak governments declared their determination to enter "into a closer political and economic association," as the nucleus of a larger regional union.[17] These efforts have since been abandoned, apparently because the Soviet Union disapproved for fear of another *cordon sanitaire*. However, now that east-central Europe is being recognized as a Russian sphere of influence, it is probable that the movement toward federation will be resumed.

If reason alone were to govern European reconstruction, we would propose that each regional federation be subdivided into its component national elements; that is, that every nationality inhabiting a given territory become a self-governing unit in the federal union. In such a scheme, Sub-Carpathian Ruthenia would be a constituent member of a Danubian federation, and Croatia would enjoy a status equal with Serbia in a Balkan federation. Thus troublesome national conflicts would be indeed solved.

However, since this is probably unattainable, it would be wiser to build less logically but more securely on the foundations of the present. In other words, the states as constituted before the outbreak of this war could combine into federations, retaining their

[17] See Holborn, *op. cit.*, pp. 452–453. Such regional federations were strongly supported by President Beneš and other leaders of the Czechoslovak Government. *Ibid.*, pp. 407–409, 417–422, 425–436, 439, 467–469.

historic unity but delegating to the central government specific functions. The structure of each state, however, must be changed: the national state in which the majority language and culture predominate should give way to the multi-national state. Each state-unit in the regional confederation would itself become a partnership of the leading nationalities (or linguistic and cultural groups) inhabiting its territory. The multi-national state would constitute national federalism.

Thus Jugoslavia (a member of the Balkan regional confederation) would consist of national territorial subdivisions like Serbia, Croatia, Slovenia, each enjoying full equality, especially with respect to language and culture. In each national subdivision (Croatia, for example) the language of the majority would be official, and this local national unit would have charge of the local administration, especially of cultural affairs, including education.

Regional confederation would help meet the economic needs of east-central Europe, while national federalism (that is, the reorganization of the state-members of the confederation into multi-national units) would eliminate many of the most acute minority problems, because cultural groups like the Sudeten Germans [18] or the Hungarians of Transylvania would cease to be minorities. They would become equal partners in the multi-national state. However, small and scattered minorities would remain in the self-governing territorial subdivisions. For such national fragments, minority rights would be necessary.

4. THE RIGHTS OF NATIONAL MINORITIES

Human Rights and National Rights

The actual freedoms which minorities require may be divided into two categories, namely, (1) human rights, and (2) national or cultural rights. The first category embraces the time-honored elementary rights of man—that is, citizenship, the protection of

[18] See below, pp. 152–154.

life and liberty, equality before the law, civil and political rights, religious freedom, and freedom from discrimination generally, including equality of economic opportunity.[19] The national or cultural rights of minorities are concerned chiefly with special safeguards against linguistic and educational discrimination which might undermine the national-cultural cohesion of the group.

Precise and emphatic in their provisions for human rights, the Minorities Treaties may serve in part as a guide for the future, except that "freedom from want" will require clear formulation. The cultural safeguards, however, were inadequate, chiefly because minorities were denied recognition as corporate or group entities. The rights of man may be assured to a member of a minority as an individual, but language and culture are essentially *group* factors which depend upon common action for their preservation. No less an authority than Georges Kaeckenbeek, President of the Arbitral Tribunal of Upper Silesia from 1922 to 1937, has reached the conclusion that "it is not probable that under existing social, political, and economic conditions minorities should prove capable of enduring, without a minimum of corporate structure and organization." [20]

Freedom of Association and Cultural Autonomy

The Geneva Convention of May 15, 1922, relating to Upper Silesia, was a considerable improvement upon the Minorities Treaties in this respect. Article 78 extended the *right of association* to members of minorities, even when the purpose was the furtherance of "the interests of minorities as regards their language, culture, religion, ethnical character or social relations." And President Calonder of the Upper Silesian Mixed Commission ruled that such minority organizations were qualified to submit petitions not only on their own behalf or in the name of specific members of a minority, but also for the purpose of defending the *general* in-

---

[19] See Commission to Study the Organization of Peace, *International Safeguard of Human Rights* (Fourth Report, Part III), May, 1944.
[20] Kaeckenbeek, *op. cit.*, p. 272.

terests of the minority; that is, to intercede on behalf of the minority *as a whole*.[21]

This "right of association" lent minorities a measure of organic existence, especially for defense against discrimination. But even the Upper Silesian régime failed to incorporate minorities as cultural units within the structure of the state. Again, the ideal of the national state hampered the realization of cultural freedom in a region of mixed nationality.

It is here proposed that the principle of "national federalism" be extended to small and scattered minorities in the form of cultural autonomy. By this means the minority would be recognized as a corporate entity and entrusted by the state with the autonomous management of its educational and cultural affairs. In other words, a council chosen democratically by the members of the minority would become the agency of the state for the administration of the educational and cultural institutions of that particular group. The government of the state should have the authority to set norms and standards for the entire population of the country, and it should exercise general supervision. But the direction and management of the minority's institutions should be in its own hands.

The financing of the educational and cultural undertakings of a minority should be the responsibility of the state. And to avoid interminable wrangling over the "equitable share," as it was called, provision should be made for an allotment *proportional* to the numbers of the minority. However, a minority should be authorized to supplement such state funds by levying taxes upon its own members, subject always to the supervision of the state authorities.

The right of membership in a minority is a crucial question. Under the Minorities Treaties attempts made by governments to establish objective criteria for admission into minority schools resulted in conflict. For example, the Rumanian Government sought to exclude children of "Rumanian origin" from minority schools, but the term "Rumanian origin" defied objective definition. In

[21] See Kaeckenbeek, *op. cit.*, pp. 272–278; Stone, J., *Regional Guarantees of Minority Rights, op. cit.*, pp. 51–52.

Upper Silesia, too, difficulties arose from the contention of the Polish Government that membership in a minority was a matter not of intention but of fact, to be determined by national origin or mother tongue. If conflict and injustice are to be avoided, there is no alternative but to recognize that fundamentally *nationality is a subjective matter:* one "feels" a sense of kinship with a particular group. Membership in a minority should, therefore, rest solely on the expressed desire of an adult to identify himself with the group. Every individual should likewise have the right of severing his connection with a minority group and of declaring himself a member of the majority or of any other nationality.

The Law of Cultural Autonomy adopted by Estonia in 1925 should serve as a guide in the reconstruction of east-central Europe. This liberal measure authorized minorities numbering not less than 3,000 persons to draw up a register of freely enrolled members for the purpose of exercising self-government in cultural affairs. An elected "Cultural Council" was then empowered to direct the educational, cultural and charitable institutions of the minority, to receive and administer public funds for their maintenance, to enact by-laws, and to tax the members of the minority for educational and cultural purposes.[22]

The Jews of East-Central Europe as Minorities.

The Jews of east-central Europe require special consideration, because there is a lack of clarity in the Western world as to the nature and character of the Jewish group. In the United States the Jews do not desire "minority rights," because they are fully identified with American cultural as well as political and economic life. Any educational or cultural agencies maintained voluntarily by them are ancillary or supplementary to the all-embracing American cultural institutions. Therefore, some Americans, including some American Jews, assume that the Jews of eastern Europe could or

[22] See Maddison, E., *Die nationalen Minderheiten Estlands und ihre Rechte* (Reval, 1930). For brief summaries, see Ammende, E. (ed.), *Die Nationalitäten in den Staaten Europas* (Vienna, 1931), pp. 6–9; Royal Institute of International Affairs, *The Baltic States* (London, 1938), pp. 36–38.

should be regarded as members of the majority or of some other nationality, rather than as an independent Jewish nationality. This is an arbitrary and doctrinaire assumption.

In the first place, a majority of the Jews of the east-central European states consider themselves a nationality, and since membership in a national minority must rest on the expressed desire of the individual, one could not deny to Jews a right deemed just and proper for other minorities.

Secondly, in the mixed population of east-central Europe the association of the Jews with a nationality other than their own would be exceedingly dangerous for themselves and troublesome for others. A few illustrations should make this point clear. In the old Austro-Hungarian Empire, the Province of Galicia contained Poles and Ruthenians in coordinate numbers,[23] with some 850,000 Jews as the balance of power. By counting the Jews as "Poles of the Mosaic Persuasion," the Polish majority was enabled to dominate and oppress the Ruthenians. This role of the Jews as an instrument of Polish nationalism provoked anti-Semitism among the Ruthenians. Similarly, in Russian Poland, prior to 1914, Jews who spoke Russian, the official language of the country, were denounced by Poles as a spearhead of Russification.

Instances can be multiplied of similar difficulties since the close of the First World War. Czechs resented Bohemian Jews who declared themselves to be of German nationality, and Rumanians hated Jewish Magyars. In fact, wherever two or more nationalities shared the same territory the Jews were under suspicion as an agent of denationalization, unless they declared themselves of Jewish nationality. Preconceived notions respecting the Jews of the national states of the West must not be allowed to determine their status in east-central Europe, where special conditions render necessary multi-national states.[24] There Jewish nationality must be reckoned

---

[23] Poles to the number of 3,864,173 and 3,186,579 Ruthenians in 1910. See Winkler, W., *Statistisches Handbuch der europäischen Nationalitäten, op. cit.,* p. 182.

[24] For an elaboration of this point, see Janowsky, O. J., "Jewish Rights in the Postwar World," *Survey Graphic,* September, 1943.

with as a fact, and assured equal status with that of other national-cultural groups.

Before the Nazi onslaught upon east-central Europe, the Jews formed large and important minorities in many of the states of that region. When hostilities come to an end, the number of Jews will be considerably reduced. Large numbers have been deliberately exterminated by the Nazis. Others have been uprooted from their homes. Inadequate nourishment, exposure and sheer human despair are unquestionably taking their toll. Many who sought refuge in flight will not return. Their possessions and means of livelihood are gone. Friends and relatives are dead or broken in spirit and scattered to the ends of the earth. The word "home" awakens only memories of humiliation and savagery. Large numbers of such uprooted and pauperized Jews, many of whom had for long been devoted Zionists, will desire to build a new life in Palestine.

Yet many Jews will undoubtedly remain in east-central Europe. Though reduced in numbers and impoverished, they should be assured not special privileges, but a status of equality with other nationality groups. If the end of the war finds some settled in compact masses on a definite territory, they should enjoy national and territorial autonomy like other similar peoples. If they survive only as small and scattered communities, national-cultural autonomy should place them on an equal footing with other minorities. In either case, they should be an integral part of the structure of the state.

The Special Problem of the German and Hungarian Minorities

National reconstruction in east-central Europe will be complicated by the presence of German and Hungarian groupings. As minorities prior to the present war they were a thorn in the flesh of the individual states. Many of them were disloyal irredentists, who used the guarantee of the rights of minorities as a shield to screen their treacherous designs. Konrad Henlein's Sudeten German Party,[25] for example, prepared the ground for the Nazi

[25] See Wiskemann, E., *Czechs and Germans* (New York, 1938), pp. 200–271.

onslaught upon Czechoslovakia. Since 1939, members of these minorities have served as the willing tools of their Nazi masters, looting and terrorizing the peoples of east-central Europe.

It is likely that areas like the Sudetenland will remain predominately German in population, and that German and Hungarian minorities elsewhere in east-central Europe will survive the defeat of Hitlerism. To assume that these people will overnight shed their Fascist propensities and be transformed into loyal citizens of their respective countries would be quixotic. Therefore, such national federalism and cultural autonomy as we have proposed cannot immediately be applied to them.

It is true that not all Germans and Hungarians in east-central Europe were or are today Nazis. It is probably true also that, with the collapse of Nazism, large numbers among the masses will attach themselves to moderate and democratic parties. However, one cannot dissociate nationalities or minorities from the crimes committed by their leaders. To be sure, only those who committed atrocities should be punished. But the masses, too, must undergo a period of tutelage.

The treatment of the German and Hungarian minorities at the close of the war should correspond to that meted out to their kinsmen in Germany and Hungary. It would be folly to turn over the local administration of the Sudeten area to the Germans or to endow smaller German and Hungarian minorities with cultural autonomy, just as it would be folly to permit Germans to take over immediately the government of the Reich. The United Nations propose to occupy and administer Germany and Hungary for a transitional period. In like manner the multi-national states of east-central Europe or the regional federations should be empowered by the United Nations to occupy and administer even the cultural affairs of their German and Hungarian minorities during the transitional period.

Permanent subjection, however, or denationalization would create more problems than it would solve. No people can be condemned to eternal servitude. After the period of transition, when reconstruction and re-education have been accomplished, the German and Hungarian nationalities and minorities ought to be admitted as the equals of all other peoples in the government of themselves and of their countries.

5. INTERNATIONAL SUPERVISION

The Problem of the Sovereign Equality of States

International supervision is indispensable if the rights of national minorities are to be enforced in practice—a fact amply demonstrated by the history of minorities protection during the past century. It is, therefore, proposed that the United Nations assume the guarantee of the rights of minorities, and reserve the prerogative to act as final arbiter in issues arising from nationality and majority-minority relationships.

This poses a difficult problem. If, in the final analysis, the adjustment of minority grievances devolves upon the international community, then the welfare and loyalty of minorities cease to be questions of purely domestic concern. But many states, including the Great Powers, do so regard their minority problems, and would reject any suggestion of foreign interference. We therefore find ourselves on the horns of a dilemma. If the sanction of international concern were removed, minority rights might prove no more than a body of principles with little effect upon the practical needs of minorities: on the other hand, if the Great Powers remained free of international obligations with respect to their minorities, while certain specified states were required to assume such obligations, then the principle of equality of all sovereign states would be violated. We have shown above that this objection was, indeed, voiced in criticism of the Minorities Treaties.

Abstract justice would no doubt require that all minorities be guaranteed equal protection, and all states throughout the world be equally subject to the control of the international community. Considerations of realism, however, require that we note several compelling distinctions.

In the first place, *equality* need not be equated with *universality*.

To say that all states should be equally subject to the supervision of the international community does not necessarily mean that precisely the same precepts or procedures must apply everywhere. Since conditions differ in various parts of the world, international government must reckon with the differences. For example, the principle of free international trade might theoretically call for the abolition of all protective tariffs. Yet variations in wages and standards of living, say between the United States and the Far East, would certainly compel adjustments. The proposal of regional federation has been put forward to provide for just such regional differences. East-central Europe has the character of a region.

Those who have dealt constructively with the future of east-central Europe agree that the area requires one or several regional federations.[26] This is predicated on the assumption that economic, political, and social conditions are sufficiently uniform to warrant confederation. We have already shown that the ethnographic, linguistic and cultural problems of the entire region of east-central Europe—stretching from the Baltic to the Aegean and from the Soviet borders to Germany and Italy—are strikingly similar. Every political or historical unit lacks national-cultural uniformity. Everywhere the population is mixed in language, composite in culture, heterogeneous in national consciousness. Nationalities and national minorities are hopelessly intermingled, and the pressures and tensions have, at times, occasioned strife, which in turn has endangered the peace of Europe and the world. Therefore, regional and world peace require a special international supervision of the nationality and minority policies of this distinctive region of east-central Europe. The principle of equality, as applied to this region, demands that every state of east-central Europe be equally subject to the international guarantee.

Secondly, realistic plans of world organization do not propose to sweep away working adjustments which have already been

---

[26] See, for example, the views of President Beneš (Holborn, *op. cit.*, pp. 417, 419, 427, 439–440), Hubert Ripka (*ibid.*, pp. 407–409), and Josef Hanč, *Tornado Across Eastern Europe* (New York, 1942), pp. 320–321.

evolved for specific regions, and then start afresh on the basis of uncompromising universal equality. The British Commonwealth of Nations and the solidarity of the Americas are cases in point. Whatever the final form of the new United Nations organization, room will unquestionably be found within its broad framework for the special needs of the British Commonwealth and the peculiarities of the Americas. In like manner, the international organization might provide for the requirements of the mixed population of east-central Europe, irrespective of the fact that it would not be immediately possible to accord protection to minorities outside of this region.

Thirdly, we must face the fact that the Great Powers will not countenance the universal guarantee and enforcement of minority rights. Whatever the theory of the equality of all states in international law, in practice all states have not been equal. The smaller and weaker countries have in the past moved as satellites in the orbits of the Great Powers, and present indications appear to foreshadow even greater dependence of the east-central European peoples upon their stronger neighbors. The issue is not the sovereign equality of the lesser states *versus* international supervision; it is really international supervision *versus* subjection to some Great Power.

Recent history has proved conclusively that the smaller states can provoke war but are incapable of maintaining or enforcing world peace. Therefore, since insurance against war is the responsibility of the Great Powers, and since minority conflicts have proved a threat to world peace, some external control over the minority policies of the east-central European states is both necessary and reasonable. The question resolves itself into the alternatives of joint action by the Great Powers, through an international agency in which the small states have some voice, or unilateral action by individual Great Powers, each exercising control in its "sphere of influence."

At the end of the First World War, when the Minorities Treaties were imposed upon the states of east-central Europe, the

"Clemenceau Letter to Paderewski" [27] argued that the recognition by the Powers of new states and the sanction of large cessions of territory to established states were matters of international concern, and that the public law of Europe required that the states affected undertake to observe certain principles of government, particularly with respect to the rights of minorities. This is a valid position which should be maintained when new states are recognized or accessions of territory sanctioned.

We are not absolving the Great Powers from the duty of rendering justice to their minorities. We merely maintain that the guarantee of the proper treatment of minorities in east-central Europe need not wait upon the time when international supervision can become universal. The ideal remains a general guarantee applicable to all states which harbor nationally conscious minorities, but the ultimate objective will have to be reached gradually in successive stages.

One legitimate grievance of the states of east-central Europe must be removed, namely, the privileged position of Germany and Italy. It was intolerable to the states subject to Minorities Treaties to be pilloried as oppressors of minorities, when their immediate neighbors, Germany and Italy, were free to perpetrate every atrocity upon their own minorities. When the brutal Nazi régime posed as protector of minorities in democratic Czechoslovakia, the whole League system of minorities protection was reduced to a mockery. In the new Europe, Germany and Italy should be required to assume the same obligations as their neighbors to the east.

The International Guarantee

The Fourth Report of the Commission to Study the Organization of Peace (Part III, the "International Safeguard of Human Rights") proposes that a conference on human rights be convened for the primary purpose of establishing a permanent United Nations Commission on Human Rights. It is here proposed that

[27] See below, pp. 179–184.

one of the functions of this Commission should be the drafting of a treaty or of a bill of associative rights for the protection of nationalities and national minorities. This instrument may be open to the signature and ratification of all states, in accord with the procedure evolved for draft conventions of the International Labor Organization. However, for certain categories of states the ratification of this treaty, or the acceptance of the bill of rights under international guarantee, should be a condition precedent to their admission as active participants in the general international organization of the United Nations. These categories should include:

(1) All states which had been subject to the régime of the League of Nations for the protection of minorities, that is, every country of east-central Europe;
(2) All states, Germany and Italy in particular, which have in recent years pursued oppressive policies toward minorities;
(3) All new states seeking recognition; and
(4) All states annexing territories which contain distinct nationalities or national minorities.

In effect, the United Nations would impose the international guarantee for the protection of minorities upon the states indicated above. All other member states of the world community would be free to accept, voluntarily, international supervision of their minority policies, by ratifying the minorities treaty or bill of rights in question. These states, including, of course, the Great Powers, would be under no international pressure to ratify such a treaty. Their decision would be determined solely by enlightened public opinion expressed through the will of their own citizens.

Enforcement Procedure

The guarantee of the rights of minorities by the United Nations will require agencies of supervision and enforcement procedure. It would, of course, be unwise to attempt at this time to draft a plan exact to the last detail. But it is important to indicate the broad outlines of enforcement, bearing in mind the experience of the League of Nations in general minorities procedure, and particularly in the more effective régime set up for the minorities of Upper Silesia. We shall discuss the aims of supervision, the requisite agencies and the relation between United Nations and local organs.

The merits and defects of the League's minorities procedure have been dealt with above.[28] Two points remain to be noted: (1) the League's procedure operated only in impending emergencies; and (2) the enforcement of minority rights (outside of Upper Silesia) was *Geneva* centered.

Always anxious to minimize the threat to world peace, the League properly sought to dispose of conflicts as they arose by means of mediation and conciliation. But attention was concentrated primarily on the offending government and on a neighboring state which evinced concern for a particular minority. In so far as minority issues affect the relations between neighboring states, this policy of impartial and impersonal adjudication should be continued. In no case should an interested individual Power be permitted to exploit minority differences to its own advantage, or to employ force to right a wrong.

However, it is not the wisest course for international agencies to remain inactive until an infraction of right has occurred, or until the danger of infraction is clearly evident, and then suddenly to bestir themselves to effect a settlement. When a conflict has arisen, a settlement must of course be found. But the aim should be pacification, so that dissension might be avoided and differences adjusted before they could harden into quarrels. This requires continuous, not sporadic, supervision. Above all, it requires a new orientation in nationality questions.

Instead of centering attention upon states which might become embroiled in war as a result of nationality disputes, the primary concern of the international agencies should be with nationality and with majority-minority relationships. In minority questions the function of international organs is to be always at hand to

[28] See pp. 123–134.

facilitate understanding and cooperation between nationalities or minorities and majorities, so that most problems might be resolved within the confines of the territory affected.

The center of enforcement of nationality or minority rights ought to be in the states of east-central Europe. It was a fundamental weakness of the League system that responsibility for the welfare of minorities was concentrated in Geneva. Governments like Rumania and Hungary, which were ill-disposed toward their minorities, felt free to adopt whatever measures they pleased, no matter how harmful to minorities. It was the League's concern to discover a wrong, to demonstrate an infraction or danger of infraction of a Minorities Treaty and to take measures to secure redress.

In a very real sense, however, the infraction of the rights of a nationality or a national minority is not an issue between the international organization and the state concerned, nor between neighboring states, nor even between the national minority and the state, for the minority is itself an integral part of the state. The conflict should be viewed as an *internal maladjustment* between two factions within the state, that is between the administrative officers, or those represented by them, and a group which is momentarily at odds with the government. The objective of the international community is to help maintain harmony within the multi-national state.

Such a function can be performed by *experts whose primary interest is minority questions,* not by busy statesmen who are distracted by multifarious problems. And it can best be performed by close contact with the situation on the spot. Writing with the wisdom gained from a wealth of experience in Upper Silesia, Kaeckenbeek gave this point classic expression: "Look at the matter from far away and high up—as a Committee of Three [a Minorities Committee] or a League Council must needs do—and you perceive nothing but dim unreasonableness. Look at the individual cases hard and near, and you perceive a tissue of little individual vexations and tragedies, the accumulation of which embitters life." [29]

The procedure in Upper Silesia had the merit of providing for *local* organs—"Minorities Offices," an "Arbitral Tribunal" and a "Mixed Commission" with a President appointed by the Council of the League. The latter was Felix Calonder, a particularly happy choice, for he was a distinguished Swiss, that is, a citizen of a traditionally neutral state, and a native of the Canton of Grisons, who understood well the complications of a multi-national state. M. Calonder dealt with individual cases—eliciting facts, conducting inquiries, allowing petitioners to submit their observations, and finally presenting his reasoned judgment in an "opinion." However, concern for state sovereignty made it impossible to give his "opinions" binding force, while fear of foreign interference prevented his colleagues, two Germans and two Poles from Upper Silesia, from sharing responsibility for his decisions.

In evolving institutions for United Nations supervision and enforcement of minority rights, the Upper Silesian procedure should serve as a guide. However, modification will be necessary. In Upper Silesia, the procedure was handicapped by the fact that two independent states, Germany and Poland, were directly involved. This condition need not obtain elsewhere in east-central Europe.

It is desirable to combine international supervision with local responsibility for safeguarding the rights of national minorities. A representatve of the international organization should always be at hand as an impartial collaborator, and the primacy of the international guarantee could be established in the right of appeal to the agencies of the United Nations. This right of appeal, however, should be exercised as a last resort. A state should be summoned before the bar of world opinion only when local institutions have failed to secure justice. Normally, it should be possible to effect a settlement through international collaboration with local agencies.

[29] Kaeckenbeek, *op. cit.*, p. 357.

In particular full use should be made of the technique of administrative handling, in a healing way, right at the point of conflict.

The following procedure for enforcement is here proposed:

1. Each nationality or national minority in a state, duly recognized as having corporate status, should be empowered to receive petitions from its members, specifying grievances. Many complaints, real or imaginary, might be disposed of through the intercession of the leaders of the nationality with the administrative authorities. An informal conference with a local official, or a protest by the responsible leader of a national minority, could accomplish much without dragging the state before an international tribunal.

2. A "Minorities Office" should be established in each state of east-central Europe, composed of representatives of all the nationalities, including the national minorities, with an impartial chairman named by the executive organ of the United Nations. This body should be authorized to receive petitions from individuals or from minorities as corporate entities, to conduct inquiries and transmit its findings to the Government.

3. If regional federations are formed in east-central Europe, a "Regional Minorities Commission" should be maintained in each federation, with an impartial chairman named by the executive organ of the United Nations. This body could have the power of reviewing, on appeal, the findings of the Minorities Office in each state. Such findings might bear on the perpetuation of an offense or failure to redress it as recommended by the Minorities Office.

4. The Commission on Human Rights, proposed by the Fourth Report of the Commission to Study the Organization of Peace, or a Sub-Commission associated with it, should be the central agency of the United Nations to deal with questions affecting nationalities and national minorities. The impartial chairmen of the Minorities Offices and of the Regional Minorities Commissions should be accountable to this body, submitting to it reports at regular intervals and transmitting the findings in each case. When the local agencies fail to settle a dispute, or to redress a wrong, the Commission on Human Rights, or the Sub-Commission, should have the power to hear an appeal, before placing the issue on the agenda of the executive organ of the United Nations.

5. The executive body of the United Nations could then take such action as it might deem proper and effective under the circum-

stances. The practice of submitting a troublesome question to the Permanent Court of International Justice for an Advisory Opinion has proved very helpful heretofore and should be continued.

It should be noted that the central idea of this procedure is not compulsion but conciliation and local efforts at peaceful adjustment. Dictation from above will not induce governments to deal justly with their national minorities. The aim is to avoid an open rupture between the national minority and its shared Government, by emphasizing the fact that the minority is an integral part of the state, and by providing for joint consideration of disputes by representatives of the various nationalities composing the state. Above all, foreign intervention would be reduced to a minimum. The national minority would appeal, in the first instance, to an agency of its own Government, and a settlement might easily and informally be reached without arousing national sensibilities. At the same time, the impartial chairman would be a permanent link with the international organs, rendering possible continuous supervision and exerting through his presence the pressure of the United Nations. The direct appeal to the United Nations is employed only as a last resort.

6. THE CRITICAL CHARACTER OF THE TRANSITIONAL PERIOD

For parts of east-central Europe, the transitional period between war and peace is about to begin: it has indeed already begun. Measures taken during this period, although termed provisional and temporary, may prove of great moment for the future. Therefore, the spokesmen of the United Nations and the local leaders should be mindful of the fact that in east-central Europe they are dealing with a heterogeneous population, each of its segments within a territory differing in language, religion, culture and national feeling. They should be careful not to view conditions through the spectacles of a Western focus.

In the first place, it must be remembered that the Minorities Treaties were never legally terminated. Until a new régime is set up, the provisions of those Treaties should be considered as in force. Equality of status and treatment should be assured to all sections of the population, regardless of differences in race, language or religion. The indiscriminate expulsion of habitual residents, whatever their national and cultural affiliation, should be rigidly barred. Care will have to be taken that the technicalities of repatriation do not operate to the disadvantage of national minorities. Relief agencies, like the UNRRA, should make provision for the religious and linguistic requirements of all groups. Even the military administration would gain in effectiveness if it could learn to treat with the various nationality groups and take advantage of their cohesion and internal organization.

Furthermore, in setting up local agencies, whether for provisional government or for relief and rehabilitation, representation should be allotted to the various nationalities and national minorities. The temptation will be strong to avoid complications by dealing solely with the dominant element. Superficial efficiency might thus be achieved, but irreparable harm would be done in storing up hatreds and resentments for the future. Given a mixed population, the effort must be made to promote collaboration at every stage of reconstruction.

CONCLUSION

The régime set up at the close of the First World War for the protection of minorities is in ruins today. But though inadequate in many ways, we must remember that it did not fall because of the weight of its own deficiencies. The entire structure of the League of Nations collapsed, reducing momentarily to rubble all mechanisms for international conciliation and cooperation. The rights of national minorities can command no more respect in a lawless world than any other rights.

International brigandage has been the enemy of minorities guarantees, as of all efforts at peace and understanding. When international anarchy yields to a reign of law, national minorities should be vouchsafed their due share of protection. The imperfections in the solutions of the past, or even inherent difficulties in the present or future, do not invalidate the principle of minority rights. However, the defects of the Minorities Treaties should be frankly noted and effectively corrected.

A quarter of a century ago the peacemakers recognized that the population of east-central Europe lacked homogeneity in language, culture and national sentiment. They wisely repudiated the Prussian ideal of the culturally uniform national state, hoping that a system of toleration of minorities would dispose of the problem. But tolerance is not enough.

The statesmen assembled at Paris thought the national problem of east-central Europe could be solved by erecting national states similar to the most tolerant political communities of the West. The majority nationalities were, therefore, permitted to assume *mastery* of the various states. But the solution found workable in the West did not apply. The mixture of population required what we have called multi-national states.

In planning for the future, the peculiar condition of east-central Europe must remain the paramount consideration. Despite Nazi efforts literally to destroy minorities, the population will inevitably remain heterogeneous. National-cultural homogeneity cannot be achieved. "Ethnic" frontiers are not attainable in east-central Europe. The transfer of many millions of minorities would be a colossal undertaking, involving incalculable suffering, and one providing, at best, no complete solution. Forcible assimilation has proved productive of hatred and strife, not unity. It is the tyrant's way, not ours. We are left no alternative but to incorporate nationalities and national minorities in the structure of the state, with respect for, recognition of, and legal protection extended to the pattern of life of every group.

This is possible only under what we have called, in Dr. Shotwell's phrase, "National Federalism," where differences in language and culture do not connote disloyalty or disunity. That such a solution is practical and feasible is attested by the fact that a number of states, including Switzerland and South Africa, have prospered under multi-national régimes. Russia, too, long an inferno of national strife, has found in Soviet federalism a solution of its nationalities and minorities problems.

National federalism offers the means of harmonizing the seemingly contradictory requirements of national freedom and economic unity. Once territorial nationalities are assured self-government in local affairs, and once national minorities enjoy national-cultural autonomy, it becomes possible to form large regional federations with resources adequate for a satisfactory standard of living. A solution of the problems of east-central Europe will require unity in economic life, democracy in government and decentralization in national-cultural affairs. In affording the possibility of realizing all these objectives, national federalism holds the promise of bringing to east-central Europe economic prosperity, national freedom and regional security.

Until the present war, it was not possible to deal organically and comprehensively with minorities questions, because an important fact was overlooked; namely, that national minorities are but a fragment of a broader problem, that of nationalities. This fundamental fact, that national minorities and nationalities constitute two aspects of the same problem, was obscured by the effort to establish national states in east-central Europe. For example, to form the national state of Jugoslavia, it was necessary to assume that the Serbs, Croats and Slovenes compose a single nationality, the ruling nationality of the state. When, however, a bitter struggle involving violence and assassination ensued between the Serbs and Croats, the League of Nations was powerless to intervene, because technically the Croats were not a "minority." Thus the need for national federalism was eclipsed by reducing the nationality problem to a segment, namely that of minorities.

During the present war, when whole countries have been overrun and enslaved, former majorities, the Poles for example, have sunk to the level of minorities of the "Greater Reich," returning thereby to the lowly status which was theirs before the First World War. The façade of national states in east-central Europe has crumbled, and the whole national question has been reduced again to its "raw" state. We are now in a position to assess the true relationship between the various nationalities of east-central Europe, and the national requirements of majorities and minorities alike. These requirements have been admirably summarized by Stefan Osuský:

Undoubtedly, the nations in Central, Eastern and South-Eastern Europe have a right to their national liberty. But the interests of the European peoples require that those nations should not be encouraged in the dream of bringing about national uniformity within their States. Not on national uniformity but on national liberty depends the existence and the future of Czechoslovakia, Poland, Austria, Hungary, Rumania, Yugoslavia, Greece and Bulgaria. It is by guaranteeing the peoples of Central, Eastern and South-Eastern Europe their freedom of national consciousness that the foundation of the peace of Europe will be laid. Furthermore, national uniformity would mean the elimination of every authority except that of the State. In countries with different religions, languages, customs and traditions, this is not desirable. For the preservation of religious, linguistic and cultural liberty means not only that individuals have a right to profess the religion of their choice, speak the language of their mothers and live according to the traditions and customs of their ancestors; it means the practical possibility of associating together and administering their own particular affairs.[1]

The opportunity beckons to start afresh and attempt a genuine solution of the nationalities problem of east-central Europe on the basis of national liberty. This time the leaders of the United Nations dare not fail.

[1] *The Contemporary Review,* November, 1941, pp. 280–281.

APPENDICES

The International Protection of Racial, Religious and Linguistic Minorities in East-Central Europe

APPENDIX I

INTERNATIONAL INSTRUMENTS UNDER THE GUARANTEE OF THE LEAGUE OF NATIONS

1. *Special Minorities Treaties* drafted and imposed by the Peace Conference:

State affected	Name and Date of Treaty	Date Entered into Force
1) Poland	Treaty between the Principal Allied and Associated Powers (the United States, the British Empire, France, Italy and Japan) and Poland, signed at Versailles, June 28, 1919.	Jan. 10, 1920
2) Czechoslovakia	Treaty between the Principal Allied and Associated Powers and Czechoslovakia, signed at St. Germain-en-Laye, September 10, 1919.	July 16, 1920
3) Jugoslavia	Treaty between the Principal Allied and Associated Powers and the Serb-Croat-Slovene State, signed at St. Germain-en-Laye, September 10, 1919. (The Serb-Croat-Slovene State acceded to it on December 5, 1919.)	July 16, 1920
4) Rumania	Treaty between the Principal Allied and Associated Powers and Rumania, signed at Paris, December 9, 1919.	Sept. 4, 1920
5) Greece	Treaty between the Principal Allied and Associated Powers and Greece, signed at Sèvres, August 10, 1920.	Aug. 30, 1924

2. *Special articles* for the protection of minorities inserted in the general Treaties of Peace:

1)	Austria	Treaty of St. Germain-en-Laye, September 10, 1919. Part III, Section V, Articles 62–69.	July 16, 1920
2)	Bulgaria	Treaty of Neuilly-sur-Seine, November 27, 1919. Part III, Section IV, Articles 49–57.	Aug. 9, 1920
3)	Hungary	Treaty of Trianon, June 4, 1920. Part III, Section VI, Articles 54–60.	July 26, 1921
4)	Turkey	Treaty of Lausanne, July 24, 1923. Part I, Section III, Articles 37–45.	Aug. 6, 1924

3. *Declarations* for the protection of minorities made before the Council of the League of Nations:

1)	Albania	Declaration of October 2, 1921.	Feb. 17, 1922
2)	Estonia	Declaration of September 17, 1923.	Sept. 17, 1923
3)	Finland (Aaland Islands)	Declaration of June 27, 1921.	June 27, 1921
4)	Latvia	Declaration of July 7, 1923.	July 28, 1923
5)	Lithuania	Declaration of May 12, 1922.	Dec. 11, 1923

4. *Conventions* for the protection of minorities:

1)	Upper Silesia	German-Polish Convention on Upper Silesia, signed at Geneva, May 15, 1922. Part III, Articles 64–158.	June 3, 1922
2)	Memel	Convention concerning the Memel Territory, signed at Paris, May 8, 1924.	Sept. 27, 1924

Appendix II

THE POLISH MINORITIES TREATY [1]

(Signed at Versailles, June 28, 1919)

THE UNITED STATES OF AMERICA, THE BRITISH EMPIRE, FRANCE, ITALY and JAPAN

The Principal Allied and Associated Powers,

on the one hand;

And POLAND,

on the other hand;

WHEREAS the Allied and Associated Powers have by the success of their arms restored to the Polish nation the independence of which it had been unjustly deprived; and

WHEREAS by the proclamation of March 30, 1917, the Government of Russia assented to the re-establishment of an independent Polish State; and

WHEREAS the Polish State, which now in fact exercises sovereignty over those portions of the former Russian Empire which are inhabited by a majority of Poles, has already been recognized as a sovereign and independent State by the Principal Allied and Associated Powers; and

WHEREAS under the Treaty of Peace concluded with Germany by the Allied and Associated Powers, a Treaty of which Poland is a signatory, certain portions of the former German Empire will be incorporated in the territory of Poland; and

WHEREAS under the terms of the said Treaty of Peace, the boundaries of Poland not already laid down are to be subsequently determined by the Principal Allied and Associated Powers;

The United States of America, the British Empire, France, Italy and Japan, on the one hand, confirming their recognition of the Polish State, constituted within the said limits as a sovereign and independent member of the Family of Nations, and being anxious to ensure the execution

[1] League of Nations, *Protection of Linguistic, Racial and Religious Minorities by the League of Nations,* Geneva, 1927 (C. L. 110. 1927. I. Annexe.), pp. 42–45.

of the provisions of Article 93 of the said Treaty of Peace with Germany;

Poland, on the other hand, desiring to conform her institutions to the principles of liberty and justice, and to give a sure guarantee to the inhabitants of the territory over which she has assumed sovereignty;

For this purpose the HIGH CONTRACTING PARTIES represented as follows:

[Here follow the names of the plenipotentiaries.]

After having exchanged their full powers, found in good and due form, have agreed as follows:

CHAPTER I

Article 1

Poland undertakes that the stipulations contained in Articles 2 to 8 of this Chapter shall be recognized as fundamental laws, and that no law, regulation or official action shall conflict or interfere with these stipulations, nor shall any law, regulation or official action prevail over them.

Article 2

Poland undertakes to assure full and complete protection of life and liberty to all inhabitants of Poland without distinction of birth, nationality, language, race or religion.

All inhabitants of Poland shall be entitled to the free exercise, whether public or private, of any creed, religion or belief, whose practices are not inconsistent with public order or public morals.

Article 3

Poland admits and declares to be Polish nationals *ipso facto* and without the requirement of any formality German, Austrian, Hungarian or Russian nationals habitually resident at the date of the coming into force of the present Treaty in territory which is or may be recognized as forming part of Poland, but subject to any provisions in the Treaties of Peace with Germany or Austria respectively relating to persons who became resident in such territory after a specified date.

Nevertheless, the persons referred to above who are over eighteen years of age will be entitled under the conditions contained in the said Treaties to opt for any other nationality which may be open to them. Option by a husband will cover his wife and option by parents will cover their children under eighteen years of age.

Persons who have exercised the above right to opt must, except where it is otherwise provided in the Treaty of Peace with Germany, transfer within the succeeding twelve months their place of residence to the State for which they have opted. They will be entitled to retain their immovable property in Polish territory. They may carry with them their movable property of every description. No export duties may be imposed upon them in connection with the removal of such property.

Article 4

Poland admits and declares to be Polish nationals *ipso facto* and without the requirement of any formality persons of German, Austrian, Hungarian or Russian nationality who were born in the said territory of parents habitually resident there, even if at the date of the coming into force of the present Treaty they are not themselves habitually resident there.

Nevertheless, within two years after the coming into force of the present Treaty, these persons may make a declaration before the competent Polish authorities in the country in which they are resident, stating that they abandon Polish nationality, and they will then cease to be considered as Polish nationals. In this connection a declaration by a husband will cover his wife, and a declaration by parents will cover their children under eighteen years of age.

Article 5

Poland undertakes to put no hindrance in the way of the exercise of the right which the persons concerned have, under the Treaties concluded or to be concluded by the Allied and Associated Powers with Germany, Austria, Hungary or Russia, to choose whether or not they will acquire Polish nationality.

Article 6

All persons born in Polish territory who are not born nationals of another State shall *ipso facto* become Polish nationals.

Article 7

All Polish nationals shall be equal before the law and shall enjoy the same civil and political rights without distinction as to race, language or religion.

Differences of religion, creed or confession shall not prejudice any Polish national in matters relating to the enjoyment of civil or political rights, as for instance admission to public employments, functions and honours, or the exercise of professions and industries.

No restriction shall be imposed on the free use by any Polish national of any language in private intercourse, in commerce, in religion, in the press or in publications of any kind, or at public meetings.

Notwithstanding any establishment by the Polish Government of an official language, adequate facilities shall be given to Polish nationals of non-Polish speech for the use of their language, either orally or in writing, before the courts.

Article 8

Polish nationals who belong to racial, religious or linguistic minorities shall enjoy the same treatment and security in law and in fact as the other Polish nationals. In particular they shall have an equal right to establish, manage and control at their own expense charitable, religious and social institutions, schools and other educational establishments, with the right to use their own language and to exercise their religion freely therein.

Article 9

Poland will provide in the public educational system in towns and districts in which a considerable proportion of Polish nationals of other than Polish speech are residents adequate facilities for ensuring that in the primary schools the instruction shall be given to the children of such Polish nationals through the medium of their own language. This provision shall not prevent the Polish Government from making the teaching of the Polish language obligatory in the said schools.

In towns and districts where there is a considerable proportion of Polish nationals belonging to racial, religious or linguistic minorities, these minorities shall be assured an equitable share in the enjoyment and application of the sums which may be provided out of public funds under the State, municipal or other budget, for educational, religious or charitable purposes.

The provisions of this Article shall apply to Polish citizens of German speech only in that part of Poland which was German territory on August 1, 1914.

Article 10

Educational Committees appointed locally by the Jewish communities of Poland will, subject to the general control of the State, provide for the distribution of the proportional share of public funds allocated to

Jewish schools in accordance with Article 9, and for the organisation and management of these schools.

The provisions of Article 9 concerning the use of languages in schools shall apply to these schools.

Article 11

Jews shall not be compelled to perform any act which constitutes a violation of their Sabbath, nor shall they be placed under any disability by reason of their refusal to attend courts of law or to perform any legal business on their Sabbath. This provision, however, shall not exempt Jews from such obligations as shall be imposed upon all other Polish citizens for the necessary purposes of military service, national defense or the preservation of public order.

Poland declares her intention to refrain from ordering or permitting elections, whether general or local, to be held on a Saturday, nor will registration for electoral or other purposes be compelled to be performed on a Saturday.

Article 12

Poland agrees that the stipulations in the foregoing Articles, so far as they affect persons belonging to racial, religious or linguistic minorities, constitute obligations of international concern and shall be placed under the guarantee of the League of Nations. They shall not be modified without the assent of a majority of the Council of the League of Nations. The United States, the British Empire, France, Italy and Japan hereby agree not to withhold their assent from any modification in these Articles which is in due form assented to by a majority of the Council of the League of Nations.

Poland agrees that any Member of the Council of the League of Nations shall have the right to bring to the attention of the Council any infraction, or any danger of infraction, of any of these obligations, and that the Council may thereupon take such action and give such direction as it may deem proper and effective in the circumstances.

Poland further agrees that any difference of opinion as to questions of law or fact arising out of these Articles between the Polish Government and any one of the Principal Allied and Associated Powers or any other Power, a Member of the Council of the League of Nations, shall be held to be a dispute of an international character under Article 14 of the Covenant of the League of Nations. The Polish Government hereby consents that any such dispute shall, if the other party thereto demands, be referred to the Permanent Court of International Justice.

The decision of the Permanent Court shall be final and shall have the same force and effect as an award under Article 13 of the Covenant.

THE PRESENT TREATY, of which the French and English texts are both authentic, shall be ratified. It shall come into force at the same time as the Treaty of Peace with Germany.

The deposit of ratifications shall be made at Paris.

Powers of which the seat of the Government is outside Europe will be entitled merely to inform the Government of the French Republic through their diplomatic representative at Paris that their ratification has been given; in that case they must transmit the instrument of ratification as soon as possible.

A procès-verbal of the deposit of ratifications will be drawn up.

The French Government will transmit to all the signatory Powers a certified copy of the procès-verbal of the deposit of ratifications.

IN FAITH WHEREOF the above-named Plenipotentiaries have signed the present Treaty.

Done at Versailles, the twenty-eighth day of June, one thousand nine hundred and nineteen, in a single copy which will remain deposited in the archives of the French Republic, and of which authenticated copies will be transmitted to each of the Signatory Powers.

Appendix III

THE LETTER OF CLEMENCEAU TO PADEREWSKI [1]
(Covering letter presented to Poland
with the Minorities Treaty.)

Paris, June 24, 1919.

Sir,—On behalf of the Supreme Council of the Principal Allied and Associated Powers, I have the honour to communicate to you herewith in its final form the text of the Treaty which, in accordance with Article 93 of the Treaty of Peace with Germany, Poland will be asked to sign on the occasion of the confirmation of her recognition as an Independent State and of the transference to her of the territories included in the former German Empire which are assigned to her by the said Treaty. The principal provisions were communicated to the Polish Delegation in Paris in May last, and were subsequently communicated direct to the Polish Government through the French Minister at Warsaw. The Council have since had the advantage of the suggestions which you were good enough to convey to them in your memorandum of the 16th June, and as the result of a study of these suggestions modifications have been introduced in the text of the Treaty. The Council believe that it will be found that by these modifications the principal points to which attention was drawn in your memorandum have, in so far as they relate to specific provisions of the Treaty, been adequately covered.

In formally communicating to you the final decision of the Principal Allied and Associated Powers in the matter, I should desire to take this opportunity of explaining in a more formal manner than has hitherto been done the considerations by which the Principal Allied and Associated Powers have been guided in dealing with the question.

1. In the first place, I would point out that this Treaty does not constitute any fresh departure. It has for long been the established procedure of the public law of Europe that when a State is created, or even when large accessions of territory are made to an established State, the joint and formal recognition by the Great Powers should be accompanied

---

[1] Miller, David Hunter, *My Diary at the Conference of Paris, With Documents* (privately printed, New York, 1925), XIII, pp. 215–222; Temperley, *op. cit.*, V, pp. 432–437.

by the requirement that such State should, in the form of a binding international convention, undertake to comply with certain principles of government. This principle, for which there are numerous other precedents, received the most explicit sanction when, at the last great assembly of European Powers—the Congress of Berlin—the sovereignty and independence of Serbia, Montenegro, and Roumania were recognized. It is desirable to recall the words used on this occasion by the British, French, Italian, and German Plenipotentiaries, as recorded in the Protocol of the 28th June, 1878:—

"Lord Salisbury recognizes the independence of Serbia, but is of opinion that it would be desirable to stipulate in the Principality the great principle of religious liberty.

"Mr. Waddington believes that it is important to take advantage of this solemn opportunity to cause the principles of religious liberty to be affirmed by the representatives of Europe. His Excellency adds that Serbia, who claims to enter the European family on the same basis as other States, must previously recognize the principles which are the basis of social organization in all States of Europe, and accept them as a necessary condition of the favour which she asks for.

"Prince Bismarck, associating himself with the French proposal, declares that the assent of Germany is always assured to any motion favourable to religious liberty.

"Count de Launay says that, in the name of Italy, he desires to adhere to the principle of religious liberty, which forms one of the essential bases of the institutions in his country, and that he associates himself with the declarations made on this subject by Germany, France, and Great Britain.

"Count Andrassy expresses himself to the same effect, and the Ottoman Plenipotentiaries raise no objection.

"Prince Bismarck, after having summed up the results of the vote, declares that Germany admits the independence of Serbia, but on condition that religious liberty will be recognized in the Principality. His Serene Highness adds that the Drafting Committee, when they formulate this decision, will affirm the connection established by the Conference between the proclamation of Serbian independence and the recognition of religious liberty."

2. The Principal Allied and Associated Powers are of opinion that they would be false to the responsibility which rests upon them if on this occasion they departed from what has become an established tradition. In this connection I must also recall to your consideration the fact that it is to the endeavours and sacrifices of the Powers in whose name

I am addressing you that the Polish nation owes the recovery of its independence. It is by their decision that Polish sovereignty is being re-established over the territories in question and that the inhabitants of these territories are being incorporated in the Polish nation. It is on the support which the resources of these Powers will afford to the League of Nations that for the future Poland will to a large extent depend for the secure possession of these territories. There rests, therefore, upon these Powers an obligation, which they cannot evade, to secure in the most permanent and solemn form guarantees for certain essential rights which will afford to the inhabitants the necessary protection whatever changes may take place in the internal constitution of the Polish State.

It is in accordance with this obligation that Clause 93 was inserted in the Treaty of Peace with Germany. This clause relates only to Poland, but a similar clause applies the same principles to Czecho-Slovakia, and other clauses have been inserted in the Treaty of Peace with Austria, and will be inserted in those with Hungary and with Bulgaria, under which similar obligations will be undertaken by other States which under those Treaties receive large accessions of territory.

The consideration of these facts will be sufficient to show that by the requirement addressed to Poland at the time when it receives in the most solemn manner the joint recognition of the re-establishment of its sovereignty and independence, and when large accessions of territory are being assigned to it, no doubt is thrown upon the sincerity of the desire of the Polish Government and the Polish nation to maintain the general principles of justice and liberty. Any such doubt would be far from the intention of the Principal Allied and Associated Powers.

3. It is indeed true that the new Treaty differs in form from earlier Conventions dealing with similar matters. The change of form is a necessary consequence and an essential part of the new system of international relations which is now being built up by the establishment of the League of Nations. Under the older system the guarantee for the execution of similar provisions was vested in the Great Powers. Experience has shown that this was in practice ineffective, and it was also open to the criticism that it might give to the Great Powers, either individually or in combination, a right to interfere in the internal constitution of the States affected which could be used for political purposes. Under the new system the guarantee is entrusted to the League of Nations. The clauses dealing with this guarantee have been carefully drafted so as to make it clear that Poland will not be in any way under the tutelage of those Powers who are signatories to the Treaty.

I should desire, moreover, to point out to you that provision has been inserted in the Treaty by which disputes arising out of its provisions may be brought before the Court of the League of Nations. In this way differences which might arise will be removed from the political sphere and placed in the hands of a judicial court, and it is hoped that thereby an impartial decision will be facilitated, while at the same time any danger of political interference by the Powers in the internal affairs of Poland will be avoided.

4. The particular provisions to which Poland and the other States will be asked to adhere differ to some extent from those which were imposed on the new States at the Congress of Berlin. But the obligations imposed upon new States seeking recognition have at all times varied with the particular circumstances. The Kingdom of the United Netherlands in 1814 formally undertook precise obligations with regard to the Belgian provinces at that time annexed to the kingdom which formed an important restriction on the unlimited exercise of its sovereignty. It was determined at the establishment of the Kingdom of Greece that the Government of that State should take a particular form, viz., it should be both monarchical and constitutional; when Thessaly was annexed to Greece, it was stipulated that the lives, property, honour, religion and customs of those of the inhabitants of the localities ceded to Greece who remained under the Hellenic administration should be scrupulously respected, and that they should enjoy exactly the same civil and political rights as Hellenic subjects of origin. In addition, very precise stipulations were inserted safeguarding the interests of the Mohammedan population of these territories.

The situation with which the Powers have now to deal is new, and experience has shown that new provisions are necessary. The territories now being transferred both to Poland and to other States inevitably include a large population speaking languages and belonging to races different from that of the people with whom they will be incorporated. Unfortunately, the races have been estranged by long years of bitter hostility. It is believed that these populations will be more easily reconciled to their new position if they know that from the very beginning they have assured protection and adequate guarantees against any danger of unjust treatment or oppression. The very knowledge that these guarantees exist will, it is hoped, materially help the reconciliation which all desire, and will indeed do much to prevent the necessity of its enforcement.

5. To turn to the individual clauses of the present Treaty. Article 2 guarantees to all inhabitants those elementary rights which are, as a

matter of fact, secured in every civilised State. Clauses 3 to 6 are designed to insure that all the genuine residents in the territories now transferred to Polish sovereignty shall in fact be assured of the full privileges of citizenship. Articles 7 and 8, which are in accordance with precedent, provide against any discrimination against those Polish citizens who by their religion, their language, or their race differ from the large mass of the Polish population. It is understood that, far from raising any objection to the matter of these articles, the Polish Government have already, of their own accord, declared their firm intention of basing their institutions on the cardinal principles enunciated therein.

The following articles are of rather a different nature in that they provide more special privileges to certain groups of these minorities. In the final revision of these latter articles, the Powers have been impressed by the suggestions made in your memorandum of the 16th June, and the articles have in consequence been subjected to some material modifications. In the final text of the Treaty it has been made clear that the special privileges accorded in Article 9 are extended to Polish citizens of German speech only in such parts of Poland as are, by the Treaty with Germany, transferred from Germany to Poland. Germans in other parts of Poland will be unable under this article to claim to avail themselves of these privileges. They will, therefore, in this matter be dependent solely on the generosity of the Polish Government, and will in fact be in the same position as German citizens of Polish speech in Germany.

6. Clauses 10 and 12 deal specifically with the Jewish citizens of Poland. The information at the disposal of the Principal Allied and Associated Powers as to the existing relations between the Jews and the other Polish citizens has led them to the conclusion that, in view of the historical development of the Jewish question and the great animosity aroused by it, special protection is necessary for the Jews in Poland. These clauses have been limited to the minimum which seems necessary under the circumstances of the present day, viz., the maintenance of Jewish schools and the protection of the Jews in the religious observance of their Sabbath. It is believed that these stipulations will not create any obstacle to the political unity of Poland. They do not constitute any recognition of the Jews as a separate political community within the Polish State. The educational provisions contain nothing beyond what is in fact provided in the educational institutions of many highly organized modern States. There is nothing inconsistent with the sovereignty of the State in recognizing and supporting schools in which children shall be brought up in the religious influences to which they

are accustomed in their home. Ample safeguards against any use of non-Polish languages to encourage a spirit of national separation have been provided in the express acknowledgment that the provisions of this Treaty do not prevent the Polish State from making the Polish language obligatory in all its schools and educational institutions.

7. The economic clauses in Chapter II of the Treaty have been drafted with the view of facilitating the establishment of equitable commercial relations between independent Poland and the other Allied and Associated Powers. They include provisions for reciprocal diplomatic and consular representation, for freedom of transit, and for the adhesion of the Polish Government to certain international conventions.

In these clauses the Principal Allied and Associated Powers have not been actuated by any desire to secure for themselves special commercial advantages. It will be observed that the rights accorded to them by these clauses are extended equally to all States who are members of the League of Nations. Some of the provisions are of a transitional character, and have been introduced only with the necessary object of bridging over the short interval which must elapse before general regulations can be established by Poland herself or by commercial treaties or general conventions approved by the League of Nations.

In conclusion, I am to express to you on behalf of the Allied and Associated Powers the very sincere satisfaction which they feel at the re-establishment of Poland as an independent State. They cordially welcome the Polish nation on its re-entry into the family of nations. They recall the great services which the ancient Kingdom of Poland rendered to Europe both in public affairs and by its contribution to the progress of mankind which is the common work of all civilised nations. They believe that the voice of Poland will add to the wisdom of their common deliberations in the cause of peace and harmony, that its influence will be used to further the spirit of liberty and justice, both in internal and external affairs, and that thereby it will help in the work of reconciliation between the nations which, with the conclusion of Peace, will be the common task of humanity.

The Treaty by which Poland solemnly declares before the world her determination to maintain the principles of justice, liberty, and toleration, which were the guiding spirit of the ancient Kingdom of Poland, and also receives in its most explicit and binding form the confirmation of her restoration to the family of independent nations, will be signed by Poland and by the Principal Allied and Associated Powers on the occasion of, and at the same time as, the signature of the Treaty of Peace with Germany. ——— I have, etc.,

CLEMENCEAU

APPENDIX IV

RESOLUTIONS OF THE LEAGUE COUNCIL RELATING TO MINORITIES PROCEDURE [1]

1. REPORT PRESENTED BY M. TITTONI AND ADOPTED BY THE COUNCIL OF THE LEAGUE OF NATIONS ON OCTOBER 22ND, 1920

The Council of the League of Nations has thought it advisable to determine the nature and limits of the guarantees with regard to the protection of minorities provided for by the different Treaties.

The stipulations of the Treaties with regard to minorities are generally defined in the following terms:

"The country concerned agrees that the stipulations in the foregoing articles, so far as they affect persons belonging to racial, linguistic or religious minorities, constitute obligations of international concern and shall be placed under the guarantee of the League of Nations."

The stipulations with regard to minorities declare further that the country concerned "agrees that any Member of the Council of the League of Nations shall have the right to bring to the attention of the Council any infraction, or any danger of infraction, of any of these obligations, and that the Council may thereupon take such action and give such direction as it may deem proper and effective in the circumstances."

The countries concerned have further agreed that any difference of opinion as to questions of law or fact arising out of these articles between the Government concerned and any one of the Powers a Member of the Council of the League of Nations shall be held to be a dispute of an international character under Article 14 of the Covenant of the League of Nations, which dispute shall, if the other party thereto demands, be referred to the Permanent Court of International Justice.

Up to the present time, international law has entrusted to the great Powers the guarantee for the execution of similar provisions. The Treaties of Peace have introduced a new system; they have appealed to the League of Nations.

[1] League of Nations, *Protection of Linguistic, Racial or Religious Minorities by the League of Nations,* Geneva, 1931 (C. 8. M. 5. 1931. I.), pp. 7–12.

The Council and the Permanent Court of International Justice are the two organs of the League charged with the practical execution of the guarantee.

It may be advisable at the outset to define clearly the exact meaning of the term "guarantee of the League of Nations." It seems clear that this stipulation means, above all, that the provisions for the protection of minorities are inviolable—that is to say, they cannot be modified in the sense of violating in any way rights actually recognized and without the approval of the majority of the Council of the League of Nations. Secondly, this stipulation means that the League must ascertain that the provisions for the protection of minorities are always observed.

The Council must take action in the event of any infraction, or danger of infraction, of any of the obligations with regard to the minorities in question. The Treaties in this respect are quite clear. They indicate the procedure that should be followed.

The right of calling attention to any infraction or danger of infraction is reserved to the Members of the Council.

This is, in a way, a right and a duty of the Powers represented on the Council. By this right they are, in fact, asked to take a special interest in the protection of minorities.

Evidently this right does not in any way exclude the right of the minorities themselves, or even of States not represented on the Council, to call the attention of the League of Nations to any infraction or danger of infraction. But this act must retain the nature of a petition, or a report pure and simple; it cannot have the legal effect of putting the matter before the Council and calling upon it to intervene.

Consequently, when a petition with regard to the question of minorities is addressed to the League of Nations, the Secretary-General should communicate it, without comment, to the Members of the Council for information. This communication does not yet constitute a judicial act of the League or of its organs. The competence of the Council to deal with the question arises only when one of its members draws its attention to the infraction or danger of infraction which is the subject of the petition or report.

The State interested, if it is a Member of the League, is informed at the same time as the Council of the subject of the petition. As a matter of fact, the Secretary-General has for some time adopted the procedure of forwarding immediately to all the Members of the League any document forwarded for the information of Members of the Council. This information, which may give the State concerned an opportunity of submitting to the Members of the Council such remarks as it may consider desirable, does not, however, partake of the nature of a request of the League for information with regard to the subject of the petition, nor yet does it imply, with regard to the State concerned, the obligation of furnishing evidence in its defence.

Any cases where, as the result of the petition, the intervention of the League seems to be urgently necessary, the Secretary-General may also adopt the above procedure, but, in view of the urgency of the case, he will forward the petition in question to the Members of the Council as soon as possible (by telegraph if he thinks it advisable).

Each Power represented on the Council may demand that an urgent Council meeting be summoned in accordance with the provisions of the regulations in force.

This precaution will have the object of preventing any sudden act of oppression of minorities.

If the Council approves of the interpretation that I have had the honour to develop, it might adopt the following resolution:

"The Council invites its Members to draw the very special attention of their Governments to the conclusions arrived at in the present report."

2. RESOLUTION ADOPTED BY THE COUNCIL ON OCTOBER 25TH, 1920

For a definition of the conditions under which the Council shall exercise the powers granted to it by the Covenant and by various Treaties for the protection of minorities, the Council approved a resolution which will be inserted in its Rules of Procedure:

"With a view to assisting Members of the Council in the exercise of their rights and duties as regards the protection of minorities, it is desirable that the President and two members appointed by him in each case should proceed to consider any petition or communication addressed to the League of Nations with regard to an infraction or danger of infraction of the clauses of the Treaties for the protection of minorities. This enquiry would be held as soon as the petition or communication in question had been brought to the notice of the Members of the Council."

3. RESOLUTION ADOPTED BY THE COUNCIL ON JUNE 27TH, 1921

With reference to M. Tittoni's report, adopted on October 22nd, 1920, at Brussels, the Council of the League of Nations resolves that:

"All petitions concerning the protection of minorities under the provisions of the Treaties from petitioners other than Members of the League of Nations shall be immediately communicated to the State concerned.

"The State concerned shall be bound to inform the Secretary-General, within three weeks of the date upon which its representative accredited to the Secretariat of the League of Nations received the text of the petition in question, whether it intends to make any comments on the subject.

"Should the State concerned not reply within the period of three weeks, or should it state that it does not propose to make any comments, the petition in question shall be communicated to the Members of the League of Nations in accordance with the procedure laid down in M. Tittoni's report.

"Should the State concerned announce that it wishes to submit comments, a period of two months, dating from the day on which its representative accredited to the Secretariat of the League receives the text of the petition, shall be granted to it for this purpose. The Secretary-General, on receipt of the comments, shall communicate the petition, together with the comments, to the Members of the League of Nations.

"In exceptional and extremely urgent cases, the Secretary-General shall, before communicating the petition to the Members of the League of Nations, inform the representative accredited to the Secretariat of the League of Nations by the State concerned.

"This decision shall come into immeditae effect for all matters affecting Poland and Czechoslovakia.

"With regard to other States which have accepted the Treaty provisions relating to the protection of minorities, the Council authorises the Secretary-General to inform them of the decision taken in the case of Czechoslovakia and Poland and to ask them to state whether they wish the same procedure to be made applicable to them."

4. Resolution Adopted by the Council on September 5th, 1923

With reference to the previous resolutions relating to the procedure to be followed with regard to the protection of minorities, dated October 22nd and 25th, 1920, and June 27th, 1921, the Council of the League of Nations decides that:

1. In order that they may be submitted to the procedure established

by the Council resolutions dated October 22nd and 25th, 1920, and
June 27th, 1921, petitions addressed to the League of Nations concerning the protection of minorities:

(a) Must have in view the protection of minorities in accordance with the Treaties;
(b) In particular, must not be submitted in the form of a request for the severance of political relations between the minority in question and State of which it forms a part;
(c) Must not emanate from an anonymous or unauthenticated source;
(d) Must abstain from violent language;
(e) Must contain information or refer to facts which have not recently been the subject of a petition submitted to the ordinary procedure.

If the interested State raises for any reason an objection against the acceptance of a petition, the Secretary-General shall submit the question of acceptance to the President of the Council, who may invite two other members of the Council to assist him in the consideration of this question. If the State concerned so requests, this question of procedure shall be included in the agenda of the Council.

2. The extension of the period of two months, fixed by the resolution of June 27th, 1921, for observations by the Government concerned on the subject of the petitions may be authorised by the President of the Council if the State concerned so requests and if the circumstances appear to make such a course necessary and feasible.

3. The communication, in accordance with the resolution of June 27th, 1921, to the Members of the League of petitions and of observations (should there be any) by the Government concerned shall be restricted to the Members of the Council. Comumnications may be made to other Members of the League or to the general public at the request of the State concerned, or by virtue of a resolution to this effect passed by the Council after the matter has been duly submitted to it.

4. The consideration of petitions and observations (should there be any) of the Governments concerned by the President and two other members of the Council, in accordance with the resolution of October 25th, 1920, shall be undertaken with the sole object of determining whether one or more Members of the Council should draw the attention of the Council to an infraction or danger of an infraction of the clauses of the Treaties for the protection of minorities. The right re-

served to all members of the Council of drawing its attention to an infraction or danger of infraction remains unaffected.

5. The present resolution shall be communicated to the Governments which have signed treaties or made declarations concerning the protection of minorities.

5. RESOLUTION ADOPTED BY THE COUNCIL ON JUNE 10TH, 1925

The Council of the League of Nations,

Considering that, by the resolution of October 25th, 1920, it was decided, with a view to assisting Members of the Council in the exercise of their rights and duties as regards the protection of minorities, that it is desirable that the President and two members appointed by him in each case should proceed to consider any petition or communication addressed to the League of Nations with regard to an infraction or danger of infraction of the clauses of the Treaties for the protection of minorities, and that this enquiry should be held as soon as the petition or communication in question has been brought to the notice of the Members of the Council,

Decides

I. If the Acting President of the Council is:

The representative of the State of which the persons belonging to the minority in question are subjects, or ,

The representative of a neighbouring State of the State to which the persons belonging to the minority in question are subject; or

The representative of a State the majority of whose population belong from the ethnical point of view to the same people as the persons belonging to the minority in question,

that the duty which falls upon the President of the Council in accordance with the terms of the resolution of October 25th, 1920, shall be performed by the member of the Council who exercised the duties of President immediately before the Acting President, and who is not in the same position.

II. The President of the Council, in appointing two of his colleagues in conformity with the resolution of October 25th, 1920, shall not appoint either the representative of the State to which the persons belonging to the minority in question are subject or the representative of a State neighbouring the State to which these persons are subject, or the representative of a State a majority of which population belong from the ethnical point of view to the same people as the persons in question.

6. RESOLUTION ADOPTED BY THE COUNCIL ON JUNE 13TH, 1929

The Council:

(a) Decides to add to the provisions contained in its previous resolutions regarding the procedure for the examination of minorities petitions the following provisions:

1. *Receivability of Petitions*

When the Secretary-General declares a petition non-receivable, he will inform the petitioner and, if necessary, will communicate to him the Council resolution of September 5th, 1923, laying down the conditions of receivability of minorities petitions.

2. *Composition of Minorities Committees.*

The President of the Council may, in exceptional cases, invite four members of the Council to examine minorities petitions instead of two as laid down in the Council resolution of October 25th, 1920.

3. *Frequency of the Meetings of the Minorities Committees.*

The Council considers that it would be desirable for Minorities Committees to take into account the possibility of holding meetings in the intervals between sessions of the Council, whenever they think it expedient for the examination of individual petitions.

4. *Communications concerning the Action taken on Petitions by the Minorities Committees.*

(i) When the members of a Minorities Committee have finished the examination of a question, without asking that it be placed on the Council's agenda, they will communicate the result of their examination by letter to the other Members of the Council for their information. The Secretary-General will keep the relevant documents at the disposal of the Members of the Council.

(ii) The Secretary-General will distribute once a year, for the information of all the Members of the Council, a document reproducing the letters addressed during the year, as described above, by the various Minorities Committees to the Members of the Council.

5. *Publication of the Result of the Examination of a Question by a Minorities Committee.*

The Minorities Committees should consider carefully the possibility of publishing, with the consent of the Government concerned, the result of the examination of the questions submitted to them. The Council earnestly hopes that the Governments will, whenever possible, give their consent to such publication. The information might be published in the *Official Journal* and might consist of the letter from the Minorities Committee informing the other Members of the Council, or any other text that seemed expedient.

6. *Regular Annual Publications concerning the Work of the League in connection with the Protection of Minorities.*

The Secretary-General will publish annually in the *Official Journal* of the League statistics of: (1) the number of petitions received by the Secretariat during the year; (2) the number of petitions declared to be non-receivable; (3) the number of petitions declared to be receivable and referred to Committees of Three; (4) the number of Committees and the number of meetings held by them to consider these petitions; (5) the number of petitions whose examination by a Committee of Three has been finished in the course of the year.

(b) The present resolution will be communicated to the States which have accepted stipulations for the protection of minorities.

(c) The report prepared by the Japanese representative, as Rapporteur, with the assistance of the British and Spanish representatives (document C.C.M.I.), including the annexes thereto, together with the Minutes of the meetings of the Council sitting in committee for the examination of this question and those of the present meeting of the Council, will be communicated to all the Members of the League and will, in accordance with practice, be published.

SELECTED BIBLIOGRAPHY

The literature on nationalities and national minorities is extensive and voluminous. Many a minority group has sought to interest world opinion in its cause or its plight, while some of the states under obligations to protect minorities have been at pains to counteract unfavorable propaganda. Scholars, too, have recognized the importance of the subject and have devoted many volumes to its elucidation. The following bibliography consists mainly of scholarly works, but some contentious and propagandistic material has been included, in order to guide the reader to a well-rounded study of the subject.

PART I

General works and those bearing on the explosive nature of the nationalities problem in the war-breeding zone of East-Central Europe

Alexander, Thomas, *The Prussian Elementary Schools,* New York, 1918.
Bauer, Otto, *Die Nationalitätenfrage und die Sozialdemokratie,* 2nd ed., Vienna, 1924.
Brackmann, Albert (ed.), *Germany and Poland in their Historical Relations,* Munich, 1934.
Brown, F. J., and Roucek, J. S. (eds.), *Our Racial and National Minorities,* New York, 1937. (This work deals with groupings in the United States.)
Buell, Raymond Leslie, *Poland: Key to Europe,* New York, 1939.
Bülow, Bernhard von, *Imperial Germany,* New York, 1914.
Bismarck the Man and the Statesman: Being the Reflections and Reminiscences of Otto, Prince von Bismarck, Written and Dictated by Himself after his Retirement from Office, 2 vols. New York, 1899.
Cambridge History of Poland, The, Cambridge, 1941. (Edited by Reddaway, W. F., Penson, J. H., Halecki, O., and Dyboski, R.)
Chartier, Pierre, *La Colonisation allemande dans l'ancienne Pologne Prussienne et ses consequences actuelles,* Paris, 1921.

Dawson, William H., *What is Wrong With Germany?* London, 1915.

Dubnow, S. M., *History of the Jews in Russia and Poland,* 3 vols., Philadelphia, 1918–1920. (The standard work on the subject.)

Dyboski, R., *Poland,* London, 1933.

Edwards, Sutherland, *The Polish Captivity:* An account of the Present Position of the Poles, 2 vols. London, 1863. (The author has a strong pro-Polish bias.)

Fischel, Alfred, *Der Panslawismus bis zum Weltkrieg,* Stuttgart, 1919. (See especially Chap. VIII.)

Geshkoff, T., *Balkan Union: A Road to Peace in Southeastern Europe,* New York, 1940.

Great Britain, Foreign Office Historical Section, Peace Handbooks (Vol. VIII, No. 43), *Poland: General Sketch of History, 1569–1815,* London, 1920.

———, Foreign Office Historical Section, Peace Handbooks (Vol. VIII, No. 44), *Russian Poland Lithuania and White Russia,* London, 1920.

———, Foreign Office Historical Section, Peace Handbooks (Vol. VIII, No. 45), *Prussian Poland,* London, 1920.

———, Foreign Office Historical Section, Peace Handbooks (Vol. VIII, No. 46), *Austrian Poland,* London, 1920.

Guttzeit, Johannes, *Geschichte der deutschen Polen-Entrechtung,* Danzig, 1927. (Pro-Polish.)

Hayes, C. J. H., *Essays on Nationalism,* New York, 1926.

———, *The Historical Evolution of Modern Nationalism,* New York, 1931.

Headlam, James W., *Bismarck and the Foundation of the German Empire,* London, 1899.

Ignatiev, P. N., Odinetz, D. M., and Novgorotsev, P. J., *Russian Schools and Universities in the World War,* Carnegie Endowment for International Peace, New Haven, 1929.

Iorga, N., *A History of Roumania: Land, People, Civilization,* London, 1925.

Janowsky, Oscar I., "Ethnic and Cultural Minorities," MacIver, R. M. (ed.), *Group Relations and Group Antagonisms,* New York, 1944.

Jászi, Oscar, *The Dissolution of the Habsburg Monarchy,* Chicago, 1929. (An excellent study.)

Jedlicki, M. Z., *Germany and Poland Through the Ages,* Cambridge,

1942. (A lecture with a pro-Polish bias, given at Cambridge University on 31 October, 1941.)

Jomard, Lucien, *Le Conflit national et l'école en Pologne Prussienne,* Dijon, 1921. (A careful doctoral dissertation.)

Joseph, Bernard, *Nationality, Its Nature and Problems,* London, 1929.

Karski, S., *Poland Past and Present,* New York, 1933.

Kohn, Hans, *The Idea of Nationalism,* New York, 1944. (This is one of the best works on the subject.)

Kosáry, D. G., *A History of Hungary,* New York, 1941.

Machray, R., *Poland, 1914–1931,* London, 1932.

Masaryk, Thomas G., *The Problem of Small Nations in the European Crisis,* London, 1916.

———, *The New Europe (The Slav Standpoint),* London, 1918.

Mears, E. G. (ed), *Modern Turkey,* New York, 1924.

Perdelwitz, Richard, *Die Posener Polen von 1815–1914,* Schneidemühl, 1936.

Poland's Case for Independence (Being a series of Essays illustrating the Continuance of her National Life), London, 1916. (Issued by the Polish Information Committee of London.)

Polish Question from the German Point of View, The, London, 1855. (By a "German Statesman.")

Renner, Karl, *Das Selbstbestimmungsrecht der Nationen* (second and revised edition of *Der Kampf der Österreichischen Nationen um den Staat*), Vienna, 1918. (This is a basic and indispensable study.)

Robinson, Jacob, *Das Minoritätenproblem und seine Literatur,* Berlin, 1928. (A very good and comprehensive bibliography, but somewhat out of date.)

Roucek, J. S., *The Politics of the Balkans,* New York, 1939.

Royal Institute of International Affairs, The, *The Baltic States,* London, 1938.

———, *Nationalism,* London, 1939. (A "Report" by a study group of members of the Royal Institute of International Affairs.)

———, *South-Eastern Europe,* London, 1939.

Seipel, I., *Nation und Staat,* Vienna, 1916.

Seton-Watson, R. W., *A History of the Czechs and Slovaks,* London, 1943.

———, *A History of the Roumanians,* Cambridge, 1934.

Toynbee, A. J., and Kirkwood, K. P., *Turkey*, New York, 1927.

Trampe, L., *Sprachenkampf und Sprachenrecht in Preussen und seiner Ostmark* (Vol. II of *Ostdeutscher Kulturkampf*), Leipzig, 1908.

Wiskemann, Elizabeth, *Czechs and Germans: A Study of the Struggle in the Historic Provinces of Bohemia and Moravia*, London, 1938. (This is an excellent book.)

PART II

The Evolution of Successful Multi-National States

Chapter IV. National Federalism in Switzerland

Adams, F. O., and Cunningham, C. D., *The Swiss Confederation*, London, 1889.

Bonjour, F., *Real Democracy in Operation: The Example of Switzerland*, New York, 1920.

Brooks, R. C., *Civic Training in Switzerland*, Chicago, 1930. (This is a very good and very useful book.)

―――, *Government and Politics in Switzerland*, New York, 1918.

Bryce, James, *Modern Democracies*, Vol. I, London, 1921. (Chaps. XXVII–XXXII.)

Bunsen, Herman, *Die Dynamik der Schweizerischen Demokratie*, Breslau, 1937.

Clerget, Pierre, *La Suisse au XXe Siècle: Etude economique et sociale*, Paris, 1908. (See especially Chap. I.)

Dändliker, Karl, *A Short History of Switzerland*, London, 1899. (This is a good general work.)

Dürsteler, J., *Die Organisation der Exekutiv der Schweizerischen Eidgenossenschaft seit 1798*, Aarau, 1912.

Friedrich, Carl J., and Cole, Taylor, *Responsible Bureaucracy: A Study of the Swiss Civil Service*, Cambridge, Massachusetts, 1932. (This is an excellent short account.)

Hilty, C., *Les Constitutions fédérales de la Confédération Suisse*, Neuchatel, 1891.

Oechsli, Wilhelm, *History of Switzerland, 1499–1914*, Cambridge, 1922. (See especially Bks. IV–VI.)

Rappard, William E., "Documents on the Government of Switzerland," in Rappard, W. E., Sharp, W. R., Schneider, H. W., Pollock, J. K. and Harper, S. N., *Source Book on European Governments*, New York, 1937, I, 122 pages.

———, *The Government of Switzerland*, New York, 1936. (This is probably the best brief work on the subject.)

Rougemont, Denis de, and Muret, Charlotte, *The Heart of Europe*, New York, 1941.

Switzerland, *Recueil des constitutions fédérale et cantonales en vigueur au Ier Janvier 1880, Edition officielle*, Bern, 1880.

Tripp, M. L., *The Swiss and United States Federal Constitutional Systems: A Comparative Study*, Paris, 1940.

Vincent, John M., *State and Federal Government in Switzerland*, Baltimore, 1891.

Weilenmann, Hermann, *Die vielsprachige Schweiz: Eine Lösung des Nationalitätenproblems*, Basel, 1925. (This is an admirable study.)

Weinmann, Ernst, *Geschichte des Kantons Tessin in der späteren Regenerationszeit, 1840–1848*, Zurich, 1924.

Winchester, Boyd, *The Swiss Republic*, Philadelphia, 1891. (The author was the United States Minister at Bern.)

Zurcher, A. J., "The Political System of Switzerland," in Shotwell, James T. (ed.), *Governments of Continental Europe*, New York, 1940, pp. 979–1039. (This is an excellent survey.)

Chapter V. Bilingualism in South Africa

Aucamp, Anna J., *Bilingual Education and Nationalism with Special Reference to South Africa*, Pretoria, 1926.

Barnouw, Adriaan J., *Language and Race Problems in South Africa*, The Hague, 1934. (This is a valuable first-hand account.)

Botha, Colin G., *Social Life in the Cape Colony in the 18th Century*, Cape Town, 1926.

Brand, R. H., *The Union of South Africa*, Oxford, 1909.

Carnegie Corporation of New York, *Report of Professor Robert Herndon Fife on Tendencies in Education in East and South Africa with Particular Reference to Language Questions*, New York, 1932.

Cory, George E. (ed.), *The Diary of the Rev. Francis Owen*, Cape Town, 1926.

———, *The Rise of South Africa*, 5 vols. London, 1910–1930. (This is a detailed and scholarly work.)

Crafford, F. S., *Jan Smuts, A Biography*, New York, 1943.

Eybers, G. W. (ed.), *Select Constitutional Documents Illustrating South African History, 1795–1910*, London, 1918.

FitzPatrick, J. P., *South African Memories*, London, 1932. (The author was a very active and prominent Uitlander.)

Hofmeyr, Jan H., *South Africa*, New York, 1931.

Jones, Thomas Jesse, *Education in Africa*, New York, 1922.

———, *Education in East Africa*, New York, 1924.

Kennedy, W. P. M., and Schlosberg, H. J., *The Law and Custom of the South African Constitution*, London, 1935.

Kiewiet, C. W. de, *British Colonial Policy and the South African Republics, 1848–1872*, London, 1929.

———, *A History of South Africa: Social and Economic*, Oxford, 1941. (This is a brilliant work.)

Kilpin, Ralph, *The Parliament of the Cape*, London, 1938.

Malan, W. de Vos, *Tendencies in Secondary Education* (With special reference to the situation in the Cape Province of the Union of South Africa), New York, 1923.

Malherbe, E. G., *Education in South Africa (1652–1922)*, Cape Town, 1925. (This is a comprehensive and important book.)

McKerron, M. E., *A History of Education in South Africa (1652–1932)*, Pretoria, 1934.

Millin, S. G., *General Smuts*, 2 vols., Boston, 1936.

———, *The South Africans*, New York, 1927.

Nathan, Manfred, *The South African Commonwealth*, Johannesburg, 1919.

Newton, A. P. (ed.), *Select Documents Relating to the Unification of South Africa*, 2 vols., London, 1924.

Smuts, Adriaan J., *The Education of Adolescents in South Africa*, Cape Town, 1937. (This is an excellent survey and analysis of South African secondary education.)

Sowden, Lewis, *The Union of South Africa*, New York, 1943. (See especially Chap. IX.)

South Africa, *Papers Relating to a Federation of the South African Colonies*, London, 1907 (Cmd. 3564).

———, *Report to the Respective Parliaments of the Delegates to the*

South African Convention, 1908–1909, London, 1909 (Cmd. 4525).

———, *Second Report to the Respective Parliaments of the Delegates to the South African Convention, 1908–1909,* London, 1909 (Cmd. 4721).

South African National Convention, Minutes of Proceedings with Annexures (selected) of the South African National Convention held at Durban, Cape Town and Bloemfontein, 12th October, 1908, to 11th May, 1909, Cape Town, 1911.

Theal, George M., *History of the Boers in South Africa,* London, 1887.

———, (ed.), *Records of the Cape Colony* (From February 1793 to April 1831), 36 vols., London, 1897–1905. (This is a collection of invaluable first-hand information.)

Union of South Africa, *Papers Relating to Constitutional Changes in the Transvaal,* London, 1905 (Cmd. 2479).

Union of South Africa, Parliament of, *Report from the Joint Committee on the Use of Afrikaans in Bills, Acts and Official Documents of Parliament, Together with the Proceedings of the Committee, Minutes of Evidence and Appendix,* March 20, 1925.

Union of South Africa, *Report of the Rehoboth Commission,* Cape Town, 1927.

Williams, Basil (ed.), *The Selborne Memorandum, A Review of the Mutual Relations of the British South African Colonies in 1907,* Oxford, 1925.

Walton, Edgar H., *The Inner History of the National Convention of South Africa,* Capetown, 1912. (This book contains material unavailable elsewhere.)

Chapter VI. National Federalism in the Soviet Union

Anglo-Russian Parliamentary Committee, The, *Soviet Progress: A Record of Economic and Cultural Development, 1917–1937,* London, 1937. (Pamphlet)

Aronson, G., *The Jewish Problem in Soviet Russia* (in Yiddish), New York, 1944.

Batsell, W. R., *Soviet Rule in Russia,* New York, 1929. (This book contains valuable documents.)

Brailsford, H. N., *How the Soviets Work,* New York, 1927.

Chamberlin, William Henry, *The Russian Enigma: An Interpretation*, New York, 1944.

———, *Soviet Russia: A Living Record and a History*, Boston, 1930.

———, *The Ukraine, A Submerged Nation*, New York, 1944.

Chekalin, M., *The National Question in the Soviet Union*, New York, 1941. (This is a laudatory brief survey.)

Chernov, Victor, *The Great Russian Revolution*, New Haven, 1936, Chap. XIV.

Davies, R. A., and Steiger, A. J., *Soviet Asia*, New York, 1942.

Elgers, A., *Die Kulturrevolution in der Sowjetunion*, Berlin 1930.

Fischer, L., *Men and Politics*, New York, 1941.

Florinsky, M. T., "Russia—The U.S.S.R.," in Shotwell, James T. (ed.), *Governments of Continental Europe*, New York, 1940, pp. 757–936.

Hans, N., and Hessen, S., *Educational Policy in Soviet Russia*, London, 1930.

Harper, Samuel N., "Documents on the Government of the Soviet Union," in Rappard, W. E., Sharp, W. R., Schneider, H. W., Pollock, J. K., and Harper, S. N., *Source Book on European Governments*, New York, 1937, V, 186 pages.

———, *The Government of the Soviet Union*, New York, 1938.

Hrdlička, Aleš, *The Peoples of the Soviet Union*, Washington, 1942. (Pamphlet)

Hrushevsky, Michael, *A History of Ukraine*, New Haven, 1941, Chaps. XXI–XXV.

Kaftanov, S., *Soviet Students*, Moscow, 1939. (Pamphlet)

King, Beatrice, *Changing Man: The Education System of the USSR*, New York, 1937. (See especially Appendix I, "National Minorities," pp. 279–310.)

Kohn, Hans, *Nationalism in the Soviet Union*, New York, 1933.

———, "The Nationality Policy of the Soviet Union," in Harper, Samuel N. (ed.), *The Soviet Union and World Problems* (Harris Foundation Lectures), Chicago, 1935, pp. 85–121.

Kunitz, Joshua, *Dawn Over Samarkand: The Rebirth of Central Asia*, New York, 1935. (See especially Chap. XII.)

Lamont, Corliss, "The Peoples of the Soviet Union," *Soviet Russia Today*, June, 1944.

———, "Union Republics and Subdivisions," *Soviet Russia Today*, July, 1944.
———, "The Russian Republic," *Soviet Russia Today*, August, 1944.
Lengyel, Emil, *Siberia*, New York, 1943.
Lestschinsky, Jacob, *Soviet Jewry* (in Yiddish), New York, 1941.
London, Kurt, *The Seven Soviet Arts*, New Haven, 1938.
Malevsky-Malevitch, P. (ed.), *Russia USSR: A Complete Handbook*, New York, 1933.
Mandel, William, *The Soviet Far East and Central Asia*, New York, 1944.
Markov, P. A., *The Soviet Theatre*, London, 1934. (See especially Chap. X.)
Mikhailov, N., *The Land of the Soviets*, New York, 1939.
Papyan, M., *Industrial Progress in the Soviet Republics of the Non-Russian Nationalities*, Moscow, 1939. (Pamphlet)
Pomus, V. I., *Buriat Mongolia*, New York, 1943.
Russia Today, New York, 1925. (The official Report of the British Trade Union Delegation.)
Stalin, Joseph, *Marxism and the National and Colonial Question*, New York, 1935. (This is an invaluable collection of papers and speeches on the national question.)
———, *The New Soviet Constitution*, New York, 1936. (Pamphlet)
Strong, Anna Louise, *Peoples of the USSR*, New York, 1944.
———, *Red Star in Samarkand*, New York, 1929.
———, *The New Soviet Constitution*, New York, 1937.
———, *This Soviet World*, New York, 1936. (See especially Chap. V.)
Taracouzio, T. A., *The Soviet Union and International Law*, New York, 1935.
Webb, Sidney and Beatrice, *Soviet Communism: A New Civilization?*, 2 vols., New York, 1938.
Williams, A. R., *The Russians: The Land, the People and Why They Fight*, New York, 1943. (See Chaps. 2, 3.)
———, *The Soviets*, New York, 1937. (See Part I.)
Yarmolinsky, Avrahm, *The Jews and Other Minor Nationalities Under the Soviets*, New York, 1928.

PART III

The Bases of a Solution of the Nationalities Problem in East-Central Europe

Ammende, E. (ed.), *Die Nationalitäten in den Staaten Europas* (published by The European Nationalities Congress), Vienna, 1931.

Auerhan, Jan, *Die sprachlichen Minderheiten in Europa*, Berlin, 1926.

Balogh, Arthur de, *L'Action de la Société des Nations en matière de protection des minorités*, Paris, 1937.

Balogh, Arthur von, *Der internationale Schutz der Minderheiten*, Munich, 1928.

Boteni, V., *Les Minorités en Transylvanie*, Paris, 1938.

Bruns, C. G., *Gesammelte Schriften zur Minderheitenfrage*, Berlin, 1933.

Bulgares et Yougoslaves, Belgrade, 1928. (This is a pamphlet issued by the Jugoslav League of Nations Association.)

Cabot, J. M., *The Racial Conflict in Transylvania*, Boston, 1926.

Cecil, Viscount of Chelwood, *Minorities and Peace* (Lucien Wolf Memorial Lecture), London, 1934.

Čermelj, L., *Life and Death Struggle of a National Minority* (The Jugoslavs in Italy), Ljubljana, 1936.

Chmelař, J., *La Minorité polonaise en Tchécoslovaquie*, Prague, 1935.

―――, *National Minorities in Central Europe*, Prague, 1937. (This is a very good brief survey.)

Clark, C. U., *Racial Aspects of Romania's Case*, n.p., 1941. (The author has a pro-Rumanian bias.)

Commission to Study the Organization of Peace, "Preliminary Report and Monographs," *International Conciliation*, April, 1941.

―――, "Second Report—The Transitional Period," *International Conciliation*, April, 1942.

―――, "Third Report—The United Nations and the Organization of Peace," *International Conciliation*, April, 1943.

―――, "Fourth Report," New York, 1943–1944. (See especially Part III, "International Safeguard of Human Rights.")

Constantopoulos, D. S., *Zur Nationalitätenfrage Südosteuropas*, Würzburg, 1940.

Dérer, I., *The Unity of the Czechs and Slovaks*, Prague, 1938.

Dragomir, S., *The Ethnical Minorities in Transylvania*, Geneva, 1927. (This is a pro-Rumanian and contentious account.)

Duparc, J. F., *La Protection des minorités, de race, de langue et de religion*, Paris, 1922.

Education in Poland, 1918–1928, Warsaw, 1929. (This is a publication of the Polish Ministry of Education.)

Engelmann, G., *Das Recht der nationalen Minderheiten in Lettland*, Riga, 1930.

Erler, G. H. J., *Das Recht der nationalen Minderheiten*, Münster, 1931.

Europäischer Nationalitäten Kongress, *Sitzungsbericht des Kongresses der organisierten nationalen Gruppen in den Staaten Europas*, Geneva, 1925–1931; Vienna, 1932; Berne, 1933–1934; Geneva, 1935–1936.

————, *Die Nationalitäten in den Staaten Europas* (Ergänzungen), Vienna, 1932.

European Nationalities Congress, *The Congress of the European National Minorities, 1937*, Vienna, 1938.

Feinberg, Nathan, *La Question des minorités a la Conférence de la Paix de 1919–1920 et l'action Juive en faveur de la protection internationale des minorités*, Paris, 1929.

Felinski, M., *The Ukrainians in Poland*, London, 1931. (This is a Polish apology.)

Fischer, P., *Rights and Safeguards of the Polish Minority in Upper Silesia*, Berlin, 1931.

Friedman, Samuel, *Le Problème des minorités ethniques et sa solution par l'autonomie et la personnification*, Toulouse, 1927.

Genov, G. P., *Bulgaria and the Treaty of Neuilly*, Sofia, 1935. (The author has a pro-Bulgarian bias.)

Gower, Sir Robert, *The Hungarian Minorities in the Succession States*, London, 1937. (This is a good example of pro-Hungarian propaganda.)

Hanč, J., *Tornado Across Eastern Europe*, New York, 1942.

Heyking, Alphonse de, *La Conception de l'état et l'idée de la cohésion ethnique*, Paris, 1927.

Holborn, Louise W. (ed.), *War and Peace Aims of the United Nations, 1939–1942*, Boston, 1943.

The Hungarian Minorities in the Succession States, Budapest, 1929. (This is Hungarian propaganda.)

James, E. H., *Crossroads in Europe* (A Word for Minorities), Geneva, 1929.

Janowsky, Oscar I., *The Jews and Minority Rights (1898–1919)*, New York, 1933.

———, "Minorities: Pawns of Power," *Survey Graphic*, February, 1939.

———, "More Minorities—More Pawns," *Survey Graphic*, November, 1939.

———, *People at Bay*, New York, 1938.

———, "Towards a Solution of the Minorities Problem," in Kingsley, J. D., and Petegorsky, D. W., *Strategy for Democracy*, New York, 1942.

Jaquin, P., *La Question des minorités entre l'Italie te la Yougoslavie*, Paris, 1929.

Jeziorancki, K., *Le Problème minoritaire en Europe*, Warsaw, 1932. (Pamphlet)

Junghann, Otto, *National Minorities in Europe*, New York, 1932.

Kaeckenbeek, Georges, *The International Experiment of Upper Silesia* (A Study in the Working of the Upper Silesian Settlement, 1922–1937), London, 1942. (This is an admirable work by the President of the Upper Silesian Arbitral Tribunal, 1922–1937.)

Kornis, J., *Ungarns Unterrichtswesen seit dem Weltkriege*, Leipzig, 1930.

Kraus, Herbert, *Das Recht der Minderheiten*, Berlin, 1927. (This is a collection of documents.)

Krofta, K., *The Germans in the Czechoslovak Republic*, Prague, 1937. (Pamphlet)

Kulischer, E. M., *The Displacement of Population in Europe*, Montreal, 1943. (This is an excellent survey.)

Ladas, S. P., *The Exchange of Minorities: Bulgaria, Greece and Turkey*, New York, 1932. (This is the best and most comprehensive work on the subject.)

Laserson, M. M., *Staat, Souveränität und Minorität*, Riga, 1927.

League of Nations, *Protection of Linguistic, Racial and Religious Minorities by the League of Nations*, Geneva, 1927. (C.L.110, 1927 I. Annexe.) (This volume contains the provisions of the various Treaties and Declarations.)

League of Nations, Council, *Protection of Linguistic, Racial or Religious Minorities by the League of Nations*, second edition. Geneva.

1931 (C.8.M.5. 1931. I.) (This volume contains resolutions and extracts from minutes of the Council and resolutions and reports adopted by the Assembly, relating to *procedure* in minorities questions.)

League of Nations, Council, *Protection of Minorities in Upper Silesia*, Geneva, 1927. (C.66. 1927. I.) (This contains an appeal of the "Deutscher Volksbund," observations of the Polish Government, the "Opinion" of the President of the Mixed Commission, and related materials.)

League of Nations, Secretariat, *Ten Years of World Co-operation*, London, 1930. (Chapter XI deals with minorities.)

League of Nations, Secretariat, Information Section, *The League of Nations and the Protection of Minorities of Race, Language and Religion*, revised edition, Geneva, 1927. (This is a convenient summary.)

Lengyel, Emil, *The Cauldron Boils*, New York, 1932. (This book describes the maltreatment of minorities in Poland.)

Lessing, O. E. (ed.), *Minorities and Boundaries*, The Hague, 1931. (This is a collection of pro-German papers on German minorities.)

Lichtträger, F., *Immer wieder Serbien,* Berlin, 1933.

Lilek, Em., *Verfolgungen der Slovenen und Kroaten in Italien*, Celje, 1935. (Pamphlet)

Lucien-Brun, J., *Le Problème des minorités devant le droit international*, Lyon, 1923.

Macartney, C. A., *Hungary*, London, 1934.

———, *Hungary and Her Successors: The Treaty of Trianon and Its Consequences, 1919–1937*, London, 1937.

———, *National States and National Minorities*, London, 1934. (This is a very good and comprehensive book.)

Maddison, E., *Die nationalen Minderheiten Estlands und ihre Rechte*, Reval, 1930.

Mair, L. P., *The Protection of Minorities*, London, 1928.

Mandelstam, A., "La protection des minorités," in *Académie de droit international, recueil des cours*, vol. I, Paris, 1925, pp. 367–519.

Martel, R., *La Ruthénie Subcarpathique*, Paris, 1935.

Miller, D. H., *My Diary at the Conference of Paris, With Documents*, 21 vols., privately printed. New York, 1925. (This is an invaluable collection of source material. See especially Vols. I, XIII.)

Nationality Policy in Czechoslovakia, Prague, 1938. (This is a collection of speeches made in parliament by Premier Hodža and Ministers Franke, Nečas and Dérer.)

Noel-Buxton, E., and Conwill-Evans, T. P., *Oppressed Peoples and the League of Nations*, London, 1922. (See Chaps. I, IV.)

Paprocki, S. J. (ed.), *Minority Affairs and Poland*, Warsaw, 1935.

The Peace Conference, Paris, 1919, *Report of the Delegation of the Jews of the British Empire*, London, 1920.

Les Polonais en Tchécoslovaquie, Warsaw, 1935.

"The Problem of Minorities," *International Conciliation*, September, 1926, pp. 313-386. (This is a collection of articles by Louis Eisenmann, William E. Rappard, H. Wilson Harris, and Raymond Leslie Buell.)

Raschhofer, H., *Hauptprobleme des Nationalitätenrechts*, Stuttgart, 1931.

Religious Minorities in Transylvania, The, Boston, 1925. (This volume was issued by the American Committee on the Rights of Religious Minorities.)

Reut-Nicolussi, E., *Tyrol Under the Axe of Italian Fascism*, London, 1930.

Roucek, J. S., *The Working of the Minorities System Under the League of Nations*, Prague, 1929.

Robinson, J., Karbach, O., Laserson, M. M., Robinson, N., Vichniak, M., *Were the Minorities Treaties a Failure?* New York, 1943.

Roumania Ten Years After, Boston, 1928. (This volume was issued by the American Committee on the Rights of Religious Minorities.)

Ruyssen, Th., *Les Minorités nationales d'Europe et la Guerre Mondiale*, Paris, 1923.

Schiemann, P., *Ein europäisches Problem*, Vienna, 1937. (Pamphlet)

Schmidt, R. and Boehm, M. H., *Materialen der deutschen Gesellschaft für Nationalitätenrecht*, Nos. 1-13, Leipzig, 1929. (This is a collection of the Minorities provisions and treaties.)

Segal, Simon, *The New Order in Poland*, New York, 1942. (This is an excellent study of Poland under Nazi rule.)

Shotwell, James T., *The Great Decision*, New York, 1944. (This is an excellent discussion of the fundamentals of world peace.)

Sipson, C. C., *La Question scolaire dans les pays à minorités*, Paris, 1939.

La Situation des Minorités Bulgares, Sofia, 1932. (This is a publication of the Bulgarian League of Nations Association.)

La Situation de la Minorité Yougoslave en Italie, Ljubljana, 1927. (This pamphlet was issued by the Minority Rights Institute of Ljubljana.)

Sobota, E., *Das Tschechoslovakische Nationalitätenrecht*, Prague, 1931. (This is an invaluable work.)

Stephens, J. S., *Danger Zones of Europe: A Study of National Minorities*, London, 1929. (This is a brief and general but good account.)

Stillschweig, Kurt, *Die Juden Osteuropas in den Minderheitenverträgen*, Berlin, 1936.

Stone, Julius, *International Guarantees of Minority Rights* (Procedure of the League of Nations in Theory and Practice), London, 1932. (This is an excellent study.)

——, *Regional Guarantees of Minority Rights*. (A Study of minorities procedure in Upper Silesia), New York, 1933. (This is an excellent study.)

Szász, Zsombor de, *The Minorities in Roumanian Transylvania*, London, 1927. (This strongly pro-Hungarian account should be balanced by Dragomir's book.)

Temperley, H. W. V. (ed.), *A History of the Peace Conference of Paris*, Vols. I, V, VI, London, 1920–1924. (See especially Vol. V, pp. 112–155, 432–466.)

Trampler, Kurt, *Staaten und nationale Gemeinschaften* (Eine Lösung des europäischen Minderheiten-Problems), Munich, 1929.

Truhart, Herbert von, *Völkerbund und Minderheitenpetitionen*, Vienna, 1931.

Türcke, K. E., *Das Schulrecht der deutschen Volksgruppen in Ost-und Südosteuropa*, Berlin, 1938.

Vichniak, M., *La Protection des droit des minorités dans les traités internationaux de 1919–1920*, Paris, n.d.

Wambaugh, Sarah, *Plebiscites Since the World War*, 2 vols., Washington, 1933. (This is the standard work on the subject.)

Wasilewski, L., *La Question des nationalités en Poméranie*, Paris, n.d.

Winkler, Wilhelm, *Statistisches Handbuch der europäischen Nationalitäten*, Vienna, 1931.

INDEX

Aegean Sea, 19, 155
Afghanistan, 84, 90
Afrikaans, Boer vernacular: cultural awakening *1870's*, 57; *1925* amendment to South Africa Act, *Article 137*, 65; use in elementary schools after *1914*, 66
Afrikander Bond: political league formed in the *1880's*, 57; "Christian National" schools, 61
Albania, Minorities Declaration, 112; Albanian Minority Schools case, 132
"Aliens": minorities in the culturally uniform national state, 27, 30, 31; Jewish "foreigners" in Rumania, 113
Alphabets, invention for backward nationalities in the Soviet Union, 101, 102
Amur River, 98
Appeasement, policy of, by the Great Powers, 139
Armenia: census *1939*, 75, 77; by *1922* allied to R.S.F.S.R., 84, 86; Transcaucasian Federation, 86; union republic, 90; Armenian language in the schools, 102
Asia, Central, in the Soviet Union, 77, 90, 99
Asia Minor, Greek invasion *1922*, 139
Assimilation, national-cultural: in the United States, 3; why it must be abandoned in east-central Europe, 4; possible with individuals, but not with conscious national communities, 4; forces of assimilation resisted as agencies of denationalization, 5; aided by circumstances in France and England, 15, 19; French Protestant refugees and Westphalians in South Africa, 47; assimilation of Dutch South African law to the law of England, 52; statements of Mello-Franco and Austen Chamberlain, 129–130, 131; east-central European heritage of forced assimilation, 133, 136; conflict resulting from efforts to impose a national state on a mixed population, 142, 143, 166
"Association for Defence of the Eastern Marches," see *Ostmarkenverein*
Assyrians in the Soviet Union, 76, 102
Atlantic Charter, statements on self-determination, 12, 106
Auflassung, German Settlers Case, 121
Ausrotten, extermination of dissident national characteristics, 29–31; *see also* Extermination
Austria, Austria-Hungary: liberation of minorities under Versailles Treaty, 11; resulting economic un-balance after dissolution, and formation of petty states, 11; economic unity and relative prosperity in XIXth century, 20; Hapsburg dynastic, rather than national, interests, 22; proposal for a federation of national-territorial units, 22; establishment of the Dual Monarchy *1867*, and ineffective efforts toward equality of various nationalities, 22, 23; Wilson and Lloyd George on the reconstruction of Austria-Hungary, 106, 107; hope for a multi-national state, 107, 108; Hapsburg proposal of self-determination, 107; collapse of the Hapsburgs, 108
Azerbaijan: *1939* census, 75, 77; *1922* treaty of alliance with R.S.F.S.R., 84, 86; Transcaucasian Federation, 86; a union republic, 90

Balkanization of east-central Europe, 9, 107, 143
Balkans, the: resistance to efforts of Young Turks at Ottomanization, 23; suggestion of a multi-national federation, 143, 146; a regional confederation, 147
Baltic, the: ethnographic, linguistic and cultural problems, 19, 155; region under Czarist Russia, 36, 84; annexation by Soviet *1939–41*, 90; States' Declarations accepting League supervision of treatment of minorities, 112
Barère, Bertrand, quoted on linguistic uniformity, 15
Bashkirs, 75, 77; oil, 99; present-day literacy, 101
Batsell, W. R., *Soviet Rule in Russia*, 78
Beck, Col. Joseph: non-aggression pact with Berlin, 127; repudiation of League supervision of Poland's minorities, 127
Beneš, Eduard, Foreign Minister of Czechoslovakia: hope for a multinational Czechoslovakia, 108; statements on national minorities, transfer of populations, 136–138; elimination of disloyal elements, 138; *New York Times* interview *1943*, 138; regional federation, 146, 155
Bern: linguistic diversity, 38; guarantee of language rights under the Constitution of *1831*, 40; *see also* Switzerland
Bessarabia, annexation by the Soviet Union, 90
Big Three, 110; *see also* Wilson; Clemenceau; Lloyd George
Bilingualism, *see* Languages
Bill of Rights for protection of minorities, 158
Binationalism, bilingualism a workable form of, 67, 68
Birobidjan, Jewish autonomous region, 98
Bismarck, Prince von: Polish problem, 25, 26; idea of a German national state, 26, 31, 145; the *Kulturkampf*: struggle with the Catholic Church, 26; peace with the Church, continued measures against the Poles, 27; retirement *1890*, 27; *Ostmarkenverein*, 28; Nazi depravity a result of Junker teaching, 31; compulsory assimilation, 123; Congress of Berlin, 180
Bloemfontein, South African National Convention *1908–09*, 62
Boer War, 59; effects, 60–62; Vereeniging Peace Treaty *1902*, 60
Boers, the: British-Boer antagonism, 46–47; popular name for South Africans of Dutch origin, 48; reaction to proclamation on the use of the English language, 50–51; trek to the interior due to deep sense of grievance, 53–55; Anglicization in Cape Colony, 56; cultural awakening *1870's*, 57; Afrikaans and the Afrikander Bond, 57, 61, 65, 66; new patriotism following the annexation of the Transvaal by the British, 58; a war lesson, that South Africa must remain composite, 60; reaction to Lord Milner's rule, and Lady Curzon's remark with reference to children, 61; "Christian National" schools, 61; unity of Transvaal British and Boers at South African National Convention, 62; *see also* South Africa; Cape of Good Hope; Orange River territory; Transvaal
Bohemia, mixed population, 138, 151
Botha, General Louis, attitude toward Anglicization of Boer children, 61
Bukovina, 90
Bulgaria: minority in the Soviet Union, 76, 91; exchange with Greece of minorities, 139–140; question of membership in a Balkan federation, 143; treaty of peace, 181
Bülow, Prince von: on the struggle of nationalities within the state, 28; "the hammer and the anvil," 28, 31; Dispossession Bill *1908*, 29;

INDEX

attempt to maintain a German national state, 29, 30; legal suppression, expropriation, and expulsion, a precursor to *Ausrotten*, 30, 31
Buryats in the Soviet Union, 77, 85
Byelo Russians, *see* White Russians

Calonder, Felix, President of the Swiss Confederation: quoted on Swiss federation, 44; Upper Silesian Mixed Commission: on the submission of minorities petitions, 148, 161
Cape of Good Hope: occupied by the Dutch *1652*, 47; Cape Colony seized by the British during the wars of the French Revolution, 47–48; Union of South Africa, from *1910*, 62; petition *1811* for asylum for people from Holland, 48; British colonists aided in settlement *1820*, 48
Capetown, 48, 49, 50, 53, 62; *see also* Charter of Justice
Caspian Sea, 76, 85
Caucasus, the: numerous nationalities, 76, 77
Centralization: rise of west-European national states, 14; unifying effect of royal power, 14, 15, 19; British policy in South Africa, 54; curbed in the Soviet Union by national federalism, 77
Chamberlain, Sir Austen, British Foreign Minister, on the assimilation of minorities, 130, 131
Charter of Justice *1827*, reconstruction of Capetown Courts, and question of language, 52, 53
Chauvinism, 28, 43; Soviet attitude toward, 96, 103
Chinese-Russian border, 77, 85
"Christian National" schools, *see* Afrikander Bond
Chuvashes, a Turko-Tartaric people within Soviet Russia, 75, 77
Citizenship: of minorities, provided for in Minorities Treaties, 112–113; under guarantee of the League, 115; a human right, 147

Civil rights: in the United States, 3; Minorities Treaties, 112; guarantee, under the League, to individuals, not groups, 132; elementary right of man, 148; *see also* Citizenship; Freedom of association, etc.; Human rights; National rights; Political rights
Civil service: bilingualism in Switzerland, 41; South Africa, 66, 67
Clemenceau, Letter of *June 24, 1919*, to Paderewski, 128; *text*, 179
Commission to Study the Organization of Peace, Fourth Report: suggested Conference and Commission on Human Rights, 157, 162
Committee of Three, *see* League of Nations: Minorities Committees
Communism: national rights harmonized with the precept and practice of Communism, 35, 77, 103; contribution of Stalin, 78; *1903* resolution of Russian Social Democrats on self-determination, 79; the class, not the nation, the fundamental unit of society, 80; self-determination, within the bounds set by communist doctrine, 82; propagation of communist ideology among non-Russian peoples, 82; hope for the achievement of an un-national society, 96; national freedom does not extend to the sphere of Communist ideology, 97; prohibition of close relations of nationalities with kindred peoples outside the Union, 100
Concentration camps, Nazi, 7; *see also* Maidanek
Conciliation: used by the League in the settlement of minorities disputes, 119, 124, 125, 159, 163, 165
Congress of Berlin, 180, 182
Congress of Oppressed Nationalities, Rome, *April 1918*, 108
Congress of Vienna, the national individuality of the Poles, 25
Cordon sanitaire, Soviet attitude toward Czech-Polish regional union, 146

Cosmopolitanism, federation rather than, 43, 44
Crimea, the: mixed population, 76, 77; Jewish national area, 98
Croats: within the Austro-Hungarian Empire, 107; in a Balkan federation, 143, 146, 147; bitter struggle within Jugoslavia, 167
Culture, national, *see* National culture
Curzon, Lady, on the Anglicization of Boer children, 61
Czechoslovakia: pre-war (World War II) strife because of minorities questions, 6; Wilson's 1917 request for liberation of Czechoslovaks, 10; Succession State, 11; truculence of Sudeten Germans, and Hitler's attack, 12, 152–153; German minorities represented in Czechoslovak Parliament, use of German language, German university, 16–17; Czech minority in Soviet Union, 76, 91; Czechoslovak element in Austria-Hungary, 107; Dr. Beneš's statement on minorities and a federated state, 108, 110; signing of Minorities Treaty, 112; transfer of disloyal minorities, 136–138; a post-war German minority, 138; statements by Osuský on population transfer and national liberty, 142, 167; Polish-Czech effort toward regional union 1940, 146; Nazi "protection" of minorities, 157; continued existence dependent on national liberty, not national uniformity, 167

Danubian region, 107, 108; suggested federation, 146
Decentralization: of government functions in Switzerland, 35, 44–45; an alternative to the break-up of Austria-Hungary in the peace settlement of World War I, 107; solution of the problem of minorities, 143, 165; *see also* Federalism
Democracy: growth in Great Britain, and the treatment of minorities, 16; Switzerland, 42–43, 45; democracy in government and solution of the east-central European problem, 166
Denationalization: minorities' resistance to assimilation, 5; German policy toward Prussian Poles, 30; Switzerland, 39; South Africa, 56; effort of Western statesmen to protect minorities, 110, 114; danger in the compulsory denationalization of minorities within a regional federation, 143; use of the Jews as a tool in denationalization, 151; problem of Germany and Hungary, following World War II, 153
Dispossession Act, 1908: expropriation by Germany of Polish estates, 29
Don, the, 76
Durban, South African National Convention 1908, 62

Economic unity: versus self-determination, 10–12; sacrificed in 1919 to the principle of nationality, 11, 12; need to harmonize with claims of nationalities and minorities in east-central Europe, 13; the multi-national state, 45, 106, 107; national federalism, 145–147, 166; regional confederation, 146, 155
Economic welfare: economic opportunity in the United States, 3; economy of Austria-Hungary, 11; no provision for economic cooperation among the Succession States, 11; economic prosperity: freedom from want, 12; Polish economic "cold pogrom" against minorities, 31; an inducement to the union of South African colonies, 62; equality of economic opportunity, 148
Edict of Nantes, 18
Education of minorities: Americanization under the public school system, 4; Britain, 16; Czechoslo-

vakia, 16–17; Ottoman Turkey, 22–23; Polish districts of Prussia, 27; religious instruction to Polish children, and ensuing school strike, 29; Switzerland, 45; South Africa, under the Dutch, 47; South Africa, under the British, 48–53, 56, 58; British educational commissions, 57; resistance of the Boers, 59, 61; Anglicizing Boer schools under Lord Milner, 61; Dutch "Christian National" schools, 61; bilingualism in South Africa, 65–67; Czarist Russia, 69; following the Revolution of 1905, 72; liberal policy of Count Ignatiev, Russian Minister of Education 1915, 72; Bolshevik national policy, 79, 102; use of the vernacular, 86, 100, 101–102; backward peoples in the Soviet Union, 101–102; four categories in Soviet school system, 101–102; minority schools in the Soviet Union, 102; scholastic rights in Poland, 113–114; state funds to be shared by minorities, 114, 133, 149, 150; Jewish "Educational Committees," 114; requirements under the Minorities Treaties, 132–133; of local interest, in a regional confederation, 147–148, 149; Estonian Cultural Council, 150

Equality: of opportunity, 3; of nationalities, 35, 98, 103, 155, 164; Switzerland, 40–42; of the sovereign republics of the Soviet Union, 88; provision for equality before the law in the Minorities Treaties, 112, 163–164; equality before the law and of economic opportunity, a human right, 148; of the Jews and other national groups, 152; international supervision of minorities, and the problem of sovereign equality of states, 154–156

Estonia: population, 76; union republic, 90; Law of Cultural Autonomy 1925, 150; Cultural Council, 150

Ethnic frontiers, impossibility of devising, 17, 20, 110, 135, 136, 142, 143, 148, 155, 166

Europe: comparison of national homogeneity in the East and in the West, 10, 107, 129, 135, 136, 142, 163; confusion of Western thought as to the Soviet Union, and nationalities of east and east-central Europe, 91, 96, 98, 99, 114

east-central: area, 19, 155; migrations and colonization, 19; division among the three great states, national enclaves, 20; paramount interest of Soviet Russia, 73, 146; disintegration following First World War, 109; national minorities in every new or enlarged state, 110; weaknesses which militated against proper functioning of Minorities Treaties, 129; a guide for reconstruction in the Estonian Law of Cultural Autonomy, 150

Exchange of populations, *see* Transfer of populations

Expropriation, policy of denationalization in the German state, 29–31; *see also* Expulsion; Transfer of populations

Expulsion: Prussian policy, 27, 31; forced migration, 140; indiscriminate expulsion should be barred under the organization of the United Nations, 164; *see also* Expropriation; Transfer of populations

Extermination: of dissident elements in Nazi Germany, 7, 31, 166; "cold pogrom" carried out by the Poles, 31; treatment of the Jews by Nazis, 152; see also *Ausrotten;* Maidanek

Far East, 76, 155

Fascism, 153; misuse of minority protection by partisan interests, 9; effect of aggression on the League of Nations, 123

Federalism, 67; *national,* 144, 167; in Switzerland, 37–45; federation rather than cosmopolitanism, 44; local government and cultural autonomy, 45, 86, 166; in the Soviet Union, 69–104, 166; nationality factor, 77, 96, 97; proposals, and original federation *1923* of the Soviet Union, 86, 90; functioning of Soviet national federalism, 91–102; comparison of American and Soviet forms of federalism, 97; national equality within the Soviet Union, 97; national federalism and economic unity, 145–147, 166; within the framework of regional federalism, 145–146, 147, 166; steps taken by governments-in-exile, 146; the multi-national state, 147; solution of acute minority problems, 147; extension to small and scattered minorities in the form of cultural autonomy, 149; should not at once be extended to German and Hungarian minorities, 153; national federalism eclipsed by reducing national problem to that of minorities, 167; *regional:* possibility within Austria-Hungary, 107, 108; in east-central Europe, 143, 145, 146, 155, 162; federation of states, 146, 147

Finland: restricted autonomy and Russification under Czarist Russia, 21; independence, 74; Karelian union republic, 85

Fourteen Points, *see* Woodrow Wilson

France: national state, 14–18; assimilation of minorities by the end of the XVIIIth century, 15; French Revolution, a unifying force, 15; present-day ideal of linguistic and cultural uniformity, 16, 18; kinship with French-speaking Swiss, 42; French Protestant refugees in South Africa, 47; attitude toward League minorities action, 116

Frederick the Great, attempt to colonize Polish areas, 24

Freedom *of association:* a human right, 3; to members of minorities, 148, 149, 158; *from want:* economic prosperity, 12, 148; *of expression,* use of minority languages, 43, 113, 133, 143; *of movement,* for the peoples of a federated area, 143; *see also* Language; Religion

Fribourg, Canton of: linguistic diversity, 38; early attempt at a uniform language, 39; language guarantee in the Constitution of *1831,* 40

Geneva, Canton of, 42

Geneva, city of: seat of the League of Nations, 129, 159, 160; center for action of the League in minorities protection, 129, 159, 160

Geneva Convention, *see* Treaties

Georgia: Soviet census *1939,* 75, 77; alliance with R.S.F.S.R., 84, 86; Transcaucasian Federation, 86, 90; schools for minorities, 102

German policy of colonization: settlement of Germans in southern Russia and Hungary, 19, 77; attempts by Frederick the Great, Bismarck and von Bülow, to "colonize" Polish estates, 24, 27; Colonization Commission, *1886,* 27, 121; colonization of Germans among the minority to hasten Germanization, 30; settlement in conquered countries by Hitler, 142

German minorities: best organized of European minorities, 8; the spearhead of Nazi aggression, 8, 152–153; anti-Nazi element, 9, 153; represented in Czechoslovakian Parliament, use of the German language, German university, 16–17; in the Soviet Union, 75; Beneš's statement regarding postwar inclusion of Germans in Czechoslovakia, and possible transfer of disloyal element, 138, 139; mistaken belief that German minorities have been transferred to the Reich, 141, 142; established in conquered territories, 142; Jews of German nationality in Czechoslovakia, 151; special problem of

INDEX

German minorities during reconstruction, 152–158; national federalism and cultural autonomy must for a time be denied them, 153; transitional administration by the United Nations, 153–154; *see also* Sudetenland; Upper Silesia; German Settlers Case

Germany, 9, 155; peace note of *1916*, 10; liberation of oppressed nationalities by Versailles statesmen, 11, 108; German national movement, and rise of the German national state *1848*, 26; proclamation of the German Empire, 26; Bismarck's struggle against Polish nationalism and the Catholic Church, the *Kulturkampf*, 26, 27; after *1890* national unity identified with the German national state, 27–29; *Ostmarkenverein*, 28; kinship with German-speaking Swiss, 42; German minority in the Soviet, 77, 102; German-Austrians, 107; transfer of populations, policy of Pan-Germanism, 140; transitional occupation by the United Nations, 153, 154; need for minority guarantees by Germany, 157, 158, 161; post-war transfer of territory to Poland, 179; *see also* Nazism; Prussia

Goebbels, Paul Joseph, 30

Great Britain: war aims, Lloyd George's address *1918* to trade unions, 10; assimilation of minorities of language and culture, 15; conflict with Ireland, 15, 16, 18; effect of growth of democracy, and public education, on attitude to language and culture of minorities, 16, 17; confused characterization of the United Kingdom as an "un-national" state, 16; tolerance of local differences, 18; South Africa of strategic importance, 46, 59; decision *1822* to transform the Cape into an English-speaking colony, 50; hesitation in London over the enforced use of English language in South African court procedure, 53; advent of the Liberals, and an end of intermeddling in internal South African affairs, 62; dominant status of majority language and culture in Great Britain, 109, 131, 145; cultural minorities, few in number and largely identified with language and customs of the majority, 133–134

Great Powers, 9; refusal to incorporate religious liberty clause in the League Covenant, 127; domination over the lesser states, 128, 129, 156; responsibility for the guarantees in the Minorities Treaties, and for the maintenance of peace, 128, 156; policy of appeasement of the Nazis, 139; control of minority policies under the United Nations, 156, 158

Great Russians, 74, 98; census (Russians) *1939*, 75, 76; union republic *1923*, 90; proportion of population, 91; repudiation of Great Russian domination, 96; aspirations of nationalities for equality with Great Russians, 103; *see also* Russian Soviet Federative Socialist Republic

Greco-Turkish War *1922*, 136, 139

Greco-Turkish Mixed Commission, 139

Greece: minorities within the Soviet Union, 75, 91, 102; signature of Minorities Treaty, 112; exchange of minorities with Turkey and Bulgaria, 136, 139; Moslem minority in Greece, 139; cost of settling Greek refugees, 140

Grisons, Canton of, 161; linguistic diversity, 38

"Hammer and anvil," von Bülow's phrase with reference to the struggle between nationalities and the State, 28, 31

Hapsburgs, *see* Austria-Hungary

Henlein, Konrad, leader of Sudeten German party, 152

Hertzog, General J. B. M., resolution of language rights in Orange Free State, 63, 64; bilingualism in the public services, 66
Hitler, Adolf: the "nation" a mystic entity, 7; extermination of anti-Nazi German element, 9; attack on Czechoslovakia, 12; foreshadowing of Hitlerism in the policies of earlier Prussian leaders, 28–32; resurgence of German strength, 30; *Ausrotten,* 29, 30; German freedom from international obligations respecting minorities, 112, 123; reshuffling of populations, 141, 142; German minorities summoned "home" by Hitler, and settled in conquered territories, 142; defeat, 142, 153
Hofmeyr, J. C., leader of the Afrikander Bond, 57, 58
Human rights: Switzerland, 42; life, liberty and religious freedom, 42, 112, 148; provided for and guaranteed under the Minorities Treaties, 112, 115, 129, 131, 148; group rights: language, education and culture, 132, 148; equality before the law, 148; rights of man, 147, 148; proposed conference on human rights, 157; United Nations Commission on Human Rights, 157, 162; *see also* Civil rights; Political rights; Religious rights
Hungary, 107; Magyarization, or forcible absorption, of minorities, 5, 131; treatment of minorities, 6, 160; German settlers, 19; a Magyar national state with a unitary and centralized administration, 22; guarantees of minorities protection after the First World War, 110, 131; champion of Hungarian irredentists, 123, 124, 138; proposed transfer of disloyal Hungarian irredentists from Czechoslovakia, 138, 139; Hungarian minority in Transylvania, 147; problem of post-war reconstruction and Hungarian minority groups, 152, 153; transitional administration by United Nations of Hungary and Hungarian minorities, 153, 154; reconstruction and reeducation, 153, 154

Ignatiev, Count Paul, attempt to modify policy of Russification in education, 72
Industrial Revolution, *1820* settlement of dislocated British in South Africa, 48
International Labour Organization, procedure for draft conventions, 158
Ireland, nationality conflict under Great Britain, 15, 16, 18
Irredentism, 130; the spearhead of Nazi and Hungarian aggression, 8, 9, 123, 138, 152
Italy, 19, 122, 155; Wilson's demand for the liberation of the Italians from foreign domination, 10; Italian-speaking Swiss, 34, 37–39; Italian, an official language in Switzerland, 38, 40, 41; kinship with Italian-speaking Swiss, 42; frontier adjustments following the First World War, 107; under no international obligation to protect minorities, 112, 128, 157; oppressive policies, 157, 158

Jacobins, the, linguistic uniformity and political centralization, 15
James I, persecution of the Puritans, 18
Jameson Raid, Transvaal *1895,* 59
Jews, the: in the United States, 3, 150; expulsion and massacre in Czarist Russia, 21; expelled from eastern provinces of Prussia, 27; extermination under the Nazis, 30, 152; in Soviet Russia, 75, 76, 91, 102; Western confusion as to whether the Jews form a nationality, 98, 150–151; Jewish national areas in the Soviet Union, 98; autonomous region, 98; Rumanian declaration as to citizenship, "for-

INDEX

eigners not subject to another power," 113; Jewish minority in Poland, 114–115, 183; League guarantee, 114; educational committees, and proportional share of public funds for education, 114; possible discrimination in observance of the Jewish Sabbath, 114, 115; Jewish minorities in east-central Europe, 150–152; desire of uprooted Jews to migrate to Palestine, 152

Johannesburg, 60

Jugoslavia: Succession State, 11; Sarajevo, 12; First World War propaganda for position as a sovereign state, 108; signing of a Minorities Treaty, 112, 126; possible membership in a Balkan regional federation, 147; Serbia, Croatia, Slovenia, 147, 167; future existence dependent on national liberty, not national uniformity, 167

Kaeckenbeek, Georges, President of the Arbitral Tribunal of Upper Silesia, *1922–1937*, quoted on minorities, 148, 160–161

Kalmuks, 76, 85

Karelians, 75, 76, 85

Karelo-Finnish union republic, 90

Katkov, M. N., demand for a unitary (Czarist) Russian national state, 21

Kazaks, 75, 77, 90, 99, 101

Kazan, 77

Khabarovsk, 98

Kirghiz, 75, 85, 90, 99

Kruger, Paul: movement for a united and independent Boerdom, 58; measures taken against "foreigners," 59; result of Jameson Raid, 59

Kulturkampf, see Germany

Ladas, Stephen P., on the exchange of Greek-Turkish and Greek-Bulgarian minorities in the *1920's,* 139, 140

Lake Baikal, 85

Lamont, Corliss, chart of Soviet nationalities, 90, 92–95

Language of minorities: positive Americanization, in requiring all to learn the English language, 3, 5; in east-central Europe, minorities' languages sufficient for their needs, 5, 8; assimilation, and survival, in Great Britain and France, 14–18, 130–131; attempted obliteration in Ireland as means of countering disloyalty, 16; Czechoslovakia, 16–17, 108; Russia, 21; Austria-Hungary, 22; Poles in Prussia, 25, 27; Nazi Germany, 30–31; linguistic equality in Switzerland, 37, 38, 40–43, 45; South Africa, 35, 46, 47; restrictions by the Dutch, 47, 55–56, 59; British measures regarding the use of the English language in South Africa, 48–53, 57; qualification for public office, 49, 65, 66; Proclamation, *July 5, 1822,* 50; Boer language demands at annexation of Natal, 54; submission of Boers in British territories, 56; bilingualism, 57, 58, 64, 65, 67, 68; stipulations in Treaty *1902,* 60; South Africa National Convention *1908–09,* 62–63; Hertzog Resolution, 63, 64; Czarist Russia, 69, 72, 103; influence of the Revolution of *1905,* 72; Bolshevik régime, 74, 77; recognition of the vernacular or dialect, 86, 100, 101, 102; enclaves, *1935,* cultivating their multiplicity of languages, 91, 101, 102; under Soviet national federalism, 97; every people having a distinct language recognized as a nationality, 98; four categories in education, according to language, 101; interest of nationalities in learning the Russian language, 103; League guarantee of language rights in the Minorities Treaties, 112-115, 129, 131-132, 133, 165; Poland, 113; Jewish minority, 114; Italy, 123; an official language permitted

under the Minorities Treaties, 132; freedom of language in a federation, 143, 144, 155
Latvians, 76, 90
Launay, Count de, 180
Law: English law in Scotland and Wales, 17; publication of Swiss federal laws in three languages, 40; British policy in South Africa as to Roman-Dutch law and Dutch language in judicial business, and the reaction of the Boers, 49, 51–54, 57, 59, 60, 64; guarantee of the rights of minorities, fundamental law under the League, 115; recognition of new states or accessions of territory, 157
Law of Cultural Autonomy, adopted by Estonia 1925, 150
League of Nations: minorities régime established at the end of First World War, 13, 107; League system of national minorities, 109; tested agencies of use in post-war planning, 109; systematic international machinery for the protection of minorities, 110–134; states accepting Council's supervision of the treatment of minorities, 112; Declarations, bi-lateral supplementary treaties and special articles in Peace Treaties, on the treatment of minorities, 112, 116, 172; enforcement of Minorities Treaties, 115–122; "racial, religious or linguistic minorities . . . obligations of international concern," 115; modification only with the approval of the Council, 115; reference to Permanent Court of International Justice, 115, 122; procedure of Council, 116, 120–122; supervision, with care not unduly to offend Minorities States, 116; receivable petitions placed before the Council, 118, 119; reference to Minorities State concerned, 118; official action, 120–122; request that Minority State desist from creating a *fait accompli,* 120, 122, 125; Committee of Jurists, 121, 122; Council's request for compensation to be paid injured minority, 122, 123; criticism of League system of protection by minorities and Minorities States, 122–123; League guarantee a restraining and pacifying influence, 123; Germany and Italy free of international obligations, 123; weakening effect of Fascist aggression, 123; weakness of League procedure for minority protection, 125, 126, 160; complaint by small states of the invasion of sovereignty, 127; ambiguity as to national-cultural individuality of a minority, or its gradual assimilation, 129–132; paradox of attempting to protect minority groups while denying group status to minorities, 131, 132; procedure, a guide for United Nations action, 158–159, 161; international supervision, combined with local responsibility, 161; resolutions of the Council relating to minorities procedure, 185–192
Minorities Petition, 115, 116, 117, 124; expedient limitations, 117; submission by individual, organization, state, those concerned, or interested third parties, 117, 121, 148–149, 161, 191
Minorities Section of the Secretariat, 117–118; preliminary consideration of a petition, 118, 121, 124; preparation of memorandum or digest, 119; effort to induce state to redress the wrong, 119
Minorities Committees to consider petitions, 117, 118–120, 124; membership, 118; effort to dispose of issues out of court, 119; negotiations with state to redress the wrong, 119; reference to Council members, 119–120, 122; "pressure behind the scenes," 120; suggestion of minorities experts as members instead of statesmen, 160;

INDEX

composition and frequency of meetings, 191
Lenin, Nikolai: on national differentiation, 78; self-determination, 79; "Declaration of the Rights of the Laboring and Exploited People" 1917, 83
Lettish schools in the Soviet Union, 102
Life and liberty, see Human rights
Lithuania: Lithuanians in Prussia, 25; independence, on the collapse of Czarist Russia, 74; Soviet union republic, 76, 90; Lithuanian schools in White Russia, 102; case of the thirty-four Russian peasants in Lithuania, 125
Little Russians, see the Ukraine
Lloyd-George, David: on self-determination, 10; regarding the break-up of Austria-Hungary, 106, 107

Maidanek near Lublin, Nazi extermination camp, 30; see also *Ausrotten;* Extermination
Majority, the ruling, in a Minorities State: a reminder of conquest and oppression, 5; "the hammer and the anvil," 31; the impersonal majority, a tyrant over weak nationalities, 43; change of attitude of the minority under national federalism, 103; attempt of Western leaders to supervise the actions of the majority against the minorities in the state, 109, 113, 131; teaching of the majority language in minorities schools, 114; majorities encouraged to believe the international régime a temporary one, 129–130; Sir Austen Chamberlain's statement, 130–131; estrangement of minorities and majorities, 131; official language, that of the majority, 132; control of state funds, 133; comparison of the West with east-central Europe, 134; solution, in the multinational state, 134, 147, 165; confused idea of the West regarding national-cultural uniformity, 135; the individual's right to ally himself with majority or minority, 150; aim of international agencies should be pacification, so that dissension may be avoided, 159–160; use of local agencies, 164
Masaryk, Thomas G.: on the multinational state, 43; Pan-Germanic transmigration of national minorities, 140
Mello-Franco, M. de, on minority protection and eventual national unity, 129–130
Memel, special convention regulating minority relations, 112
Middle Ages, the ideal of universalism, 14, 19
Migration, mass: Boer trek due to British policy of Anglicization, 54, 55; see also Transfer of population; Expulsion
Milner, Lord, attempt to rule South African Dutch Republics as conquered provinces, 58, 61
Minorities: problems involving human and national rights, 3–4, 112–113, 129, 131, 147–148, 168; masses involved, not individuals, 4; conditions before the Second World War, 6; partisan interest in minorities by neighboring states, 6, 116, 123–124; reasons for present unpopularity of small political units, 6, 8, 9; right to maintain mother tongue and native culture, 8; attempt to settle minorities questions after the First World War, 11, 13, 106, 107, 109, 110–125, 161; definition of a national minority: difference in language, religion and culture, 14, 17, 112, 132; religious minorities, 17–18, 22–23, 113, 114; "aliens" in the culturally uniform national state, 30, 31; census figures on east-central European states, 111; no guarantees of minority protection required of certain Powers, 112, 123, 128, 157; consideration by

the League as a possible source of international strife, 116, 124, 125, 126, 128, 155, 156, 159; complaint of minorities regarding League régime, 122; need for protection procedure that affords continuous supervision with a minimum of friction, 126; precedent of minorities protection in the XIXth century, 127–128; individual rights and group rights, 131, 132, 148; recognition as a corporate entity, 132, 148, 149, 162; theory of the divorcement of the territorial state from the "religion" of nationalism, 144; right of membership in a minority, 149–150, 151; guarantee of rights under the United Nations, 154, 156, 157–158; relation between the supervising international organization and local organizations, 159, 161–163; conflict viewed as an internal maladjustment, 160; suggested procedure, 161–164; international brigandage, the enemy of minorities guarantees, 165; toleration of minorities not enough, 165; national minorities a fragment of the broader problem of nationalities, 167; resolutions of the League Council relating to minorities procedure, 185–192

Minorities States (states harboring minorities), 9. efforts of League Council to retain goodwill when considering minority petitions, 116, 124, 125; League discouragement of partisan interest in another state's minorities, 116, 123–124; notification, by Council, in preliminary procedure, and period of grace, 118; Council procedure in case of negative reply by state, 118, 121, 122; request by Council to desist from creating a *fait accompli*, 120, 122, 125; infringement of Minorities Treaties, 121; League request for compensation in case of injury to minorities, 122, 123; unequal international obligation attacked as negation of sovereignty, 126–128; appeal to the principle of equality of all states, 128, 129; ambiguity as to permanence of League guarantee, 129–131; failure of states to win the loyalty of their minorities, 145–146; proposed position under the United Nations, 158

Moldavian Republic, 76, 90, 91
Montenegro, recognition of, 180
Moravia, 138
Moslems, Bolshevik proclamation of religious liberty to minority in Soviet Union, 99; *see also* Turkey
Mussolini, Benito: the "nation" a mystic entity, 7; freedom from international obligations with respect to minorities, 123; compulsory assimilation in the South Tyrol, 123

Natal: Roman-Dutch law established 1845, 53; annexed by British, question of language, 54, 55, 66; predominantly English, 55, 56, 60; increase of Boer civil servants, 67

National culture: national rights, 4, 147, 148; homogeneity in the United States, 5; assimilation in England and France, 15, 16, 18, 109, 131, 133, 145; kinsmen beyond geographic boundaries, 15, 42, 100, 116, 143; efforts at uniformity under Czarist Russia, 20, 69, 103, 113; Bismarck's policy of uniformity, 27, 31, 109, 113, 133, 145, 165; "alien" minorities in the culturally uniform national state, 30, 113; national-cultural equality, example of three multi-national states, 34–35, 37–45, 46–68, 69–104, 166; "cultural affinities and essential political loyalties," 42; Bolshevik policy, 77; Austria-Hungary, 107; safeguards under the Minorities Treaties, 113, 148; Jewish minority, 114, 150–

152; régime required by east-European states radically different from that of the West, 129, 131–132, 135, 155, 163; Mello-Franco and Sir Austen Chamberlain on cultural assimilation, 130, 131; federation (the multi-national state) and national-cultural diversity, 143, 147, 166; divorcement of national culture from the territorial state, 144, 145; "cultural pluralism," 145; Upper Silesia, 149; Law of Cultural Autonomy, and the Cultural Council of Estonia, 150; application of cultural autonomy to German and Hungarian minorities, 153

National federalism, *see* Federalism

National rights, 147; recognition of minority languages and separate schools, 4, 148

Nationalities: national groupings in United States, 3; organized segments of nationalities, the European problem, 4, 8, 142, 163; national consciousness stimulated by persecution, 5, 21, 23; Western aversion due to excesses of nationalism, 6–8, 34, 91; Allied attitude to the recognition of the principle of nationalities *1916*, 10, 11, 106, 110; nationality conflicts, the cause of two World Wars, 12; national freedom and economic unity, 12, 35, 166; peculiar nature of nationalism in east-central Europe, 13; nationally mixed areas in east and east-central Europe, 19; national enclaves, 20, 84, 91, 135; national antagonisms a threat to political security, 20; concepts of national uniformity, 21, 23, 103, 129–131, 165, 167; Bülow's statement, that state boundaries do not separate nationalities, 28, 31; plural nationalism, 35; equality of nationalities, 35, 97–98, 103, 155, 164; nationality rights, and the practice of communism, 35, 36, 77–81, 97; mistaken reasoning that cosmopolitanism can supplant national loyalties, 43; Bolshevik theory regarding the withering of nationalism with the achievement of the equality of peoples under socialism, 78, 79; Soviet application of the term "nationality" only to the laboring masses, 80; mistaken statements regarding Soviet dissociation of state from nationality, 91, 96; each territory in east-central Europe considered a national homeland by several peoples, 135; the territorial state, and the "religion of nationalism," 144; sentiment of nationality intertwined with language and historical tradition, 144; national rights, 147–148; a subjective matter, 150; United Nations Commission on Human Rights: bill for the protection of nationalities, 158, 162; enforcement of nationality rights, 160, 162; nationalities and national minorities, two aspects of the same problem, 167; *see also* Federalism

Native problems: the Boers and the natives in South Africa, 46, 47, 54, 62; fraternal collaboration of nationalities and tribes of the Russian Soviet Republic, 82; Soviet efforts on behalf of primitive nationalities, 98, 99, 101–102

Nazism: exploitation of the minorities issues, 6, 8, 12, 121–123, 152, 153, 157; misuse of the term "nationalism," 6–7; opposed by anti-Nazi German minorities, 9; onslaught against petty states of east-central Europe, 9, 123, 152; efforts to destroy minorities, extermination camps, *Ausrotten,* Maidanek, 29–31, 152, 166, 167; savagery of Nazism rooted in the teachings of the *Junkers,* 30–31; defeat of Nazism and possible Polish reaction, 31; requested shift of Russian border populations, 103; Nazi-Soviet Pact *1939,* 103;

appeasement policy of Great Powers, 139; Nazicism inspired by Pan-Germanism, 140; extermination of the Jews, 152; "protector" of German minorities in Czechoslovakia, 157
Near East, experiments in population transfers, 140
Netherlands, the: settlement of Cape of Good Hope *1552*, 47; British desire to break connection of the Cape with Holland *1821*, 49; Afrikaans vernacular an offshoot of the Dutch language, 57

Orange River territory: independent in the *1850's*, 55; primacy of Dutch language and usages, 55; Roman-Dutch law, 55; Jameson Raid, 59; Boer War, 59 60; predominantly Boer, 60; rule of Lord Milner, 61; post-convention legislation on the use of languages, 66
Ossets, 75, 77
Ostmarkenverein (Association for the Defense of the Eastern Marches), 28
Osuský, Štefan: "the map of Europe cannot be ethnographically remade," 142; on freedom of national consciousness by national minorities, 167

Paderewski, Ignace, Clemenceau's letter of *June 24, 1919, see* Clemenceau
Palestine, 152
Pan-Germanism, policy of the transfer of populations, 140
Pan-Slavism, policy of Czarist Russia, 20-21
Paris Peace Conference, *see* World War I, peace settlement
Peace, a responsibility of the Great Powers, smaller states incapable of maintaining or enforcing it, 128, 156; *see also* World Wars I and II, peace settlement
Permanent Court of International Justice: advisory opinions on minorities questions, 115, 121, 122, 163; German Settlers Case, 121-122; Albanian Minority Schools Case, 132
Persia, 90
Phillimore, Captain, determination of compensation in the German Settlers Case, 122
Plebiscite, resort to the, following the First World War, 110
Pobyedonostsev, K. P., on expulsion and massacre of the Jews, 21
Pogrom, cold, by the Poles against minorities, 31
Poland, and Polish minorities: restoration of sovereignty as a Succession State, 11, 106, 107; XVIIIth century dismemberment, 19, 24; Poles in Prussia, 20, 24; Russification of Poles in Russia, 21, 151; efforts of Prussians to compel allegiance of Polish upper classes, 24; Congress of Vienna, and attempt to respect national individuality, 25; uprising against Russia *1830*, 25; vacillating policies of Germanization and conciliation, 25; *1848* combat for mastery of Prussian eastern provinces, and resulting anti-Polish policies, 25-26; the German national state, 25-27, 29; the *Kulturkampf*, 26-27; Prussian restrictions on the use of the Polish language, 26, 27; Bismarck's belief in the concurrence of Polish and "Romish-clerical" interests, 26; Prussian restrictions *1880* on education, 27; Prussian Colonization Law *1886*, 27, 121; purchase of Polish estates, 27, 121; expulsion of Poles from the eastern provinces, 27; organization of the *Ostmarkenverein*, 28; *Ausrotten*, extermination of Polonism, 29-31; ban on religious instruction in Polish, 29; school strike, 29; Dispossession Act *1908*, expropriation of Polish estates, 29; post-war Polish ideal of a national state of Poland, 30;

attack by Hitler, 30; Polish use of the "cold pogrom," 31; defeat of Nazism and possible reaction of the Poles, 31; Poles in the Soviet Union, 75, 76, 91, 102; annexation of eastern Poland (Western Ukraine and Western White Russia), by Russia *1939-1941*, 90; *1944* reports of Russian exchange of populations in Polish territories, 103; signing of the Minorities Treaty, 112, 113, *text*, 173-178; Treaty provisions on the use of national languages, 113; Jewish minority, 114-115; German Settlers Case, 121-122, 123, 125; repudiation of League supervision of minorities, 127; Hitler's colonization of invaded territory, 142; proposal of a regional federation with Czechoslovakia, 146; Upper Silesia, 150, 161; existence dependent on national liberty, not national uniformity, 167
Political rights: in the United States, 3; Minorities Treaties, 112; elementary rights of man, 148
Political unity: theoretical unity of political and cultural allegiance in Great Britain and France, 18, 109; in the East, political centralization deferred to the XIXth century, 19-20; threatened by national antagonisms, 20; Swiss ability to differentiate between cultural affinities and political loyalties, 42; an attribute of the multi-national state, 45; Soviet Russia, 97; political relation of a minority and its state under the Minorities Treaties, 117; possibility of regional confederation, 155
Population: mixed, in east-central Europe, 19, 104, 106, 110, 129, 130, 135, 136, 166; nationalities of the USSR, census of *1939*, 75, 76, 91; *see also* Transfer of populations
Principal Allied and Associated Powers, World War I; reply to German peace note *1916:* no peace without the recognition of the principle of nationalities and of the free existence of small states, 10; self-determination, principle of nationalities, the right of minorities, 106; propaganda of the Eastern nationalities, and consideration of the nationalities question, 108
Protocol of *June 28, 1878*, Congress of Berlin, 180
Prussia: iron-clad uniformity and intolerance of differences, 5, 34, 109, 110, 123, 165; Polish minority, 20, 24; uneasiness caused by Polish uprising in Russia, 25; Germanization, 25, 29, 30; national upheavals of *1848*, 25; leader in the German national movement and unification, 25, 26, 28; German-Polish combat for mastery in the Prussian eastern provinces, 25, 27; law, *1886*, establishing the Colonization Commission, 27, 121; *Junkertum*, 29, 31; Dispossession Act, expropriating Polish estates, 29; Prussianism carried to extremes resulted in Hitlerism, 31; suppression of minorities languages, 113; Prussian Colonization Law, *1886*, 121; forced cultural assimilation, 131, 133, 145

Reconstruction: in Soviet Russia, 103; the problem of minorities, 137; suggestion of regional federations, 146; Germany and Hungary, 153-154; collaboration of a mixed population, 164
Reformed Church in South Africa, Synod of *1824*, the question of language for religious instruction, 51
Reichstag *1871*, protest of the Poles against Bismarck's measures for a German national state, 26
Relief and rehabilitation, 106; local agencies to deal with representatives of the various nationalities and national minorities, 164
Religious rights: a human right, 3,

112, 132, 148; an all-embracing faith before the rise of the national state in Great Britain and France, 15, 17, 18; struggle of religious non-conformists culminating in legalization of religious pluralism, 18, 144; demand for a common faith under the Russian Orthodox Church, 21; Ottoman Turkey, a religious state, 22; organization of groups in *millets*, 23; inequality of non-Moslems, 23; equality extended to Christians and Jews under the Young Turks, 23; religious instruction of children, Polish Prussia, 27, 29; Switzerland, religious liberty to all, 37–39; British clergy sent to South African Dutch congregations, 48, 49; British policy after *1822,* 50–55; language for the religious instruction of Dutch children, 51, 52, 53; uniformity in Russia, 69; freedom under the Communists, 77; early Soviet efforts to combat religion, 96, 99; rights under the Minorities Treaties, 112, 113, 114, 133; Jewish minority, 114–115; refusal to incorporate a religious liberty clause in the League Covenant, 127; League guarantee to individuals, not groups, 132; Upper Silesia, 148; under the United Nations, 163, 164

Romansch adopted by Switzerland as a national language, 37, 38

Royal Institute of International Affairs, report on League settlement of minorities questions, 126

Rumania: national strife due to minorities problems, 6; Wilson's demand for liberation of the Rumanes from foreign domination, 10; signer of Minorities Treaty, 112; declaration regarding the citizenship of Jewish inhabitants, 113; possibility of an east-central European federation, 143; effort to exclude children of Rumanian origin from minority schools, 149; ill-disposed toward minorities, 160; existence dependent on national liberty, not national uniformity, 167; recognition by the Congress of Berlin, 180

Russia, see Union of Socialist Soviet Republics

Russian Soviet Federative Socialist Republic (R.S.F.S.R.), 101; Constitution, *Article 11,* provision for regional union of soviets "stretched" to include autonomous national units, 82, 85; a federation of national soviet republics, 83; treaties of alliance with border nationalities, 84; the bulk of the pre-war Russian Empire a single entity, the R.S.F.S.R., 84; union republics independent of the R.S.F.S.R., 85; autonomous republics and regions listed by the Constitution of *1936,* 85; status of a nationality in the federation, 85; federalism of the R.S.F.S.R.: local government by the native population, and cultural autonomy, 86; *see also* Great Russians; Union of Socialist Soviet Republics and regions by name

Sarajevo, assassination of the Grand Duke *1914,* 12

Saratov, 77

Scotland: use of Gaelic, 16, 17; instruction in local history and literature, 16; English laws, customs and language paramount, 17, 130–131; no minority conflicts, due to British tolerance of local peculiarities, 18; appointment of clergy of the Scottish church to South Africa, 50, 53; local cultural freedom, 131

Self-determination: declaration by Lloyd George *1918,* 10; Woodrow Wilson, 10; east-central European settlement after the First World War, 10–11, 107; Teheran Declaration, 12, 106; danger of irrational and airtight national compartments, 12; in the XIXth century, pre-

INDEX

sumed to be the birthright of the people, 20; Switzerland, 43; Soviet Union, 78; Lenin *1903,* 79; bounded by Communist doctrine, 82; a right only of the "laboring masses," 100; clarification needed under new world organization, 106
Self-government, and conduct of local affairs: broad powers of local self-government in Switzerland, 37; South Africa, 62, 67; latitude of regional and local self-government by nationalities in the Soviet Union, 86, 89, 97; promise of Lloyd-George to Austria-Hungary's nationalities, 106–107; a prelude to regional federation, 47, 166
Serbia: First World War propaganda for a Greater Serbia, 108; possible member within Jugoslavia of a Balkan regional federation, 143, 146, 147, 167; bitter struggle with the Croats, 167; recognition by the Congress of Berlin, 180
Shotwell, James T., "National Federalism," 145, 166
Siberia, 76
Slavs: Pan-Slavism, 20, 36; proportion in the Soviet Union, 74; Allies' promise of freedom from German and Austrian rule, 108
Slovaks: united with kindred nationalities to form Czechoslovakia, 11
Slovenes: united with kindred nationalities to form Jugoslavia, 11, 147, 167
Smuts, General Jan C., resistance to Anglicization of Boer children, 61
South Africa and Union of South Africa, 34; multi-national state, 13, 35, 166; bilingualism, 35, 46–68; white population originally Dutch in language and national sentiment, 47; petition *1811* for asylum of Hollanders, 48; British colonists, 48; first steps toward Anglicization, 48; arrival of British clergy and teachers to spread a knowledge of the English language, 48; proficiency in the English language a qualification for public office, 49; schools conducted in English, 49; British measures taken in behalf of security, and opposed by the Dutch as a threat to Boer security, 49, 54; Dutch law held to be inadequate, 49, 52; British opinion that connection with Holland must be destroyed as soon as possible, 49; all official proceedings *1822* in the English language, 49, 50; Anglicization and its effects, 50–53; Proclamation, *July 5, 1822,* on the use of the English language, 50; the courts, 50, 52, 53; resignation of justices, 51–52; stand of the Reformed Church, 51; religious instruction permitted in Dutch, 52; Commission of Inquiry in favor of introduction of English law, 52; Charter of Justice *1827,* reconstructing the courts, 52, 53; British legal procedure adopted, but Dutch-Roman law still in force, 52; Roman-Dutch law established in Natal *1845,* 53; annexation of Natal, and question of language, 54, 55; achievement of independence, 55–60; Transvaal and Orange River territory, 55; cultural awakening of the Boers *1870's,* 57; Afrikander Bond, 57; use of Dutch in parliamentary debates and courts legalized *1882–1884,* 57; choice of language in elementary education, 58; Transvaal annexed *1877,* 58; trend toward national separatism, 58; Boer War, 59; lesson, that South Africa must remain composite, 60; South African National Convention *1908–09,* 62–65; Draft Act for South African Union, 62; Union of South Africa effected *May 31, 1910,* 62; bilingual sessions of Convention, 63; South Africa Act, *Article 137,* bilingualism, 63, 65; Hertzog's resolution on bilingualism, 63–64; *Article*

INDEX

145, on public service and language, 65; Union Parliament, 65–67; equality in practice, 65–67; bilingualism a workable form of binationalism, 68; no deliberate British attempt to stamp out the individuality of the Boer, 69

Stalin, Joseph: contribution to the theory and practice of national question, 78; on the right of a nationality to secede, 81; Commissar of Nationalities, 81, 82; President of the Soviet of Nationalities, 83; fashions the structure of Soviet national federalism, 83; "Declaration of the Rights of the Laboring and Exploited People" *1917*, 83; resolution in favor of union, *December 23, 1922*, 86; criticism of draft of terms of union, 86–87; bicameral central agency favored, 87; revision incorporating plan for a soviet of nationalities, 87; creates Soviet or Council of Nationalities, 88; qualifications of an independent or union republic, 90; not a "one-nation state," but a "multi-national state," 97; culture "national in form and Socialist in content," 100; denunciation of national intolerance as "Pan-Russian chauvinism," 103; shift of border population, 103

State, the: multiplicity of small sovereign states at the close of the First World War, and resulting political and economic difficulties, 9–11; League care in safeguarding sovereign dignity of states in minorities questions, 116, 161; recognition of new states and large accessions of territory, 127, 157, 158; financing of educational and cultural undertakings, including those of minorities, 149;

Multi-national state, 3, 34, 36; union of majority and minorities within the state, 5; experiments in Switzerland, South Africa and Soviet Union, 13, 34–35, 37–45, 46–68, 69–104, 166; national state of the West unsuited to the multi-national population of east-central Europe, 14–32, 165; east-central Europe prior to the First World War, 19–32; tolerance and respect for differences, 32; neither a rigid formula nor a Procrustean remedy, 35; pillars of the multi-national state: democracy, cultural federalism, decentralization, 42–45; Masaryk on human rights in multinational regions, 43; political unity and cultural freedom possible, 45; Stalin's reference to the USSR as a multi-national state, 103; Austria-Hungary, 107, 108; Minorities Treaties, 133; position of minorities, 145, 147; status of Jewish minorities, 151; post-war administration of German and Hungarian minorities, 153; harmony, the international objective, 160

Nation-state (the national state), 11; Great Britain and France, 15, 17, 18, 145; difficulties in nationally mixed areas, 18, 31–32, 142, 149, 167; Germany, 26, 30, 145; Poland, 30; abandoned by Switzerland, South Africa and the Soviet Union, 35, 96–97; post-war planning, national states or multi-national states, 106, 143; states of the Western type, 107, 108, 165; Minorities Treaties, 133; the tolerant national state not enough, 134, 145

Un-national state, 16; characterization of the United Kingdom, 16; Soviet Union, so regarded by the Webbs, 91–96; Communist hope of eventual achievement, 96

Steyn, M. T., on the use of Dutch as an official language (bilingualism), 64

Sudetenland: truculence of German minority an excuse for dismemberment of Czechoslovakia by Hitler, 12, 123, 152

Supervision, international, of minorities: compromise with the rights of national sovereignty, 116; League provision for permanent supervision, 124; protest of small states at special commitments required, 127, 157; problem of sovereign equality of states, 154–157; international guarantee, 157–158; enforcement procedure, 158–163; need for continuous supervision, 159; international supervision combined with local responsibility, 161

Switzerland, 46; a multi-national state, 13, 34, 35, 37, 39, 45, 166; situation in the heart of Europe, 34, 42; plural nationalism, 34, 35; linguistic and cultural freedom with democratic decentralization, 35, 38, 40, 41, 44; national federalism, 37–45, 67; proportion of French- German- Italian- and Romansch-speaking populations, 37, 38, 40, 41; religions, 38; originally a Germanic country, 39; liberation of French- and Italian-speaking districts influenced by the French Revolution, 39; cantonal constitutions of Bern, Fribourg and Valais, and linguistic guarantees, 40; equality in law and fact, 40–41; new Swiss Federal Constitution *1848*, 40; national languages, 40; present Swiss Constitution *1874*, 40; language provision, 40; provision for the election of the federal judiciary, 40; parliamentary committees and civil service, 41; organic unity within the cantons, 42; ability to distinguish between "cultural affinities" and "essential political loyalties," 42; democracy, 42–43; cultural federalism, 43–44; union of nationalities, 44–45; federation, rather than cosmopolitanism, 44; safeguard of cantonal and communal institutions, 44; proposed as a model for Czechoslovakia, 108

Tadjik Republic, 75, 77, 90
Tariffs: by the new states after the First World War, 11; influence on the union of the South African colonies, 62; adjustment to varying standards of living, 155
Tartar, 75, 77, 101
Taxation: levies by minorities on their own members, for educational and cultural purposes, 149, 150
Teheran Declaration on self-determination, 12, 106
Territorial expansion: accessions by established states contingent upon the acceptance of certain principles of government, 128, 157, 179; military might of Great Powers in behalf of small states, 128; Clemenceau's letter to Paderewski, 157; Commission to Study the Organization of the Peace, 157–158
Ticino, Canton of, 41
Tien-Shan, Soviet union republic, 85
Tittoni, Tommaso, Report on Minorities Procedure presented to the League and adopted, *text*, 185–187, 188
Titulescu, Nicholas, 133
Transcaucasian Federation: *December 13, 1922*, Georgia, Armenia and Azerbaijan, 86; union republic *1823*, 90; federation dissolved and component states declared union republics, 90
Transfer, or exchange, of populations: not resorted to in the Soviet Union as a solution of the nationality problem, 103; for punitive or defense purposes, 103; border shift following the Nazi-Soviet pact *1939*, 103; question as to solution of minority problems in east-central Europe, 136–143; Beneš quoted, 136–138; Greek-Turkish and Greek-Bulgarian exchange *1920's*, 139; policy of Pan-Germanism, 140; ineffective and painful settlement of minorities problem, 141–143, 166; out of har-

mony with the spirit of federal union, 142; *see also* Expulsion

Transmigration, see Transfer of populations

Transvaal: independent in the *1850's,* 55; primacy of Dutch language and usages, 55; Roman-Dutch law, 55; discovery of gold, 46, 55, 59; Dutch language official, 55-56; annexed by Great Britain *1877,* 58; mounting antagonism under Paul Kruger to the British, 58, 59; Jameson Raid *1895,* 59; Boer War, 59, 60; treaty stipulation as to language, 60; rule of Lord Milner, 61; unity of British and Boers at the South Africa National Convention *1908-09,* 62; legislation on the use of languages, 66

Transylvania; possibility as a multinational unit within a federation, 143, 147

Treaties:
1878 Treaty of Berlin, equality of religious minorities, 113
1902 Vereeniging Peace Treaty, 60
1919 Treaty of Versailles, 8, 179, 181
1920-24 Treaties with the defeated states after the First World War, minorities articles, 112, 172, 181
1920-24 Declarations, Conventions, and bilateral supplementary treaties, on the treatment of minorities, 112, 116, 172
1920-24 Minorities Treaties, 156; human rights, citizenship, 112, 148; language rights, scholastic rights, 112; not required of Germany or Italy, 112, 123, 128, 157; Jewish minority, 114; guarantee, 115; enforcement by the League, 115-122, 160; condemned as a failure, 122, 124; any infraction an offense against the international community, 124; attacked by small states as a negation of sovereignty and equality, 126-129, 154; no time limit and no provision for renunciation, 129; on the use of languages, 132; corporate entity of minorities, 132, 149, 162; education, 132, 149; public funds for educational, religious and charitable purposes, 133; recognition of the national, rather than the multinational, state, 133; right of membership in a minority, 149; under the United Nations, 158, 165; never legally terminated following the collapse of the League, 163-164; international instruments under League guarantee, 171
1920 Polish Minorities Treaty, first to be drafted and the model for all subsequent engagements, 112-115, 157, 171; repudiated *1934,* 127; *text,* 173-178; covering letter of Clemenceau to Paderewski, 179-184
1922 Treaties of alliance of Soviet nationalities with the R.S.F.S.R., 84
1922 Geneva Convention, Upper Silesia, 148
1934 German-Polish non-aggression pact, 127
1938 Pact of Munich, 8
1939 Nazi-Soviet Pact, 103

Turcomans, 75, 77, 90

Turkestan, 76, 99

Turkey: First World War aim, to free minorities, 10; XIXth century history of the Ottoman Empire, 20, 22-23; communal autonomy under Moslem religious groups, 22-23; *millets* and the *Millet-Bashy,* 23; inequality of non-Moslems, 23; Young Turks, 23; disintegration due to inability to harmonize minorities, 23; Russian proclamation to the Moslems in the Soviet Union, 99; Turkish language schools in the Soviet Union, 102; minorities exchange with Greece, 136, 139; Greek invasion *1922,* 139

Tyrol, South, compulsory assimilation by Mussolini, 123

INDEX

Ukraine, the: Russification, 21; within the Soviet Union, 74, 75, 76; alliance with R.S.F.S.R., 84, 86; union republic, 90; Western Ukraine, a portion of Eastern Poland, 90; Jewish national area, 98; minorities' freedom to use languages, 100; minorities schools, 102

Uniate Catholics compelled to unite with the Russian Orthodox Church, 21

Union of Socialist Soviet Republics, and Czarist Russia: Russification of minorities under Czars, 5, 20, 22, 69, 103, 110, 113, 131; alienation of western borderlands, 11, 36, 74; multi-national state of the Soviet Union, 13, 34, 35; heterogeneous population, 19, 23, 34–35, 74, 77; Pan-Slavism, and its influence in the Balkans, 20, 36; Holy Russia, the "saviour" of civilization, 21; demand for a uniform national state, 21; expulsion and massacre, 21; Revolutions, *1905*, 72, *1917*, 22, 73, 81, 84, 99; inability to harmonize interests of various nationalities, 23; Polish uprising *1830–31*, 25; proscription of private capitalism, 35, 77; *map*, 70–71; reaction after *1907*, 72; hopes for modification of Russification during the First World War, 72; Social Revolution, 73, 78–79; Bolshevik task of reconstruction after *1917*, 73, 79; failure and abolition of Russification, 73, 74, 82; territorial distribution, 73, 74; *chart* of nationalities, 75–76, 92–95; proportion of Slavs, 74; census *1926*, 74; census *1939*, 75–76; Bolshevik, or communist, policy regarding nationalism, 77–81; Soviet Union a federation, 77, 90, 91; ruled by a dictatorship, 77, 97, 98, 102; the class, rather than the nation, the basis of social differentiation, 77, 80; self-determination within the bounds of communist doctrine, 78, 79, 82; equality of nationalities under socialism to attain class solidarity, 78; theoretical right of secession, 78, 80, 81, 90; abolition of classes, 79; liberation of the working class, 79; term "nationality" applied only to the laboring masses, 80; need by the masses of guidance and enlightenment, 80; Peoples Commissariat of Nationalities, 81–83, 85; Constitution *1922*, 81; Soviet of Nationalities, 81, 87; decree, *1920* reorganizing the Commissariat of Nationalities, 82; constitutional provision for regional unions "stretched" to include *national* units, 82, 85, 87, 88, 89; regionalism a concept of nationality as well as of geography, 82, 83, 85; propagation of communist ideology among non-Russian peoples, 82; structure of Soviet national federalism (R.S.F.S.R.), 83–86, (U.S.S.R.), 86–91; Declaration of the Rights of Laboring and Exploited People *1917*, 83; First All-Russian Congress of Soviets, *January 1918*, 83; Fundamental Law of *July 1918*, 84; Bolshevik civil war, 84; relationship of autonomous republics and regions, to all-Russian central authorities, 85; variation in the number of national units, as additional peoples achieve national status, 85; relation *1922* of five republics to central authorities, 86; proposals for a federal union, 86; draft of terms of union, 86, 87; First Congress of Soviets, 86, 87; Stalin's report to All-Russian Congress of Soviets, *December 26, 1922*, 87; bicameral central agency, 87; revised constitution ratified by Central Executive Committee *July 6, 1923*, 87; confirmed by second Congress of Soviets, *January 31, 1924*, 87; prescribed organs of government, respective powers of union and constituent republics, 87; All-Union

INDEX

Congress of Soviets, supreme organ of the U.S.S.R., 87, 88; Central Executive Committee (TSIK) a bicameral assembly, 87, 88; Presidium of the Central Executive Committee, 88; Council of Peoples Commissars (Sovnarkom), 88; Central Executive Committee eliminated, 88; Council of the Union and Council of Nationalities, 88, 89, 97; Presidium elected by both chambers, 88; representation of nationalities in the Council of Nationalities under the Constitution of *1936,* 88; division of powers, 89, 97; welfare and health, 89; All-Union Commissariats or Ministries, 89; Soviet Union created *1923,* 90; admission of union **republics in** *1923, 1924, 1929, 1936,* 90; increase in the number of constituent republics by the Constitution of *1936,* 90; national counties, districts and villages, 90–91; 5,000 national soviets in *1935,* 91; meaning and functioning of Soviet national federalism, 91, 96, 97; regarded, mistakenly, as an unnational state, 91–96; a multinational, federal state, 96, 97; chart of Soviet nationalities, 92–95; religion discountenanced, 96, 99; nationality an important factor in the practice of Soviet federalism, 96; aversion to "bourgeois nationalism," 96; repudiation of Great Russian predominance, 96; equal rights to all citizens under the Constitution of *1936,* 97–98; no favorites among the nationalities, 98; training of natives, and modernization on the borderlands, 99; cultural freedom, 99; proclamation on religion to the Moslems of Russia, 99; collectives, 99; restriction on contact of nationalities with kindred peoples outside the Union, 100; precedence of class aims over national purposes, 100; freedom of language, 100, 101; four categories for the education of nationalities, 101–102; case of the Russian peasants in Lithuania, 125; fear of another *cordon sanitaire,* 146; federalism a solution of nationalities and minorities problems, 166

Allied republics, *see* Union republics *below*

Autonomous regions, 84, 85; elevation to autonomous republics, 85; listed in the Constitution of *1936,* 85; represented on the Council of Nationalities, 88, 89; Jewish autonomous region, 98

Autonomous republics, 82; republics with large populations, territories, and greater economic and cultural assets, 84; elevation of autonomous regions to autonomous republics, 85; elevation to union republics, 85; listed in the Constitution of *1936,* 85; represented on the Council of Nationalities, 88, 89; subdivisions of the union republics, 90; minorities schools, 102

National areas, 82; delegations to the Soviet of Nationalities, 83, 89; introduced *1929,* a grade below the autonomous region, 89; subdivision of the union republics, 90; authority of Moscow, 97; Jewish national areas, 98

Union republics (constituent, independent), proposals for a federal union, 86; powers and functions, under the Constitution, of the constituent republics, 87; represented on the Council of Nationalities, 88, 89; share in administration, 89; four republics at the inception of the Soviet Union, *1923,* 90; admissions *1923, 1924, 1929,* 90; increase in number of constituent republics under the Constitution of *1936,* 90; annexations of *1939–41;* increase in number of union republics, 90; freedom of language, 100; autonomy in education, 102

INDEX

Union of South Africa, *see* South Africa
United Nations, 8, 168; need of attention to nationalities and national minorities by world organization, 106; assumption of the guarantee of minorities rights, 154, 158; Commission on Human Rights, functions, 157-158, 162; supervision and enforcement procedure, 158-159, 161, 162-164; guard against exploitation of minority differences, 159; right of appeal, 161-163; administrative handling in the area of conflict, 162, 163; Minorities Office, 162; Regional Minorities Commissions, 162; Permanent Court of International Justice, 163; provisional government, 163, 164
United Nations Relief and Rehabilitation Administration (UNRRA), 164
United States of America, unique character, 3-5; immigration, and national-cultural assimilation, 3; minority problems involving human rights, not national rights, 3-4; a national state, 4; the immigrant considered as an individual, not as a unit in a national community, 4; Americanization, the means of the advancement of the immigrant, 4; use of the English language without complete abandonment of supplementary languages or traditions, 5; social processes and promotion of cultural homogeneity, 5; "federalism," implying a clear division of the Powers, 97
Universalism: Middle Ages, 14; no need for universality under international supervision of minorities, 154
Upper Silesia: special convention to regulate minorities, 112; League minorities procedure, and guide to United Nations action, 125, 160, 161; minorities guarantee, 128, 159; Arbitral Tribunal *1922-1937*, 148, 161; Geneva Convention *May 5, 1922*, 148; Upper Silesian Mixed Commission, 148, 161; "right of association" for minorities, 148; failure to incorporate minorities as cultural units, 149; question of membership in a minority, 150; Minorities Offices, 161
Uzbeks, 77, 90, 99

Valais, Canton of, linguistic diversity, 38; language guarantee in the Constitution of *1844*, 40
Vaud, Canton of, 41

Wales: use of the Welsh and English languages, 16, 17; practical tolerance of the English in cultural matters, 18
War-breeding zone of east-central Europe, 12, 136
Webb, Sidney and Beatrice, *Soviet Communism*, the Soviet an unnational state, 91, 98
Western Ukraine (Eastern Poland), 90
Western White Russia (Eastern Poland), 90
White Russians (Byelo Russians), 74; census *1939*, 75, 76; treaties of alliance with R.S.F.S.R., 84; independent in *1922*, but allied with R.S.F.S.R., 86; union republic *1923*, 90; schools, 102
Wilson, Woodrow: Fourteen Points, *January 8, 1918*, 10; nationality and self-determination, 10, 107; Austro-Hungarian reconstruction, 106-108; on the relation of the Great Powers to world peace, 128
Winchester, Boyd, on the political unity of the Swiss, 41
Woldemaras, Augustus, Lithuanian spokesman before the Minorities Committee investigating Lithuanian treatment of thirty-four Russian peasants, 125
World War I: multiplication of small sovereign states, 9; war aims, 10; Prussian-Polish question, 26, 30;

hope for modification of Czarist policy of Russification, 72; armistice, 121; Masaryk on the transfer of national minorities, 140

Peace settlement: self-determination, principle of nationalities, rights of minorities, 10–11, 106, 107; liberation and guarantees of protection for national minorities, 11, 110, 115; Succession States, 11, 108, 167; concentration on nationality, 12, 166–167; minorities régime, 13, 156, 165; Poland, 106–107; Austria-Hungary, 106–107, 108; Italy, 107; Paris Peace Conference *1919,* 109, 110, 127, 131, 132, 165; international instruments under League guarantee, 171–172

World War II, 98; condition of minorities at the outbreak, 6

Peace plans, 6, 12; problem of international security, 106; Beneš's statement on need for careful consideration of minorities question, 136, 138; steps toward federation, 146; treatment of German and Hungarian minorities pending reeducation, 153; critical character of the transitional period, 163–164; consideration of the true relationship of nationalities in east-central Europe, 167; *see also* United Nations

Yakuts, 77

Young Turks, *see* Turkey

Zionism, 152